Academic Advancement in Composition Studies: Scholarship, Publication, Promotion, Tenure

Academic Advancement
in Composition Studies:
Scholarship, Publication,
Promotion, Tenure

Edited by

Richard C. Gebhardt

Barbara Genelle Smith Gebhardt

PE
1405
.U6
A32
1997

LAWRENCE ERLBAUM ASSOCIATES, PUBLISHERS
1997   Mahwah, New Jersey

Lawrence Erlbaum Associates, Inc., Publishers
10 Industrial Avenue
Mahwah, NJ 07430

Cover design by Kristin Alfano

Library of Congress Cataloging-in-Publication Data

Academic advancement in composition studies : scholarship,
    publication, promotion, tenure / edited by Richard C.
    Gebhardt, Barbara Genelle Smith Gebhardt.
        p. cm.
    Includes bibliographical references and indexes.
    ISBN 0-8058-2101-5 (alk. paper). — ISBN 0-8058-
2102-3 (pbk. : alk. paper)
    1. English language—Rhetoric—Study and teach-
ing—United States—Vocational guidance. 2. English
language—Rhetoric—Study and teaching—Authorship.
3. English language—Rhetoric—Study and teaching—Research. 4. English teachers—Employment—United States. 5. College teachers—Tenure. I.
Gebhardt, Richard C. II Gebhardt, Barbara Genelle
Smith.
PE1405.U6A32   1996
808'.042'07073—dc20   96-18456
                                             CIP

Books published by Lawrence Erlbaum Associates are printed
on acid-free paper, and their bindings are chosen for strength
and durability.

Printed in the United States of America
10 9 8 7 6 5 4 3 2 1

Contents

Preface

In his December 1993 *CCC* Editor's Column, "Scholarship, Promotion, and Tenure in Composition Studies," Richard Gebhardt sketched a number of issues confronting rhetoric and composition at a time when most faculty in the field were assistant professors approaching tenure review or associate professors working toward promotion. These issues centered on the diversity of research and scholarly publication in composition studies; the fact that composition studies faculty are often evaluated by personnel committee members, department chairs, and deans unfamiliar with the nature and demands of the field; the way that American higher education is rethinking scholarship and the role it plays in the work and the evaluation of faculty members; and the role composition studies faculty can play in this review of scholarship and professional advancement. Such issues, Rick said at the end of his column, "will be high on my professional agenda over the next few years" (442).

Pursuing this agenda, Rick recruited wife Barbara as collaborator and co-editor, then issued a widespread invitation for proposals for chapters to be included in a collection of essays dealing with scholarship, its evaluation, and related issues of academic advancement. Detailed proposals, informal inquiries, and letters suggesting topics or possible authors came in, and follow-up letters and editorial responses went out. Some potential chapters did not work out, and some changed direction over the next year. But gradually *Academic Advancement in Composition Studies* evolved in the direction we had imagined for it.

We have tried, in this book, to keep a flexible focus on a timely topic—understanding the nature of and evaluating the work of composition studies faculty members—and to speak, as well, to broader issues of scholarship and professional advancement. After all, composition studies is a field with many focuses—expository and argumentative writing, personal essay, literary nonfiction, technical and business writing, historical rhetoric, empirical research, and more. It also encompasses an array of settings, including first-year composition classes, whether basic or regular, at four-year and two-year institutions; writing centers; intermediate and advanced courses; ESL and skills-development programs; and classes and programs preparing writing teachers, writing program administrators, and writing researchers. Then, too, research in composition is deliberately interdisciplinary, so that some of its scholarship has much in common with literary theory, while some of it draws on approaches from anthropology, education, linguistics, psychology, and other fields. And, of course, many issues of scholarship, promotion, and tenure in composition studies—the comparative weighting of research and teaching, for instance, and the special problems women face in personnel review—are matters of concern in English studies as a whole and, indeed, throughout American higher education.

The breadth of composition studies as a field and the range of issues it faces involving scholarship and professional advancement are reflected in the Table of Contents. The book opens with Richard Gebhardt's discussion of how ideas of scholarship, promotion, and tenure are evolving in composition studies and across higher education, and it ends with an Afterword in which Elizabeth Tebeaux, a long-time leader in the Association of Teachers of Technical Writing, presents her prediction that tenure will wane in the years to come.

A number of chapters focus on the nature of scholarship in composition studies and consequent difficulties in evaluating it during personnel reviews. Lynn Z. Bloom, Aetna Chair of Writing at the University of Connecticut, addresses these issues in the context of external reviewing of scholarly accomplishments. John Schilb of the University of Maryland explores comparisons between scholarship in composition and literature. Douglas Hesse, editor of *Writing Program Administration*, and Barbara Genelle Smith Gebhardt discuss nonacademic publication as scholarship. Writing program administration, Arizona State University's Duane Roen shows, is both teaching and scholarship. And Nancy Roundy Blyler, Margaret Baker Graham, and Charlotte Thralls of Iowa State University write about scholarship and its evaluation in professional communication in a way that illuminates how both are influenced by the particular department and institution in which a faculty member works.

Several chapters focus on important sites of teaching and scholarship within composition studies. Keith Kroll of Kalamazoo Community College and Barry Alford of Mid Michigan Community College propose ways for two-year college faculty to enhance their teaching and their professional influence through research and publication. Purdue University's Muriel Harris, founding editor of *Writing Lab Newsletter*, outlines central issues in writing center scholarship and strategies that writing center faculty can use when presenting evidence of scholarship to personnel committees. Nancy Duke S. Lay of CUNY's City College pursues a similar task with regard to the work of ESL and basic-skills faculty.

Several chapters deal with issues of mentoring and faculty development that are important in all departments and institutions. Janice Neuleib of Illinois State University sketches some special challenges women face in personnel review. Theresa Enos, the founding editor of *Rhetoric Review*, writes on mentoring and (wo)mentoring of graduate students and faculty. Susan McLeod, Associate Dean of Liberal Arts at Washington State University, takes a dean's view of mentoring and faculty development, and Richard Gebhardt explores the chair's role as mentor as well as evaluator.

Many of the chapters have a definite how-to quality. They make suggestions—for new faculty, personnel committee members, chairs, and departments—about how composition studies scholarship can be understood and how composition studies faculty should be evaluated. And one chapter focuses specifically on ways probationary faculty members can prepare for successful personnel reviews.

We hope that the range of topics and the depth of the professional and personal experience shared by the authors will make *Academic Advancement in Composition Studies* useful to many readers: graduate students in composition studies reading on their own or in appropriate graduate courses; probationary faculty looking toward tenure evaluation and associate professors concerned about promotion; senior rhetoric faculty involved in teaching graduate courses, mentoring junior colleagues, educating literature faculty in their departments, or changing department approaches to merit, promotion, and tenure; and department chairs working to evaluate their composition studies faculty accurately and fairly.

ACKNOWLEDGMENTS

We would like to thank the chapter authors whose insights and experiences made this book possible. We also thank Mark Reynolds, editor of *Teaching English in the Two-Year College*, and Michael Mendelson of Iowa State University who helped us identify authors for two of the chapters, and Phyllis Franklin, Executive Director of the MLA, who made available to us a pre-publication copy of the Report of the MLA Commission on Professional Service. Ardella Pierce and Jessica Wade, staff members in the Bowling Green State University English Department, provided behind-the-scenes assistance at several points in this project. Amy Olener and other editors and staff of Lawrence Erlbaum Associates contributed significantly to the book, both by early support for the project and by the care and efficiency brought to its publication.

—*Barbara Genelle Smith Gebhardt*
—*Richard C. Gebhardt*

About the Authors

Barry Alford (PhD, Michigan State University) teaches at Mid Michigan Community College. He is co-editor of *Literacy Networks*, a journal of literacy providers. With Keith Kroll, he is co-editor of *Two-Year Colleges and the Politics of Writing Instruction,* forthcoming from Heinemann-Boynton/Cook.

Lynn Z. Bloom, professor of English and Aetna Chair of Writing at the University of Connecticut-Storrs, is on the Board of Directors of the National Archives of Composition and Research. A past president of the Council of Writing Program Administrators, she has led WPA Summer Workshops and, with Donald Daiker and Edward White, organized the 1993 conference out of which grew *Composition in the 21st Century: Crisis and Change* (Southern Illinois University Press, 1995). She was writing director at the University of New Mexico and the College of William and Mary, and English Department Chair at Virginia Commonwealth University.

Nancy Roundy Blyler (PhD, University of Iowa) teaches in the rhetoric and professional communication program at Iowa State University. With Charlotte Thralls, she founded and edited the *Journal of Business and Technical Communication.* Also with Charlotte Thralls, she edited *Professional Communication: The Social Perspective*, which won the 1993 NCTE award for Best Collection of Essays on Technical or Scientific Communication. Her article, "Theory and Curriculum: Reexamining the Curricular Separation of Business and Technical Communication," won the 1994 NCTE award for Best Article on Methods of Teaching Technical or Scientific Communication.

Theresa Enos, of the University of Arizona English Department, is the founder and editor of *Rhetoric Review* and a leader in the Council of Writing Program Administrators. She has published articles on rhetorical theory and issues in composition and is the author of *Gender Roles and Faculty Lives in Rhetoric and Composition* (Southern Illinois University Press, 1996). She is general editor of the *Encyclopedia of Rhetoric* *and Composition* (Garland, 1995) and the editor of other books, including *A Sourcebook for Basic Writing Teachers* (Random House, 1987) and *Learning from the Histories of Rhetoric* (Southern Illinois University Press, 1993).

Barbara Genelle Smith Gebhardt (MA in English, Northwestern University, and EdD in Higher Education Administration, University of Kentucky) taught writing and literature at Findlay College and later served with the Kentucky Council on Higher Education, the state's governing board for higher education, and in the President's Academic Planning Office at the University of Kentucky. Her publications include articles in *College Composition and Communication, College English,* and *Research in Higher Education.*

Richard C. Gebhardt, English Department Chair at Bowling Green State University, previously served as Humanities Division Chair and Assistant Dean at Findlay College. He organized the first WPA Summer Conference and served as president of the College English Association of Ohio. From 1987 to 1994, he was the editor of *College Composition and Communication.* His articles have appeared in *ADE Bulletin, College English, Hemingway Review, Rhetoric Review, Teaching English in the Two-Year College,* and other journals. His *CCC* article "Balancing Theory with Practice in the Training of Writing Teachers" won the 1978 Richard Braddock Award for the best article on composition in an NCTE journal.

Margaret Baker Graham (PhD, University of North Carolina-Chapel Hill) is an associate professor of English at Iowa State University, where she teaches in the Rhetoric and Professional Communication program and directs the first-year writing program. Her research interests include gender studies, power in organizational communication, and the training of writing teachers. She has published recently in *Journal of Advanced Composition, Technical Communication Quarterly,* and *Journal of Business and Technical Communication.*

Muriel Harris, professor of English and Director of the Writing Lab at Purdue University, is the editor of the *Writing Lab Newsletter.* She has authored a book on conferencing with students, *Teaching One-to-One* (NCTE, 1986), as well as a brief grammar handbook, *The Prentice-Hall Reference Guide to Grammar and Usage* (3rd ed., 1996), and numerous articles, book chapters, and reviews. The National Writing Centers Association has presented her with several awards for scholarship and service. She is currently involved in the development of Purdue University's OWL (Online Writing Lab), with World Wide Web and gopher sites.

Douglas Hesse, professor of English and Director of Writing Programs at Illinois State University, has published chapters on literary nonfiction, rhetorical theory, and narrative theory in several books, including, most recently, *Writing Theory and Critical Theory*, *Composition Theory for the Postmodern Classroom*, *Rebirth of Rhetoric*, and *Essays on the Essay*. His articles have appeared in *College Composition and Communication*, *Rhetoric Review*, *Journal of Advanced Composition*, and elsewhere. He is currently editor of *WPA: Writing Program Administration*.

Keith Kroll is a professor of English at Kalamazoo Valley Community College, where he teaches courses in writing, American literature, and popular culture. With Barry Alford, he edited *Two-Year Colleges and the Politics of Writing Instruction* forthcoming from Heinemann-Boynton/Cook, and he is editor of the Jossey-Bass book *Maintaining Faculty Excellence*.

Nancy Duke S. Lay, a professor and former chair in the ESL Department at City College of New York, has been teaching ESL and conducting teacher-training workshops in the United States and abroad for 20 years. She has served on the executive committee of the Conference on College Composition and Communication and on the editorial advisory boards of *College Composition and Communication* and of the *Journal of Second Language Writing*. Her recent publications include articles in *Teaching English in the Two-Year College* and *College ESL*.

Susan H. McLeod is Associate Dean of the College of Liberal Arts and a professor of English at Washington State University, where she also runs the WAC Faculty Seminars. She is the editor or co-editor of *Strengthening Programs for Writing Across the Curriculum* (Jossey-Bass, 1988), *Writing Across the Curriculum: A Guide to Developing Programs* (Sage, 1991), and *Writing about the World* (2nd ed., Harcourt 1994). Her journal articles have focused on writing across the curriculum, writing program administration, and the affective dimension of composing, and she has written a monograph on affect and writing, *Notes from the Heart*, which is forthcoming from Southern Illinois University Press.

Janice Witherspoon Neuleib is a professor of English at Illinois State University, where she directs the Center for Learning Assistance, the Writing Assessment Program, and the Illinois State Writing Project. Her publications include three textbooks, among them *Inside Out: A Guide to Writing* (with Maurice Scharton), and articles in such journals as *College Composition and Communication*, *College English*, *Journal of Teaching Writing*, *Writing Center Journal*, and *Writing on the Edge*. She received the James Britton Award for Inquiry in English Language Arts for her 1992 *CCC* essay "The Friendly Stranger: Twenty-Five Years As Other."

Duane H. Roen is Director of Composition at Arizona State University. Previously, he served at Syracuse University as Director of the Writing Program, and at the University of Arizona as Director of Rhetoric, Composition and the Teaching of English, and later as Coordinator of Graduate Studies in English. His research interests include gender and written language, collaboration, audience, and writing across the curriculum. He has published many articles and several books, including *A Sense of Audience in Written Communication* (with Gesa Kirsch) and *Becoming Expert: Writing and Learning in the Disciplines* (with Stuart Brown and Robert Mittan).

John Schilb, an associate professor of English at the University of Maryland-College Park, is especially interested in the relationships of writing, rhetoric, and literary theory. He has co-edited three volumes: *Writing Theory and Critical Theory*, *Contending With Words: Composition and Rhetoric in a Postmodern Age*, and *Constellations: A Contextual Reader for Writers*. And he is the author of *Between the Lines: Relating Composition Theory and Literary Theory* (Heinemann-Boynton/Cook, 1996).

Elizabeth Tebeaux is a professor of English at Texas A&M and a professor of Managerial Studies at Rice University. She has served on the CCCC Committee on Technical Communication and, from 1992 through 1995, was president of the Association of Teachers of Technical Writing. In addition to writing three technical communication textbooks and numerous articles on issues in technical communication, she is the editor of *Issues in Promotion and Tenure for Faculty in Technical Communication* (ATTW 1995) and the author of *Emergence of a Tradition: Technical Writing in the English Renaissance, 1475–1640* (Baywood, 1996).

Charlotte Thralls (PhD, Purdue University) is an associate professor of English at Iowa State University, where she teaches graduate and undergraduate courses in rhetoric and professional communication. She cofounded, with Nancy Blyler, the *Journal of Business and Technical Communication*. With Blyler, she co-edited *Professional Communication: The Social Perspective*, winner of the 1993 NCTE award for Best Collection of Essays on Technical or Scientific Communication. Her research specializations are contemporary rhetorical theory and rhetorical criticism.

1 Evolving Approaches to Scholarship, Promotion, and Tenure in Composition Studies

Richard C. Gebhardt
Bowling Green State University

In 1987, representatives of 80 PhD English departments attended a conference on doctoral studies sponsored by a commission of the Modern Language Association, with funding by the Ford Foundation and the University of Minnesota. As the Introduction of *The Future of Doctoral Studies in English* reported it, conference participants "rejected historical coverage along with canonical unity as the invariable reference points that could guide our conceptualization of curricula" and sensed the need to find "an alternate way of conceptualizing what we do" (Lunsford, Moglen, and Slevin vi). Some discussions saw in rhetoric "a model for investigations of discourse broadly conceived—beyond the narrower concerns with canonical texts and forms that seem unnecessarily limiting to contemporary scholarship and criticism" (vii). Other discussions did "not so much argue for adopting rhetoric as our organizing principle . . . as . . . urge that reading and writing be reintegrated at all levels in theory and practice" (ix)—an integration that "would challenge curricular and institutional hierarchies at every turn and would demand basic renegotiation of disciplinary turf" (xi).

A few years later, George Levine of Rutgers University warned in the pages of the MLA's *Profession 93* that the "future of English, as a profession sustained by publicly and privately endowed institutions," is at risk

1

because the two functions of English departments that institutions and the culture as a whole endorse, and pay for, are perhaps the two to which we as research faculty members are least committed. One is the teaching of writing as a basic skill that all educated people need to acquire, and the other is the teaching of literature as it is widely understood by those who don't make the study of it their profession. (44)

If they want to survive, Levine wrote, English departments "should be rethinking their teaching responsibilities. They should be taking far more seriously than they at present do the disparity between their sense of what constitutes useful work in English and what the state and most people who send their children to universities think such work is." Indeed, Levine wrote, "[o]ne of the most difficult questions the profession will have to face is whether the now prevalent model of the research-oriented career can (or even should) be sustained . . ." (44).

About the time MLA members were reading those words, AAUP members opened their Winter 1994 copies of *Academe* and found "The Work of Faculty: Expectations, Priorities, and Rewards." This was a detailed report with much analysis and many tables by an interdisciplinary AAUP committee on teaching, research, and publication. Toward the end, in the fifth of the committee's eight Conclusions and Recommendations, was this passage:

Research, generally undertood to mean discovery and publication, should be related to a broader concept of scholarship that embraces the variety of intellectual activities and the totality of scholarly accomplishments. Though discovery and publication are the core of scholarly endeavor, scholarship seen in its many forms offers a wider context within which to weigh individual contributions.

Innovative and integrative research are essential to research and graduate institutions as well as the capstone of many faculty careers. But scholarship can also mean work done to further the application and integration or synthesis of knowledge, and new directions in pedagogy clearly fall on both sides of the line between what we see as teaching and what can be classified as scholarship. In addition, work in the creative and performing arts, in applied fields of academe, and in areas that demand practical training is also . . . often best classified as research. By enlarging the perspective through which we judge scholarly achievement, we more accurately define the many ways in which intellectual inquiry shapes . . . our complex and interrelated roles as teachers and researchers in a multitude of institutional and disciplinary settings. (AAUP Committee 47–48)

No trio of prefatory paragraphs can adequately introduce a subject as broad and complex as scholarship, promotion, and tenure in composition studies. But those last three paragraphs should help establish some background for this chapter—and for this book—by reminding us all that many of our profession's assumptions and practices are under review or revision. For this is a time of evolution in our field (English studies as a whole, composition studies, and the role of composition within English studies), in the role scholarship plays in the work and rewards of faculty members, and in ideas of scholarship and the way it should be evaluated.

Any responsible discussion of scholarship and its role in the job description and evaluation of college and university faculty members during the decade surrounding the year 2000 must be marked by awareness of and openness to change. This is especially true when the subject is scholarship and professional advancement in composition studies. For ours is a broad and evolving field that is, at once, part of English studies—with all its complexities and evolutionary tendencies—and part of a system of American higher education that is reappraising the work and evaluation of faculty members.

SCHOLARSHIP IN COMPOSITION STUDIES

Diversity of Scholarly Concerns

Composition studies is such a diverse field that, in Lester Faigley's words, "[i]n some departments we now find scholars studying topics ranging from pre-Socratic rhetoric to interactive computer networks . . . " (48). A pamphlet issued by the Conference on College Composition and Communication notes that composition research "has taken as its subject the production, exchange, and reception of texts in a variety of settings," and that it is concerned with reading and writing instruction at all levels" and with "the practice and uses of writing both inside and outside the academy . . ." (CCCC Executive). In the field's oldest and largest journal, to quote a history of *College Composition and Communication*, articles on these subjects appeared between 1980 and 1994:

> (a) assessment, both from political and practical perspectives; (b) cognition, particularly as it applies to the composing process or to the development of the student writer and thinker; (c) the composing process; (d) basic writers; (e) the state of the profession or discipline; (f) interaction among writing, reading, and speaking; (g) political or ideological concerns, such as the nature of literacy, pluralism in the classroom, or women as writers and/or teachers; (h) professional concerns, such as the exploitation of part-time faculty or the marginalizing of the discipline; (i) rhetorical concerns of the writer, specifically choices in invention, arrangement, and style; (j) textbooks; and (k) writing in disciplines other than English, both as it applies to specific composing processes and rhetorical choices, and as a program or curriculum. (Phillips, Greenberg, and Gibson 457–58)

In the program of the 1995 meeting of the Conference on College Composition and Communication, these subjects, among others, were listed in the Topic Index to Concurrent Sessions: teaching of writing and rhetoric, nonfiction and creative writing, writing in professional and technical environments, teaching in the two-year college, institutional contexts for writing and literacy, teaching and learning in a global context, writing and difference, and computers and writing.

Diversity of Scholarly Approaches

Lists of scholarly topics—pre-Socratic rhetoric, workplace writing of software developers, tutorial instruction in writing centers, and what have you—may suggest the range of composition studies. But the diversity of the field involves more than that. To begin with, scholars investigating the same subject may employ very different research strategies or scholarly approaches. "To study the complex domain of rhetoric and composition," wrote Janice Lauer and Andrea Lunsford, "scholars engage in multiple modes of inquiry, including historical scholarship, rhetorical or theoretical inquiry, and empirical research" (106). And in conducting these inquiries, scholars draw on anthropology, education, linguistics, literary theory, philosophy, psychology, and other disciplines.[1]

Another dimension of the field's diversity is the fact that composition studies encourages—and honors—the whole range of scholarly endeavor outlined in the Carnegie Foundation's much-quoted *Scholarship Reconsidered*: the scholarship of discovery, the scholarship of integration, the scholarship of application, and the scholarship of teaching (see Boyer 16–25). Janet Emig's *The Composing Process of Twelfth Graders* is a work of discovery scholarship that has significantly influenced the way scholars view student writing and methods for studying writing. Just as influential, perhaps, is Emig's "Writing As a Mode of Learning," a work of integration and application scholarship that draws on research and insights from education, psychology, medicine, and other fields to enlarge understanding of writing and the relationship of writing to learning.

Both of Emig's works—representing very different goals or motives in research—have been widely cited by scholars. For the field of composition studies understands that scholarship can pursue various ends and that the relationship between teaching and scholarship is both close and mutually supporting.[2] In this regard, composition studies is far ahead of the AAUP effort (mentioned in a prefatory paragraph) to enlarge "the perspective through which we judge scholarly achievement" (AAUP Committee 47–48) and even ahead of the effort of the Institutional Priorities and Faculty Rewards Project to expand the scope of scholarly and professional work to include such things as course development, K to 12 curriculum projects, and community outreach (see Diamond and Adam).

Yet another aspect of the diversity of composition studies is the fact that the field has no single form of scholarship. A few illustrations:

> Scholars conducting empirical research may prepare research reports (abstract, introduction, research methods, results, and discussion) heavy with tables and statistical tests of significance.
>
> Scholars studying written texts or historical topics may prepare books and articles containing many citations, block quotes, and analysis/commentary (which may be more or less textual, deconstructionist, feminist, Marxist, etc.).
>
> Scholars using the methods and terminology of linguistics may explore written texts of various kinds (including transcripts of group discussions or comments individuals make while they are writing).
>
> Scholars who take an anthropological approach may provide long passages of exacting detail about the activities of the professional or student writers they are studying.

Finally, composition scholars using almost any research strategy may use innovative personal approaches in their publications. Women and men committed to collaboration—in research and in writing—sometimes try to efface individual roles in coauthored works (as Lisa Ede and Andrea Lunsford do on the title page of *Singular Texts/Plural Authors*—"RDLISAEDEANDREALUNSFORDLIS . . ."). Or they may use type styles, by-lines, or other means to emphasize the individual voices of multiple authors (see Gebhardt, "Diversity" 8–9). Increasingly, too, composition scholars use their own experiences as illustrations, or as "personal validation and expression of knowledge" (Branscomb 477), or even as the central focus of scholarship. With regard to this personal focus, composition scholarship participates in a growing trend within English studies as a whole—a trend of "sharing and confiding, or even analytically exploring, our feelings and thoughts"—and a "recent increase in public interest in the theory and practice of autobiographical writing" (Bleich 44–45; also see Atkins 635–36).

Diversity—A Strength and a Problem for the Field[3]

When scholars discuss the diversity of composition studies, they usually see it as a source of the field's strength and vitality. For instance, in a discussion of the field's developing bibliography, Patrick Scott notes that "composition is a much more creatively heterogeneous discipline" now than in the 1970s and that this heterogeneity may be "the source of the field's continuing intellectual interest" (91). And Andrea Lunsford writes that composition studies tends "to look well beyond its own borders and to challenge divisions between disciplines. . . . Thus a scholar may draw on anthropology, psychology, philosophy, literary theory, neurobiology, or other disciplines in studying the creation and dissemination of written texts" (9).

Diversity, however, can be a source of difficulty for scholars in the field. For instance, glance again at the last quotation of Lunsford's, and then read her next few sentences:

> The blurring of disciplinary boundaries raises a number of difficulties for graduate students and scholars in the field. How can any one person master the discourses of multiple fields? How viable and valid is the use of one discipline's methodology transferred to another field? (Lunsford 9)

The two sides of diversity show, too, in Gesa Kirsch's discussion of research methodologies in composition studies. She states that the "diversity of research questions raised by scholars, the broad territory encompassed by rhetoric and composition, and the multidisciplinary backgrounds of researchers all invite the use of multiple research methods" (255). But such methodological diversity, Kirsch immediately adds, "is not unproblematic":

> Researchers steeped in different research traditions often speak different languages and describe their observations with different sets of vocabulary. Anne Herrington suggests that "embedded in these languages are different views of issues to investigate, ways of defining the phenomena to be studied, and, more generally, valid ways of knowing. These differences make it all the more difficult to appreciate the value of other approaches, especially when one is struggling to authorize one's own approach." (Kirsch 255–56)

And Janice Lauer describes composition studies as a "multimodal discipline" that works "[t]hrough the use of at least three modes of inquiry—rhetorical, historical, and empirical" (44). But she also emphasizes the costs of multimodality: How the difficulty of studying several "forms of inquiry" can lead people "to ignore or marginalize a mode or two" (50), for instance, or the fact that, during review for promotion and tenure, faculty in composition studies "often face a double task—to produce first-rate scholarship and to explain its nature and value" (51).

It is a matter of real consequence for composition studies—and especially for faculty members preparing for personnel review—if a defining quality of the field undermines understanding among scholars, promotes privileging of some scholarly approaches by people who ignore other approaches, demands extraordinary efforts of scholars who want to do multimodal research, and burdens faculty preparing for tenure and promotion with the need not only to do good research but also to explain its nature and its value. To an extent, these problems affect all scholars in composition studies because so much effort and time are required just to stay generally in touch with research of several different kinds. But, as Cheryl Geisler's "Exploring Academic Literacy" makes clear, the costs are much higher for those who try to use multiple approaches in their scholarship:

> When I'm done [with a multimodal text analysis], I'm fairly sure of my conclusions and I can explain and defend them, both to people who want numbers and those who want exegesis. But people who want numbers don't care about exegesis and those who want exegesis don't understand the numbers. Sure, I can talk to both, but it takes twice as long to get something to say.
>
> The second highest cost comes in terms of comprehensibility. In building an argument across multiple methods and traditions, some parts of the logic are simply incomprehensible to some of the people to whom I think the argument should be important. (47)

Evolving Views of Composition Studies

The previous passage deals with audience issues (whether readers want statistical or textual analysis, for instance, or whether a reader oriented to one research tradition can follow an argument based in other methods and traditions) that spring from the diversity of composition studies. Such things can reduce the impact of published scholarship, even for readers within the field. So it should not be a surprise, during tenure and promotion review, to find that composition scholarship sometimes causes questions and confusion among nonspecialists on English department personnel committees. On the other hand, specialists in composition studies in the 1990s have every reason to expect their work to receive serious and honest evaluation, in the same way that linguists, theorists, American studies scholars, feminist critics, poets—and all the other specialties of English studies—expect their work to be reviewed seriously for tenure and promotion.

It may be true, as Richard Miller wrote in a lead article in the leading journal in composition studies, that "English studies [has long] taken for granted that meaningful work occurs in the realm of literary studies and menial labor takes place in the composition classroom" (165). But it is equally true—as the prefatory paragraph about MLA's conference on doctoral English studies suggests—that rhetoric's stock has risen considerably during two decades of theoretical and curricular debates that made it clear to thoughtful scholars that English studies needs to find "an alternate way of conceptualizing what we do" (Lunsford, Moglen, and Slevin vi).

Jonathan Culler, for instance, writes that if English studies is

> particularly interested in integrating the teaching and study of composition with the study and teaching of literature, then this integration needs at least to be posited as a matter of theory. . . . We already have a name—rhetoric—for such a perspective of integration, and it is striking that such different literary theorists as Paul de Man and Terry Eagleton have proposed that literary studies be reconceived as (or give way to) an expanded rhetoric. . . . (80)

And Gary Waller advocates an approach to doctoral education that, it seems clear, could eventually reshape English studies. Central to this conception of the English doctorate

> is the need for interaction between reading and writing—between the theories and methodologies, say, of empirical research and cultural criticism. . . . Such dialogues require, at the very least, that students in literature, literary theory, or literary and cultural studies share, at key points in the curriculum, seminars or colloquia with students whose focus is rhetoric, communication, or composition studies. (118)

In such visions of a field where "reading and writing [can] be reintegrated at all levels in theory and practice" (Lunsford, Moglen, and Slevin ix), composition studies has a significant voice in an ongoing dialogue about the theory and the content of English studies.

There are, of course, those who disagree with that last statement, or deplore it. Some in English studies continue to see composition studies faculty as a sort of fringe group engaged in practical—and so less worthy—efforts of scholarship and teaching. But others have a very different view of practical scholarship and teaching, and of the importance of such work for the future of English studies. Speaking at an MLA-FIPSE conference on English curriculum review, for instance, Don Bialostosky cautioned that many English faculty

> have learned to deprecate those whose work gives us the strongest claim on public support and to treat them as if their work on literacy, writing, and teaching were inferior to the pure love of literature or the pure life of theory. We still invite our graduate students to look down on the work of elementary instruction in literacy and liberal education . . . and we encourage them to aspire to the fast-disappearing pure life of letters. . . . (21)

Similarly, in the second introductory paragraph of this chapter, Levine worries that English, "as a profession sustained by publicly and privately endowed institutions," is at risk because many scholars are so little committed to "the two functions of English departments that institutions and the culture as a whole endorse, and pay for"—"the teaching of writing as a basic skill that all educated people need to acquire" and "the teaching of literature as it is widely understood by those who don't make the study of it their profession" (44).

The principle operating here is that English studies should relate to the world beyond the academy and to the values of that world. As the next section suggests, this principle is becoming increasingly important for the evaluation and professional advancement of faculty in all disciplines as legislatures and governing boards scrutinize the reward system of higher education. In such a climate, taking seriously the practical scholarship of composition studies makes a lot more sense for most English departments than trying to disregard what Levine sees as a troubling disparity between the "sense of what constitutes useful work in English and what the state and most people who send their children to universities think such work is" (44).

EVOLVING VIEWS OF
FACULTY WORK AND REWARDS

The Changing Role of Scholarship
in Academic Advancement

Until the year 2000 and beyond, American higher education will be engaged in significant reappraisal of faculty work and rewards, particularly the role of scholarship in the context of faculty responsibilities for teaching and public leadership. This review of policies and practices regarding the work, evaluation, and professional advancement of faculty members grows from three recent and connected trends.

First, there is the dramatic increase in the role published scholarship plays in faculty evaluation. In 1969 and again in 1989, the Carnegie Foundation's National Surveys of Faculty asked this same question: "In my department, is it difficult for a person to achieve tenure if he or she doesn't publish?" In 1969, just 21% of faculty surveyed strongly agreed, but in 1989 the response doubled to 42%. The response from faculty in PhD-granting departments almost tripled (from 27% in 1969 to 71% in 1989); it quadrupled at liberal arts colleges (from 6% to 24%); and it increased seven times (from 6% to 43%) at comprehensive institutions (Boyer 12). And it is not surprising, given this increasing role of scholarship in tenure review, that publication is an important factor in faculty salaries. A study of data from the 1988 National Survey of Postsecondary

Faculty revealed that "the more time faculty spend on teaching . . . the lower the pay"; "[c]onversely, the more time spent on research and the greater the scholarly productivity . . . the greater the pay" (Fairweather 46).

The second trend is that, even as the importance of publication has increased on all types of campuses, many faculty members have grown unhappy with the extent to which scholarship and publishing form the basis of faculty rewards. Some of this resistance comes from heartfelt faculty desires, such as higher education scholar Clara Lovett has described: "At every type of institution, faculty express a longing for an older and spiritually richer academic culture, one that placed greater value on the education of students and on the public responsibilities of scholars . . ." (3). Much of the unhappiness reflects faculty preferences for more accurate or meaningful ways to evaluate their work as scholars. For instance, one large-scale national survey of faculty attitudes found that 68% of faculty at all types of institutions—and 77% of faculty in doctoral departments—agreed that "we need better ways, besides publications, to evaluate the scholarly performance of faculty" (Boyer 34). Similarly, a study focused on humanities faculty found that "the overwhelming majority of . . . informants expressed dissatisfaction with reward structures emphasizing research as the sine qua non" (Jarvis 11). This was true of junior faculty—who were "extremely interested in better rewards for teaching" and often "bemoaned the corrosive cynicism toward teaching that the present system engenders"—and of senior professors: "About half of the most cited scholars asked for more emphasis on teaching, and nearly a fifth felt that more careful evaluation of publication quality was in order" (Jarvis 11).

Faculty disenchantment with the emphasis on scholarship may be surprising to some people, but the third trend—public dissatisfaction with the academic reward system—is obvious. "Interest in faculty workloads intensified in the early 1990s," reported the *Chronicle of Higher Education,*

> when lawmakers across the nation began to press for a renewed emphasis on undergraduate education at public universities. They wanted to know why so many classes were being taught by teaching assistants and expressed shock at findings . . . that a typical professor spent less than nine hours a week in a classroom. (Cage 30, 33)

In the same article, the chair of Colorado's Senate Education Committee said what many politicians feel: that " 'research has become the predominant enterprise at the research institution' " but that " 'instruction [should] be the predominant enterprise' " (Cage 33). Underlining the public view of faculty work, of course, is concern about higher education's cost, which, wrote James Fairweather of the Penn State University

Center for the Study of Higher Education, "has led academic leaders and their critics alike to examine how faculty spend their time and the concomitant institutional rewards for doing so" (44).

With incentives for change coming from within higher education as well as from the public, serious review of faculty work and rewards was inevitable. And so *Scholarship Reconsidered: Priorities of the Professoriate* was warmly received when it was published in 1990 because it brought a message many people wanted to hear:

> We believe the time has come to move beyond the tired old "teaching versus research" debate and give the familiar and honorable term "scholarship" a broader, more capacious meaning, one that brings legitimacy to the full scope of academic work. Surely, scholarship means engaging in original research. But the work of the scholar also means stepping back from one's investigation, looking for connections, building bridges between theory and practice, and communicating one's knowledge effectively to students. Specifically, we conclude that the work of the professoriate might be thought of as having four separate, yet overlapping, functions. These are: the scholarship of *discovery*; the scholarship of *integration*; the scholarship of *application*; and the scholarship of *teaching*. (Boyer 16)

Since 1990, *Scholarship Reconsidered* has served as a catalyst or a frame of reference for many attempts to reform the way faculty work is defined and evaluated. One good example is the AAUP's effort (noted in my third introductory paragraph) to enlarge "the perspective through which we judge scholarly achievement" to "more accurately define the many ways in which intellectual inquiry shapes . . . our complex and interrelated roles as teachers and researchers" (47–48). But even before Boyer's book became a best-seller, efforts were underway to broaden the definition of scholarship.

During the 1980s, for instance, the National Endowment for the Humanities published *Humanities in America*, which, among other things, critiqued the way "achievements in the classroom have counted less than scholarly monographs and articles" (10) in tenure and promotion, and emphasized that "research and learning need not always involve publication" (11). About the time the NEH booklet came out, William Schaefer, a former Executive Director of the MLA, wrote an essay—"Publishing, Perishing: They Also Serve Who Only Teach"—in which he said that "publication, while one way to evaluate faculty members, is only one way, and the humanities have got to find other and more realistic means of evaluation if they are going to preserve their vitality" (106). And Earlham College English professor Paul Lacey argued in 1990 that only "the small number of faculty at research institutions" really need to publish "work expected to make original contributions and additions to the body of knowledge"; instead, most faculty members need "writing and other professional activities" that are "appropriate to our work and our own inclinations as teachers" (91–92). Lacey went on to advocate faculty evaluation focused less on published research and more on "quality of mind":

> We would examine intellectual activities that have outcomes in teaching, looking especially for evidences of breadth and connectedness, raising value questions in relation to our discipline, and encouraging cooperation in learning. . . . Materials that in a more rigid system of classification would be considered only under assessment of teaching . . . can equally well be considered as evidence of the faculty member's quality of mind. . . . Does the faculty member think a lot about pedagogy and the defining terms of the subject? If so, writing on teaching issues can as readily be examined for quality of mind and evidences of intellectual growth as can a piece of traditional research. (96–97)

Lacey's suggestion is similar to the first step *Scholarship Reconsidered* advocates to help higher education's "reward system become more flexible and more vital." This is to "take into account a broader range of writing" (Boyer 35).

For some years, the Modern Language Association has been providing leadership in this direction. In 1988, the MLA Commission on Writing and Literature issued guidelines indicating that textbooks and faculty development workshops are, in some specialties, fully appropriate evidence of scholarship, and in 1993, the MLA Executive Committee approved the recommendation of the Committee on Computers and Emerging Technologies in Teaching and Research that

> [f]aculty members who develop computer-based educational applications and scholarly works should be recognized for their curricular, pedagogical, and scholarly contributions. Electronic material should be evaluated as other comparable materials would be, through external reviews by experts as part of the review process. (MLA Committee 45)

The MLA's Association of Departments of English has spoken more broadly:

> Publication need not be the only or even the most important measure of a faculty member's accomplishments. In evaluations of scholarship, different kinds of activities and products should be given credit. Suitable measures of excellence should be developed for nontraditional as well as for traditional forms of scholarship. ("ADE" 44)

And the MLA Commission on Professional Service, in a report accepted by the MLA Executive Council in 1996, has suggested a thorough reconceptualization of the nature of faculty work—and its evaluation. "Making Faculty Work Visible" sets aside the traditional Teaching–Research–Service criteria and describes an approach in which *Professional*

Service, Teaching, and *Research / Scholarship* are " 'sites' and occasions of faculty work" (11) bearing on two "central values of the academy," *Intellectual Work* and *Academic and Professional Citizenship* (10). In this approach, research "is no longer the exclusive site of intellectual work" (14); instead, a faculty member's professional service, teaching, and research and scholarship are each evaluated for the quality of its intellectual work and of its academic and professional citizenship.[4]

The approach of the MLA Commission on Professional Service—in which "the quality, significance, and impact of work . . . is more important than its label as teaching, service, or research and scholarship" (16)—has many implications for the way faculty are evaluated for reappointment, merit, tenure, and promotion. So does the approach of the Institutional Priorities and Faculty Rewards Project. Over several years, representatives of 16 scholarly and professional associations—including MLA and CCCC—worked their way to "general agreement about the characteristics of scholarly, professional, or creative work" (Diamond and Adam 13). These included whether an "activity requires a high level of discipline-related experience," whether it "breaks new ground," whether it "can be replicated or elaborated," whether the "work and its results can be documented" and reviewed by peers, and whether the "activity has significance or impact" (14). Significantly, the Project's 1995 report makes clear, a wide range of faculty work can be judged using such criteria:

> Whether it be publishing the results of one's scholarly research, developing a new course, writing an innovative textbook, implementing an outreach program for the community, directing a student production, or assisting in a K–12 curriculum project, faculty on the discipline task forces agreed that there are many activities in which faculty engage that satisfy the scholarly, professional, or creative dimensions associated with promotion, tenure, and merit recognition. (Diamond and Adam 13–14)

Anticipating Future Developments in Scholarship and Its Evaluation

By 1996 the ADE saw that "[p]ublication need not be the only or even the most important measure of a faculty member's accomplishments" ("ADE" 44); a consortium of scholarly and professional associations developed a definition of scholarly activity broad enough to include course design, textbooks, and outreach into the community; an AAUP committee had concluded that pedagogical work can "fall on both sides of the line between what we see as teaching and what can be classified as scholarship" (AAUP Committee 47); and the MLA Commission on Professional Service had predicted that it may "become increasingly less crucial and perhaps even irrelevant for individual faculty reward whether a particular activity or accomplishment is 'counted as' teaching, service, research and scholarship, or more than one of these" (16).

Given such reappraisals, it is reasonable to expect that by 2006 the scholarship of discovery will be much less dominant in faculty evaluation and rewards than it was in 1989, when 73% of faculty at PhD-granting institutions reported that the sort of scholarship most valued and rewarded was traditional academic work published in refereed journals and books of high reputation (Boyer Appendix A–10). Scholarship of integration and application almost certainly will become more respected as we move toward and into the 2000s, and there will be fewer colleges and universities than in the 1980s or 1990s where "writing about teaching and a number of other activities that keep teachers intellectually alive and effective in the classroom . . . are excluded from consideration by definition" in tenure and promotion reviews (Lacey 95).

Two motifs run through those extrapolations—and through most of the many recent efforts to rethink faculty work and evaluation. One of these is *broadening the definition of scholarly activities*, and the second is *enhancing the relationship of scholarship to other dimensions of faculty work*. The American public, many scholars and teachers, and leading professional organizations seem committed to both goals. So it makes sense to anticipate those motifs as we think about the role of scholarship in the work and professional advancement of faculty members.

For instance, we should expect that in 2006, publications will not just be evaluated against these criteria that I found in a 1991 survey of faculty in composition studies:

> *Object of Scholarship*: A rough hierarchy ranging from arcane or theoretical topics, through more applied topics, down to explicitly pedagogical matters.

> *Manner of Scholarship*: A rough hierarchy from rigorous "original" research, through rigorous secondary or summarizing research, to work with a more personal or informal slant.

> *Genre of Publication*: A rough hierarchy in which university press books and "major" refereed articles are more important than less specialized publications, and textbooks and other pedagogical materials bring up the rear. (See Gebhardt, "Editor's Column: Scholarship" 440–41.)

Clearly, the evolution now underway in how *scholarship* is defined will mean changes in all three of those criteria. Broadening the meaning of *scholarship* to include integrative work as well as pedagogical and other applied efforts undermines the hierarchical organization of the first two criteria. Expanding the idea of scholarship to include such things as curriculum development materials, faculty development workshops, and electronic materials challenges and complicates the third criterion.

Expanded and complicated in this way, object, manner, and genre can continue as useful criteria for evaluating faculty publications.[5] After all, faculty members interested in classroom-centered research, studies of workplace writing, connections of writing and learning, and other applied and pedagogical objects of scholarship often report on their work in conference papers, articles, and books that will continue to be evaluated against such standards as significance, clarity, professional influence, and reputation of publisher or conference. When scholarship appears in internal study documents, curriculum development materials, and other untraditional genres of scholarship, it can be evaluated against traditional standards appropriate for the writer's methodology, and submitted for peer review along with more traditional work. And notes and materials developed for a workshop can be evaluated (for the effectiveness with which theories and research are integrated and clarified for others, for instance), and participants can be asked for comments about the usefulness and significance of the workshop.

Tweaking traditional criteria is a start—already well underway—toward broadening the definition of *scholarly activities* and enhancing the relationship of scholarship to other dimensions of faculty work. In addition, several new criteria are likely to evolve: the relationship of scholarship to the faculty member's work as a teacher, the relationship of scholarship to the mission of the institution and department, and the relationship of scholarship to the needs and expectations society has of higher education.

The *relationship of scholarship to teaching*—a criterion destined to evolve, if an article in *Change* is right and "attention to the quality of teaching . . . will be the main area of public attention and debate for the next decade" (Platter 28)—could apply during personnel reviews of various kinds. Department chairs, personnel committees, external evaluators, and deans could look for evidence—in course outlines, lecture notes, handouts, assignments, tests, and the like—that a professor's scholarship influences what she teaches and how she teaches. They also could look, in faculty publications, for evidence that teaching has influenced scholarship—for such things as quotations from student papers, references to course activities or class discussions, and treatment of the pedagogical implications of research. Shallow articles and vanity-press books, of course, would not provide much support for promotion just because they relate to a faculty member's teaching. But solid articles that relate to their author's teaching could well count as stronger evidence in promotion review than solid articles without such a connection.

The second criterion, *the relationship of scholarship to institutional mission,* relates to the first in that a department could give the teaching–scholarship relationship more or less weight in evaluating publications, depending on the importance of teaching in the mission of the university, college, or department. The relationship to teaching criterion probably would have less influence in doctoral departments than at two-year colleges, liberal arts colleges, and comprehensive universities. Even PhD English departments, though, have complex undergraduate missions—teaching undergraduate English majors, preparing future teachers of high school English and elementary language arts, and offering general education and basic-skills education—that are quite relevant in evaluating faculty scholarship.

The third criterion, *the relationship of scholarship to social needs and expectations,* relates to the second. General education, basic skills of thinking and communicating, and the preparation of teachers for public schools are results society expects from higher education and for which colleges and universities receive tuition payments and state support. The public has many needs, as well as expectations of how higher education should meet them. Some are broad and social, such as the need for research to broaden literacy, increase America's competitiveness and productivity, and address widespread social inequities. Some are felt personally by the public, by politicians, by parents of college students, and by students themselves—that faculty members should be teaching college classes, that undergraduates should have close contacts with faculty, and that students should leave college with the education and values to succeed in a good job.

The public perception that we are not meeting those needs is at least part of the reason American higher education faces criticism and economic constraints as it approaches the next century. So there are advantages to being seen as a discipline that is responsive to society's expectations rather than aloof from them. This, I think, was on Levine's mind when he said that "[w]e must learn to build departments whose interests and objectives are less at odds with their immediate public responsibilities" (45). And it is one of the reasons our field should broaden the definition of *scholarly activities* and enhance the relationship of scholarship to other dimensions of faculty work.

NOTES

[1]Three collections that illustrate and clarify the methodological diversity of composition research are Enos and Brown, *Defining the New Rhetorics;* Kirsch and Sullivan, *Methods and Methodology in Composition Research;* and Lindemann and Tate, *An Introduction to Composition Studies.*

[2]*Scholarship in Composition,* a pamphlet issued by the CCCC Executive Committee, states that the field "has traditionally used the classroom and student writing as material for the study of more general problems in language use and language development. In addition, it has traditionally valued projects that move back and

forth between theoretical discussion and practical application. Many journals, in fact, insist that articles be written to illuminate or comment on current practice in the classroom, in our institutions, or, more generally, in culture."

[3]This section is a revision of a portion of "Scholarship, Promotion, and Tenure in Composition Studies" published in *Rhetoric, Cultural Studies, and Literacy*.

[4]*Intellectual Work,* as defined by the MLA Commission on Professional Service, refers to "the various ways faculty members can contribute individually and jointly to the collective projects and enterprises of knowledge and learning undertaken to implement broad academic missions" (11–12). Among the Commission's examples of such work are "[c]reating new questions, problems, information, interpretations, designs, products, frameworks of understanding, etc., through inquiry . . ."; "[c]larifying, critically examining, weighing, and revising the knowledge claims, beliefs, or understanding of others and oneself;" "[c]onnecting knowledge to other knowledge"; "[p]reserving, restoring, and reinterpreting past knowledge"; "[a]pplying aesthetic, political, and ethical values to make judgments about knowledge and its uses"; "[m]aking specialized knowledge broadly accessible and usable, e.g., to young learners, to nonspecialists in other disciplines, to the public"; "[h]elping new generations to become active knowers themselves . . ."; and "[a]pplying knowledge to practical problems in significant or innovative ways" (12). As those examples suggest, intellectual work occurs in teaching and in professional service as well as in research and scholarship.

Academic and Professional Citizenship includes many tasks beyond "the explicitly . . . intellectual elements of faculty work." This work is "grounded in professional expertise and . . . directed toward the health and maintenance of academic communities and institutions" (14). And such work "can be found in any category or site of faculty effort": research and scholarship (e.g., "promotion and tenure reviews," "manuscript reviewing," or "collection and distribution of information through electronic means"); teaching (e.g., "work on institutional retention programs," "major advertising," or "advisor to field–specific student organizations or projects"; and professional service (e.g., "committee work for one's institution or professional organizations" or "representing the institution or field on external task forces" (14).

I am citing the report of the Commission on Professional Service (accepted by the MLA Executive Council in February 1996) which MLA Executive Director Phyllis Franklin very helpfully shared with me in advance of its publication in *Profession 96*.

[5]This and the next five paragraphs are a revision of a portion of "Avoiding the Teaching vs. Research Trap: Expanding the Criteria for Evaluating Scholarship" in *The Politics and Processes of Scholarship*.

WORKS CITED

AAUP Committee C on College and University Teaching, Research, and Publication. "The Work of Faculty: Expectations, Priorities, and Rewards." *Academe* Jan/Feb 1994: 15–48.

"ADE Statement of Good Practice: Teaching, Evaluation, and Scholarship." *ADE Bulletin* No. 105 (Fall 1993): 43–45.

Atkins, G. Douglas. "Envisioning the Stranger's Heart." *College English* 56 (Oct. 1994): 629–41.

Bialostosky, Don. "Toward a Rhetoric for English Department Curricular Debates." *ADE Bulletin.* No. 105 (Fall 1993): 20–22.

Bleich, David. "Collaboration and the Pedagogy of Disclosure," *College English* 57 (Jan. 1995):43–61.

Boyer, Ernest. *Scholarship Reconsidered: Priorities of the Professoriate*. Princeton: Carnegie Foundation for the Advancement of Teaching, 1990.

Branscomb, H. Eric. "Shadows of Doubt: Writing Research and the New Epistemologies." *College English* 57 (Apr. 1995): 467–80.

Cage, Mary Crystal. "Regulating Faculty Workloads." *Chronicle of Higher Education* 20 Jan. 1995: 30, 33.

CCCC Executive Committee. *Scholarship in Composition: Guidelines for Faculty, Deans, and Department Chairs*. Urbana:NCTE, n.d. n. pag.

Culler, Jonathan. "Imagining Changes." Lunsford, Moglen, and Slevin 79–83.

Diamond, Robert M., and Bronwyn E. Adam. "Describing the Work of Faculty." *The Disciplines Speak: Rewarding Scholarly, Professional, and Creative Work of Faculty*. Ed. Diamond and Adam. Washington: American Association for Higher Education, 1995. 1–14.

Ede, Lisa, and Andrea Lunsford. *Singular Texts/Plural Authors*. Carbondale: Southern Illinois U P, 1990.

Emig, Janet. *The Composing Process of Twelfth Graders*. Urbana: National Council of Teachers of English, 1971.

———. "Writing As a Mode of Learning." *College Composition and Communication* 28 (May 1977): 122–28.

Enos, Theresa, and Stuart C. Brown, eds. *Defining the New Rhetorics*. Newbury Park: Sage, 1993.

Faigley, Lester. *Fragments of Rationality: Postmodernity and the Subject of Composition*. Pittsburgh:U of Pittsburgh P, 1992.

Fairweather, James, S. "The Nature of Tradeoffs." *Change* Jul./Aug. 1993: 44–47.

Gebhardt, Richard C. "Avoiding the Teaching vs. Research Trap: Expanding the Criteria for Evaluating Scholarship." *The Politics and Processes of Scholarship*. Ed. Joseph M. Moxley and Lagretta Lenker. Westport: Greenwood, 1995. 9–17.

———. "Editor's Column:Diversity in a Mainline Journal." *College Composition and Communication* 43 (Feb. 1992): 7–10.

———. "Editor's Column: Scholarship, Promotion, and Tenure in Composition Studies." *College Composition and Communication* 44 (Dec. 1993): 439–42.

———. "Scholarship, Promotion, and Tenure in Composition Studies." *Rhetoric, Cultural Studies, and Literacy*. Ed. John Frederick Reynolds. Mahwah, NJ: Lawrence Erlbaum Associates, 1995. 177–84.

Geisler, Cheryl. "Exploring Academic Literacy:An Experiment in Composing." *College Composition and Communication* 43 (Feb. 1992): 39–54.

Herrington, Anne. "The First Twenty-Five Years of *RTE* and the Growth of a Research Community in Composition Studies." *Research in the Teaching of English* 23 (1989): 117–38.

Jarvis, Donald K. *Junior Faculty Development: A Handbook*. New York: MLA, 1991.

Kirsch, Gesa. "Methodological Pluralism." Kirsch and Sullivan 247–69.

Kirsch, Gesa, and Patricia A. Sullivan, eds. *Methods and Methodologies in Composition Research*. Carbondale: Southern Illinois U P, 1992.

Lacey, Paul A. "Encouraging and Evaluating Scholarship for the College Teacher." *Excellent Teaching in a Changing Academy*. Ed. Feroza Jussawalla. New Directions in Teaching and Learning No. 44. San Francisco: Jossey-Bass, 1990. 91–100.

Lauer, Janice. "Rhetoric and Composition Studies: A Multimodal Discipline." Enos and Brown 44–54.

Lauer, Janice, and Andrea Lunsford. "The Place of Rhetoric and Composition in Doctoral Studies." Lunsford, Moglen, and Slevin 106–110.

Levine, George. "The Real Trouble." *Profession 93*. New York: MLA, 1993. 43–45.

Lindemann, Erika, and Gary Tate, eds. *An Introduction to Composition Studies*. New York: Oxford UP, 1991.

Lovett, Clara M. "Listening to the Faculty Grapevine." *AAHE Bulletin* 46. 3 (Nov. 1993): 3–5.

Lunsford, Andrea A. "The Nature of Composition Studies." Lindemann and Tate 3–14.

Lunsford, Andrea, Helene Moglen, and James F. Slevin, eds. *The Future of Doctoral Studies in English*. New York: MLA, 1989.

MLA Commission on Professional Service. "Making Faculty Work Visible: Reinterpreting Professional Service, Teaching, and Research in the Fields of Language and Literature." 1995; accepted by the MLA Executive Council 1996.

MLA Commission on Writing and Literature. "Report on the Commission of Writing and Literature." *Profession 88*. New York: MLA, 1988. 73–74.

MLA Committee on Computers and Emerging Technologies in Teaching and Research. "Statement on Computer Support." *ADE Bulletin* No. 109 (Winter 1994): 44–45.

Miller, Richard E. "Composing English Studies: Towards a Social History of the Discipline." *College Composition and Communication* 45 (May 1994): 164–79.

National Endowment for the Humanities. *Humanities in America*. Washington: NEH, 1988.

Phillips, Donna Burns, Ruth Greenberg, and Sharon Gibson. "*College Composition and Communication*: Chronicling a Discipline's Genesis." *College Composition and Communication* 44 (Dec. 1993): 443–65.

Platter, William. "Future Work: Faculty Time in the 21st Century." *Change* May/June 1995: 22–33.

Scott, Patrick. "Bibliographical Resources and Problems." Lindemann and Tate 72–93.

Schaefer, William D. *Education without Compromise*. San Francisco: Jossey-Bass, 1990.

Waller, Gary. "Polylogue: Reading, Writing, and the Structure of Doctoral Study." Lunsford, Moglen, and Slevin 111–20.

2 Scholarship in Composition and Literature: Some Comparisons

John Schilb
University of Maryland

Imagine that you teach literature in a university English department. Let's say that you specialize in the American novel. For years, you have taught both halves of the American literature survey, along with the occasional seminar on Henry James or Edith Wharton. Moreover, you have published several articles on James's major phase, as well as a book about it. And you have always felt able to chat with colleagues about their own literary interests.

But now you find yourself saddled with a task for which you feel wholly unprepared. Despite your initial refusal, your department head insists that you serve on Pam Talbot's tenure committee. You have been on such committees before; you think kindly of Pam. Nevertheless, you wonder how you can fulfill this assignment, for Pam is a composition specialist, and you know nothing about composition. You are especially anxious about having to evaluate the articles she has published. Although you do feel able to evaluate the scholarship of your literature colleagues, composition scholarship is, for you, an alien world.

This alien world includes hundreds of publications (some of which are mentioned in the appendix to Richard Gebhardt's chapter "Mentor and Evaluator"). In fact, over the last two decades, composition journals and books have absolutely proliferated. Such an increase is, of course, indicative of composition studies' growing professionalization. So is your department's creation of Pam's tenure-track job. Until recently, many

21

English departments relegated composition specialists to part-time posts or limited-term instructorships. Even today, legions of writing teachers are ghettoized in this way. But more and more Pam Talbots are coming up for tenure in English departments. At the same time, more and more teachers of literature find themselves in your situation. How can you evaluate someone in a field you have pretty much ignored?

Here I offer you, and others like you, a rudimentary guide to composition scholarship. Specifically, I emphasize ways in which it differs from scholarship in literary studies. The comparisons I draw are necessarily broad and brief. They will leave you needing to learn still more about Pam's field—a process that will involve, I trust, your consulting various other people in composition. Also, I offer relatively few criteria for judging her particular contributions to her field. Composition studies is now a melange of theories, methodologies, issues, and projects; without knowing Pam's own scholarly interests, I hesitate to declare how you should assess her pursuit of them. Nevertheless, I hope that from the comparisons I make, you can begin contextualizing what she does.

BEYOND THE LITERARY CANON

Probably both Pam and you write about texts. In fact, this connection may help you start building a framework for evaluating her scholarship. Yet her approach to texts and yours may differ in a number of respects. For one thing, she may study writings that you have never thought worthy of sustained contemplation.

True, in recent years, the literary canon has expanded. Perhaps you yourself are now willing to include in it works you once utterly disregarded: for example, a play or two by Aphra Behn, *Incidents in the Life of a Slave Girl, The Awakening, Their Eyes Were Watching God,* and *The Woman Warrior.* And perhaps, like the New Historicists, you enjoy tying literary classics to other types of discourse produced around the same time. (For example, Stephen Greenblatt relates *King Lear* to exorcism manuals). Surely you know that many scholars trained in literature have made a dramatic shift, self-consciously moving into cultural studies. Although you may not have changed as much as they, you may tolerate their interest in popular culture, and you may think it fine that they study visual and oral texts as well as books.

But composition scholars have never really had a canon in the first place. Admittedly, certain essays have been reprinted with increasing frequency in freshman composition readers. Moreover, if you look at composition articles, you will see that their bibliographies repeatedly cite certain names. Nevertheless, it would be misleading to say that composition studies has revolved around a finite corpus of certified masterpieces. Members of the field have written about many different kinds of discourse—the majority of which are still ignored by people trained in literature.

Most often, composition scholars have studied texts written by students. This practice is uncommon in literary studies. Although literature specialists do ask their students to write papers and then spend time in their offices examining the results, relatively few go so far as to publish analyses of their students' writing. Thus, although your latest article may deal with the role of capitalism in *The Golden Bowl*, Pam's is more apt to explore how her students use sources in their written arguments.

Not that she focuses on their final drafts alone. Probably Pam analyzes her students' entire composing process, paying attention to their goals in writing, their prior knowledge, their changing thoughts, their cultural backgrounds, and how they negotiate ideological assumptions embedded in the course itself. Although quite a few literary critics basically explicate finished, published artifacts, many composition scholars trace how their students' texts evolve.

If Pam has indeed written about her students' texts, probably she has presented them as case studies to illustrate larger phenomena, principles, and issues. Interestingly enough, the term *case study* is seldom used by scholars of literature, and perhaps you hesitate to give any of your own writing this label. True, some pieces of literary criticism and theory appear to employ case study methods when they use particular texts as springboards for much wider ranging discussion. Yet if you skim most journals in literary studies, you will find article after article that does little more than interpret whatever texts it considers. Despite the New Criticism's alleged demise, literary studies has hardly abandoned hope that close reading of literary works can be an end in itself.

Furthermore, much composition scholarship has an interventionist slant that I do not find pervasive in literary studies. Many a piece of literary criticism winds up confirming the power (positive or negative) of whatever works it analyzes. On the other hand, many a piece of composition scholarship aims to determine appropriate future action. Do not be surprised if Pam's articles discuss how students can improve their writing. Perhaps Pam's articles address how to strengthen the teaching of writing, too.

A FOCUS ON TEACHING

Much composition scholarship is, in fact, grounded in pedagogy. Here is another significant difference between your field and Pam's. Perhaps you have never written about your teaching; only a minority of literature specialists have described theirs in print. A recent move by *PMLA* is symptomatic: By announcing that it will now do an issue on the teaching of literature, this journal implicitly acknowledges that pedagogy has not been central to literary scholarship. Yet the teaching of writing has long been the core topic of scholarship in composition. Quite possibly, Pam's articles treat her own classes as places for generating and implementing ideas.

My use of the word *generating* is pointed. To much of the academy, teaching is merely the practice of disseminating or applying previously established knowledge. Even when colleges aim to integrate teaching and research, they tend to assume that the latter drives the former. But actually, the two can be in reciprocal relation. Think of classrooms as sites where knowledge is produced as well as deployed. Given its tight connection to teaching, composition studies is well-positioned to explore this prospect.

Of course, if composition classes are to be seen as intellectually fertile, the image of composition students will have to rise. Traditionally, English departments and the rest of the academy have defined composition as a service program. Far from conceiving it as a significant, expansive body of scholarship, departments have viewed composition merely as an attempt to remedy first-year students' verbal deficiencies. Obviously such a conception amounts to a reductive image of Pam, for it denies that she may have multiple interests and talents. At the same time, this conception denigrates freshman writing students, seeing them as hapless recruits, not full-fledged contributors, to intellectual life.

Unfortunately, numerous composition specialists have subscribed to this thinking. Nowadays, though, more and more of them resist it. In their publications, they do not settle for depicting freshmen as apprentices needing their guidance; rather, they note how these students have provided them with insights. Also, quite a few composition scholars refuse to keep freshman composition merely a linguistic boot camp. Many of them, for example, write about how freshman composition courses might help students address civic issues.

A DIVERSITY OF CONCERNS

To be sure, Pam may have written about topics other than composition teaching. Let me return to the matter of her field's diversity. I suspect you can easily associate literary studies with that word; long ago, probably, you recognized literary scholarship as a field of specializations and subspecializations. And in recent years, I imagine, you have found your field teeming with conflict. In your own department, perhaps you have argued with colleagues in literature about the canon's virtues or a certain theory's merits. Perhaps you have debated whether to engage in theory at all. Whatever the case, you would doubt that any single scholar represented the scope of literary studies, its various topics and creeds.

Some English departments do seek generalists in literature. But more look for specialists in a period, genre, region, or theoretical approach. Quite possibly your department hired you as a specialist in the American novel. If it was able to hire literature faculty along with Pam, quite possibly it defined them as specialists, too: identifying them with feminist criticism, or postcolonial literature, or some other specialty within literary studies.

But your department may very well have hired Pam as an expert simply in composition, as if her field were monolithic and she embodied its essence. This assumption, however, is just as faulty as it is when made about a teacher of literature. You can expect Pam to be familiar with various trends in composition studies, especially if she has a doctorate in the field. As a scholar, however, probably she contributes to only a few of its areas. These days, no one in composition studies works in all its zones, and no one is thoroughly versed in each. As with literary studies, composition studies is now too diverse for one person to represent. Consider that the program proposal form for the 1995 meeting of the Conference on College Composition and Communication lists 100 different topics.

Even scholars who write about freshman composition may study different aspects of it. Several discuss the challenges of administering freshman writing programs. Others analyze various kinds of interaction in freshman writing classes, including peer review groups, student–faculty conferences, networked (online) discussions, and collaborative projects. Also, unlike the vast majority of their colleagues in literature, several composition scholars write about who teaches introductory courses in their field. They deal, too, with the circumstances under which those teachers toil. Much of the freshman composition labor force consists of graduate students, and plenty of articles explain how to prepare them for their task. This labor force also includes vast numbers of part-timers and limited-term faculty. Increasingly, composition scholarship describes how these writing instructors and teaching assistants get exploited, treated by "regular" English faculty as a lesser breed.

Back to Pam. Looking beyond English departments, she may analyze writing done in some wholly other sphere: say, in another discipline, a professional firm, an entire community, or a certain social movement. Or, she may devote herself to elaborating a general theory of literacy. Then again, she may look to the past rather than the present: studying certain rhetorical traditions, discursive practices of a now-defunct group, or the ways that writing has been taught in previous ages.

Furthermore, in her scholarly projects, Pam may use any number of research methods. Perhaps she does semantic, rhetorical, or linguistic analyses of texts, relying on computer-generated statistics in the process. Perhaps she has done ethnographic investigations of groups. Perhaps she pores over transcripts, looking for themes and recurring conversational moves. Perhaps she has extensively interviewed certain writers, tracking them over weeks or months or years.

Some of these research methods may strike you as well outside your purview, even foreign to the discipline of English. Indeed, while scholars of literature exhibit some affinities with other fields—history being the chief one at present—composition studies has always been profoundly interdisciplinary. Note that English is hardly the only department that hires scholars of writing. Plenty of composition specialists teach in departments of rhetoric, linguistics, education, communication, sociology, psychology, and anthropology. Plenty of them are located, too, in autonomous composition departments. If Pam teaches or administers in an English department's first-year writing program, she may develop interdisciplinary interests as a result of this very assignment. After all, students from throughout the university take freshman composition, and instructors often allow them to write about topics in their intended majors.

In particular, Pam may resemble a social scientist more than she does a literary critic. As I have indicated, composition specialists often make use of statistical analysis, interviews, ethnography, and longitudinal studies in their research projects, all of which are still more common in the social sciences than in literary studies. Also, Pam may have done collaborative research and writing, practices again more typical of social scientists than scholars of literature.

Worth noting, too, are the conventions of style and format in Pam's articles. A number of composition journals and publishers require APA-style documentation, whereas literary studies remains loyal to MLA. Furthermore, like a social scientist, Pam may often end her articles by identifying limits of her current work and directions for future research. Observe, for instance, how composition scholar Christina Haas concludes a recent article in *Written Communication*. After chronicling one student's experience with biology courses throughout her college career, Haas makes statements like the following: "We need to know more about the kinds of theories of discourse that students hold when they arrive in college and how these theories are reinforced or challenged by the instruction they receive across the university" (79). Rarely do literary critics or theorists end a piece in this way; instead, they tend to reiterate claims they have supposedly proven. Hence, if Pam concludes by calling for further inquiry, you may read her as declaring her incompetence. For a sociologist or a psychologist, however, this move is routine, a mark of intellectual rigor.

SCHOLARLY PUBLICATION

In discussing Pam's writing, I have repeatedly referred to her articles. I have not assumed that she has published what you would consider a scholarly book. In this respect, she would be a typical composition specialist. As far as its written scholarship is concerned, the field of composition studies has been predominantly article-driven. This situation reflects the habits of academic presses: Although many presses have regularly published books of literary criticism, only some of them have published volumes on composition theory and research. In the last few years, things have improved, with several composition series being launched and an increasing number of collections and monographs being published. Also, because the number of dissertations in composition studies has increased exponentially in the past decade, there are more potential composition books around. Still, if Pam has published only articles, consider the long-term history of her field.

Actually, within that history, a certain kind of book has forever been prominent. I am thinking of composition textbooks: rhetorics, readers, and handbooks expressly designed for freshman writing or more advanced classes. If Pam has published such a volume, you may be tempted to dismiss it. What, you may say, is scholarly about a commercial product created for students? I myself would never claim that every composition textbook blazes with sagacity. All too many of them simply recycle pedagogical platitudes. But some should be respected, and Pam's may be one. Her textbook deserves much credit if, for example, it eschews cliches, promotes sound practices, features thought-provoking material, builds on developments in her field, and still proves accessible to students.

Whether or not it does all this, you may continue to dislike her textbook's whiff of commercialism—especially if Pam's advance was much bigger than the one you got for your book on James! Yet, given that society at large increasingly distrusts the academy, more than ever colleges need people who can reach a larger public. Bear in mind, too, that Pam may not be as well-off as you think. When doing a textbook, writers often incur lots of uncompensated expenses. Moreover, because the market for textbooks like hers is incredibly crowded, Pam may fail to earn any royalties at all. Besides, whatever her financial gains in the short run, authors like you tend to make out better over time. Often, a book of literary criticism sells only a few hundred copies and yet ultimately earns the writer a secure, remunerative departmental berth. Rarely have composition textbooks reaped for their authors the same fate. In Pam's tenure case, you may be deciding whether to endorse or resist this tradition.

OTHER KINDS OF SCHOLARSHIP

It is also traditional for the academy to define scholarship in terms of written artifacts alone. But such a view can obscure Pam's other intellectual feats. Earlier, I noted that composition specialists often write about pedagogy, and I suggested this topic deserves more respect from their counterparts in literary studies. Here I want to make a further proposal. If Pam helps her classes both acquire and produce knowledge, why not consider her teaching itself a form of scholarship?

I can imagine at least three objections to this idea. First, you may argue, one cannot be sure that Pam's teaching actually generates knowledge. And I admit you have no objective way to determine whether or not it does. Ultimately, you must use your own judgment. Nevertheless, there are several ways you can become more informed about Pam as a teacher. Obviously, you can talk with her and her students about what goes on in her classroom. Furthermore, you can observe her classes, even analyze videotapes of them. Also, you can encourage all members of your department to meet periodically for discussions about their teaching. Finally, you could have at your disposal various written documents that bear on Pam's teaching. Consider asking her to compile a teaching portfolio consisting of syllabi, assignments, student evaluations, examples of student writing, examples of her comments on that writing, and an essay in which she articulates an overall philosophy of education.

Your second possible objection to evaluating Pam's teaching as scholarship concerns the parochial nature of classroom-produced knowledge. When faculty members publish, you may argue, their ideas broadly circulate and receive public scrutiny, whereas the kind of knowledge I am talking about stays close to home. I can appreciate such a concern. Certainly colleges should not insist that their teachers' work remain on campus. If anything, the academy must gain wider support than it now enjoys, as I pointed out when discussing textbooks. In keeping with this principle, however, let us not exaggerate the impact that published scholarship currently has. Most books and articles in literary studies are read only by coteries, specialists in whatever topic is being addressed. Meanwhile, as a teacher, Pam may have a substantial audience, with her students representing various segments of the public. Furthermore, her audience may be quite discriminating, pushing her to make her ideas useful as well as sound.

Your third possible objection concerns taxonomy. Even at research universities, teaching plays a role in the tenure process, considered along with scholarship and service. With Pam's case, you probably do intend to examine thoroughly all parts of this familiar triad. Hence, you may doubt the wisdom of mixing categories. What harm is there in distinguishing between Pam's scholarship and Pam's teaching, as long as you cover both? But rarely do colleges give these two categories equal weight. If your department is one of the many that esteems scholarship more than teaching, it is especially important for you to see how, for Pam, they may be integrated.

The remarks I have just made about Pam as a teacher may also apply to her as an administrator. Historically, composition specialists have had to perform a lot of administrative work. Of course, plenty of specialists in literature have done administrative work, too. But they have not had to treat it as an inevitable part of their professional destiny, whereas tenure-track people in composition are bound to direct (or assist in directing) a writing program or center some day. In fact, it is common for newly hired composition specialists to assume such duties immediately, an obligation that new teachers of literature rarely face. Besides teaching and writing, Pam (like Hanna in Duane Roen's chapter "Writing Administration As Scholarship and Teaching") may spend many hours each week chairing staff meetings, consulting with her department head, meeting with other college officials, designing course manuals, supervising placement exams, training new instructors and advising old ones, visiting classrooms, handling students' grade appeals, and corresponding with other institutions. These kinds of administrative tasks require a composition specialist not only to forge and articulate ideas about writing, but also to persuade others of their validity. Hence, Pam's administrative work can be said to involve scholarship, even if it is traditionally categorized as service.

CONCLUSION

In comparing composition scholarship with scholarship in literary studies, I have mostly called attention to their differences. I have done so because I think composition scholarship does not always square with English department value systems. Pam's case is an opportunity for you to review, even revise, principles that your department may be taking for granted. Perhaps, through serving on Pam's committee, you will newly appreciate certain actions that your literature colleagues perform. In particular, you may come to see that they, too, do significant intellectual work when they teach.

Still, composition studies and literary studies are not completely dissimilar worlds. In the last few years, they have pursued some of the same issues. For one thing, both fields have turned in their research to social constructionist epistemologies. More than ever, each examines how notions of truth, knowledge, identity, and value are shaped by specific discourses, ideologies, and practices. Both also study the influence on this shaping of variables like gender, race, and class. In conducting such research, each field is brooding about the powers and the limits of theory, wondering how to define it and how to deploy it. Both fields are keenly aware, too, that they must come to terms with new social forces: the ever-expanding information highway and the ever-increasing charges that English departments are rife with political correctness. Yet even as they acknowledge constraints of social context, both fields seek a role for human agency. Each tries to imagine what writers, readers, teachers, and students can achieve.

Thus, you may find that Pam's scholarship does resonate with yours. If it seems exotic to you, however, do not panic. Through talking with Pam, consulting with other composition specialists, and reading volumes like this, you can do much to bridge the gulf. I say this in part because my own professional orientation once resembled yours. In graduate school, I was committed to literary studies; my dissertation was, in fact, on Henry James. Over the intervening years, however, I have moved more and more into composition studies. Not easily, of course: My training in this emerging field has been necessarily stumbling, ad hoc, and autodidactic. But ultimately I feel able to say that I am a composition scholar. Although you yourself may have no such ambition, perhaps my experience will give you heart as you pursue the more modest goal of learning about Pam Talbot and her qualifications for tenure.

ACKNOWLEDGMENTS

I thank my colleagues Jeanne Fahnestock and Nancy Shapiro for their helpful advice about this chapter.

WORKS CITED

Gebhardt, Richard C. "Article Publication in Composition Studies—Some Notes for Evaluation Committee Members." Appendix to "Mentor and Evaluator: The Chair's Role in Promotion and Tenure Review." *Academic Advancement in Composition Studies*. Ed. Richard C. Gebhardt and Barbara Genelle Smith Gebhardt. Mahwah, NJ: Lawrence Erlbaum Associates, 1997. 147–65.

Greenblatt, Stephen. "Shakespeare and the Exorcists." *Shakespearean Negotiations: The Circulation of Social Energy in Renaissance England*. Berkeley: U of California P, 1988. 94–128.

Haas, Christina. "Learning to Read Biology: One Student's Rhetorical Development in College." *Written Communication* 11 (1994): 43–84.

Roen, Duane. "Writing Administration As Scholarship and Teaching." *Academic Advancement in Composition Studies*. Ed. Richard C. Gebhardt and Barbara Genelle Smith Gebhardt. Mahwah, NJ: Lawrence Erlbaum Associates, 1997. 43–55.

3   Nonacademic Publication As Scholarship

Douglas Hesse
Illinois State University

Barbara Genelle Smith Gebhardt
Findlay, OH

In his 2 July 1995 *Washington Post* column, "Teach Johnny to Write," George Will warns that "the teaching of writing has been shaped by 'an indigestible stew of 1960s liberationist zeal, 1970s deconstructionist nihilism, and 1980s multicultural proselytizing,'" resulting in teachers trading standards and responsibilities for "academic fads."[1] Will concludes that "the smugly self-absorbed professoriate that perpetrates all this academic malpractice is often tenured and always comfortable" (C7).

Our purpose here is not to contest Mr. Will's claim of malpractice in writing classrooms. (We do not concede, however, that doctoral candidates in English at Illinois State who teach two sections of English 101 for $800 a month are "always comfortable.") Instead, we want to focus on the forum for Will's remarks and their implications for rhetoric and composition studies teachers and scholars.[2]

Will's column is widely syndicated, and when it appeared in the Bloomington, Illinois *Pantagraph* on July 3, I knew at least one topic of future conversations with business friends in town. After all, Will's topic entered the public domain and the national conversation at our breakfast tables from our local newspaper via Washington, D.C.'s local paper. Rarely is the professional research or theoretical literature on the teaching of composition—now vast and significant for writing scholars

31

and teachers—reported in the *Washington Post* or Bloomington's *Pantagraph*. So, unaware of that disciplinary knowledge and theory, and already concerned about the literacy crisis, my Bloomington friends, I understood, would be willing to accept, unexamined, Will's assertion that the teaching of writing is infected with academic fads. An occasion like this, in my own hometown and in yours, serves—I have come to recognize and now recommend to you—as one more opportunity to consider how legitimate professional work can be more broadly and more flexibly defined for rhetoric and composition studies faculty.

Opinions shaped in popular media (as the spectacle of political correctness has shown) do most certainly affect college teachers, their academic advancement, and the public's perceptions of their careers regardless of how the professional literature presents the case for tenure and merit reviews. Thus, the argument of this chapter has four parts. First, those of us teaching in rhetoric and composition studies should write for a range of nonacademic audiences and in genres other than the scholarly article, academic essay, or monograph. Second, such writings do constitute a valid form of professional publication, especially for those of us who are writing program administrators. Third, there are plausible ways to evaluate such publishing activity to ensure that traditional tenure and promotion concerns are not cheapened. Fourth, even if the first three arguments prove to be persuasive, the nature and strangeness of nonacademic forums for publication will make it difficult for us to write for them, although we do offer some suggestions for widening our comfort zones in the milieu of nonacademic publishing.

WHY PUBLISH IN NONACADEMIC FORUMS?

Rhetoric and composition specialists should publish in nonacademic forums for two reasons. One is pedagogical, affecting both the classrooms in which we teach and the broader classrooms in the public sphere beyond the academy. The second reason is scholarly, as there are necessary kinds of knowledge that are produced only by writing for nonexpert audiences.

Lynn Bloom has written that "we teachers of writing should write literary nonfiction, assuming that that is what we teach" (143). While creative writing teachers publish fiction and poetry, Bloom thinks it odd, at least, that most advanced composition teachers restrict their publishing to academic articles in professional journals. Bloom values writing "belletristic nonfiction in a persona . . . that is our own" because it might engage "not only the mind but the heart" of readers, and because such writing could "enliven and enhance the genre, our teaching, and our profession. And we'd have more fun" (144).

We extend Bloom's argument by returning to the broader stance of her title, "Why Don't We Write What We Teach? And Publish It?" The assumption that "we teachers of writing" teach literary nonfiction is too narrow in these days of rhetorical and cultural studies. Yes, there has been a renewed interest in literary nonfiction, especially the essay, and Bloom may have described correctly the main focus of advanced composition courses as belletristic nonfiction. But what about those many courses in which argument is the primary focus? If we are having students write about public issues for various public audiences, should we not do so, too? Such writing may or may not be fun, to mention one of Bloom's justifications, but doing it can enhance teaching and the profession.

Recently, I taught freshman composition for the first time in the eight years since I became a writing program director (thus upholding the ironic tradition in large university writing programs that administrators rarely teach the courses they coordinate). During my absence from teaching English 101, I had observed hundreds of hours of 101 classes, and I had read thousands of pages of student essays and portfolios. But these were not *my* classes, not *my* students, and the confident advice I was accustomed to giving to TAs waned a bit in the bright fluorescent light of *my* MWF, 11:00 to 11:50 writing classroom.

A similar dislocation exists when we recommend to students writing that we do not occasionally do ourselves. A common tenet of composition teaching is that students should write for a variety of rhetorical situations or forums, from a variety of subject positions to readers similarly diverse, expecting different discourse conventions and different topics to be relevant or persuasive. And yet, the traditional, academic publication record expected for tenure and promotion in rhetoric and composition studies entails writing for a relatively constrained discourse community. Even keeping in mind the fact that English studies is anything but a unified and simple discourse community, still the act of writing as compositionist to other compositionists is qualitatively different from, say, writing as public citizen (or even compositionist) to parents outraged at whole language first grades or to members of the Montana Militia. (I am regularly amazed at how Letters to the Editor that I consider paragons of good sense and good will are misread or dismissed.)

Writing teachers at least occasionally ought to participate in the frustrations and difficulties that students experience. Writing beyond the academy offers such particular, even parallel, challenges. Even if writing program administrators (WPAs) do not regularly teach composition, they should practice a variety of writings for reasons of promoting informed pedagogies. Both explicitly and implicitly, WPAs help construct for classroom teachers what writing is, what writers do, and how writing should best be taught.

Nonacademic publication enhances teaching in ways even more subtle and profound than shaping the experiences and assumptions of teachers; it helps construct the environment in which writing programs exist. If there has ever been a time when writing programs have been able to ignore answering to anyone outside themselves, it surely is not the present. In these days of national economic competitiveness, of students as customers and education as commodity, of tenured radical PC-mongering humanist atheist Marxist professors making good money for a mere 9-to-15-hour-a-week job, various publics suspect that college writing teachers—or any college faculty, for that matter—do not truly have at heart the best interests of students and American society. Rarely do these publics openly seek to direct policies and practices in the writing program (although one may recall the fate of English 306 at Texas). Instead, these societal influences are diffuse, affecting everything from how education is funded, to what programs administrators choose to champion, to the kinds of attitudes that students bring to writing courses. Obviously, no writing program or classroom exists in splendid disinterested academic isolation.

Consider, briefly, three intersections of the public realm with college writing programs: staffing issues, colleagues' opinions, and students' attitudes and expectations. First, consider staffing issues. The decline in state support for higher education over the past 20 years makes it even less likely that lecturers or adjunct faculty (euphemistic names for limited-term and part-time instructors) will gain tenure-line positions in college composition classrooms.[3]

Second, consider colleagues' opinions. For most faculty members outside English departments, any sense of what is or should be happening in freshman composition comes from their own experiences as undergraduates and from popular representations, *qua* Will's, of a shallow touchy-feely curriculum, of barbaric deconstructionism, or of shamelessly politicized multiculturalism, all of which, they believe, have little to do with what a writing course ought to be.[4] Of course, composition studies is hardly alone in being defined for others by popular media. A longstanding avocation of mine has been reading popularized physics, astronomy, and biological sciences—the Quality Paperbook Book Club shaping my knowledge and beliefs far more than the Q section of the university library. The difference is my (perhaps misguided) sense that Stephen Jay Gould's writing, for example, has some standing among paleontologists, but that composition studies has no similar figures. Imagine Andrea Lunsford writing a monthly column about issues in rhetoric for—*Harper's*? *The New York Review of Books*?

A third example of how public spheres affect college writing programs is through the expectations and attitudes of students. What a writing class should be (and most certainly what it should not be—that is, indoctrination in political correctness) as well as what writing itself should be are expectations created in students through the popular media far more extensively than through other means. Thus, to some large extent, what writing teachers are able to do, and how, depends on the sense of writing that students bring to the classroom.

To say that teaching and writing and the teaching of writing occur only in the classroom or on campus is potentially to limit our effectiveness as teachers and scholars. Medical analogies applied to the teaching of writing trouble us—for example, the idea that students' errors should be diagnosed and cured. However, to see the place of teaching as only the classroom would be akin to a physician's dealing with patients only as they present themselves in the office, thereby forfeiting those larger public efforts beyond the physician's private domain (public health campaigns on smoking, cholesterol, or what have you) that, nonetheless, shape the environment in which medicine is practiced and health is understood.

Our argument, to summarize briefly, is that we stand to be better teachers if we write for nonacademic audiences because such practices allow us to be less complacent and rutted about writing and because we more overtly shape the environment in which teaching occurs.

CAN NONACADEMIC WRITING BE PROFESSIONAL DISCOURSE?

Traditionally, professional writing is distinguished from other writing, such as journalism, according to the specialized knowledge and expectations presumed of its readers. However much social constructivism has vexed such concepts as *an original contribution to knowledge*, we still count as the mark of the academic-working-as-academic a body of work that only a specialist could have produced (writing as research or writing as scholarship of discovery, according to Ernest Boyer's categories in *Scholarship Reconsidered*); work that, further, constitutes some extension of thinking on a problem or issue of interest to the profession. We know when such work counts because peers have accepted it as counting, and the sign of this acceptance is publication in the right kinds of journals or by the right university or academic presses. Nonacademic publications—appearing, by definition, outside such journals or presses—bear no such imprimaturs, yet.

These fairly obvious assertions seem less definitive after analysis, a fortunate situation that suggests that our publishing in public forums can be counted as professional discourse. Note up front that we are not arguing that faculties and departments making hiring, tenure, or promotion decisions should count anything written as professional discourse or that the very category of professional discourse should disappear. We judge a surgeon by her stitches in flesh, not linen, and we judge a lawyer by his performance before the bar, not the footlights. Our point is that we accept the value of some professional distinctions, and in the next section we offer some guidelines for making distinctions that count. However, our further point is that the boundaries between professional and nonprofessional discourse are porous ones, both in the features of such writings and in their effects—actual and potential—on academic disciplines. This becomes most true, especially in fields like rhetoric and composition studies, when we suspend the too-easy measure of where a given piece of writing has been published.

IF "YES, IT'S PROFESSIONAL DISCOURSE," THEN WHAT IS ITS "SCHOLARLY WORTH"?

The mere fact of being published does not make all writings of comparable length, say, equally meritorious. Therefore, if nonacademic publications are going to count toward tenure and promotion, then the academic professions—with rhetoric and composition studies faculty in the lead—will have to devise some new ways of counting. In relative terms, the terms in which one article or essay or editorial is deemed more significant than another of its kind, the problem is not a huge one. For academic publications, the twin axes of measure have been, traditionally, the prestige of the publication and peer review of the work itself. In absolute terms—in which realm exist such questions as "Does one *CCC* article equal a dozen newspaper guest commentaries, or what?"—the task is somewhat trickier.

Many traditional principles of scholarly worth can be applied to nonacademic publication. For example, publishing a book with a major nonacademic publishing house, such as Penguin, should at least carry more weight at the outset than a book published with a vanity press. An article in *Harper's* probably should be considered more prestigious than an article in the Bloomington *Pantagraph*. Many departments and institutions rate journals and presses as Category I, Category II, and so on, so it should be possible to establish locally meaningful categories for types of nonacademic publication.

In principle, having a publication accepted and published in *College Composition and Communication* is supposed to happen, and therefore to count fully, because the article has been determined by blind refereeing to be of sufficient merit; so must a version of peer review pertain to nonacademic publication, with a slight twist on tradition. For the most part, and whether out of faith or sloth, departments judging scholarly credentials are willing to assign much value to the place of publication, so that whether a tenure and promotion committee actually reads a particular article is less important than their knowing where the article has been published. The assumption is a reasonable one in many ways because it operates on the belief that the piece has already met the standards of expert peer review.

The same cannot be assumed of nonacademic publications. Editors of popular periodicals, however good they may be, are not necessarily experts (perhaps even by definition are never experts) in any given academic discipline, especially rhetoric and composition studies. What we propose, then, as a principle or a standard for evaluation, is a kind of peer-review-after-the-fact. Faculty members could submit nonacademic publications to academic peers and external evaluators to be read against their own knowledge of the field and questions such as:

- Is this writing consistent with current theory and research?
- How are the disciplines of rhetoric and composition studies and the teaching of writing furthered by such a piece's publication?
- To what extent would other professionals find this piece useful, perhaps as a reprint, even, in their own teaching or for circulation to audiences important to them?

HOW DO WE PUBLISH NONACADEMIC SCHOLARSHIP?

Perhaps more than others in rhetoric and composition, writing program administrators recognize the apparently transparent external realities that help shape course contents and pedagogies. They understand the relationships of teaching to scholarship to administration and how these, in turn, relate to broader concerns of public opinion, politics, and funding for education. And yet, direct discursive involvement in that external sphere is rare, usually restricted to Letters to the Editor after some troubling piece has been published.

There are two components to the dearth of public publications by those of us in composition studies. One is the lack of desire, spurred by the lack of incentives in a professional world in which tenure and promotion depend on refereed publications in academic forums. The other is a lack of access, as we do not just decide to publish, next month, an article in *Time* magazine in which we explain why sophistic rhetoric is the best theoretical basis for freshman composition. Charles Schuster has observed that many attempts by rhetoric and composition specialists to place articles on the field in national periodicals have failed. These have included his own efforts, as well as NCTE-sponsored ones.

Even if the desire exists to publish in a more accessible-to-the-public forum, in the spirit of Mike Rose's *Lives on the Boundary*, a Penguin paperback rather than a university press hardcover, the lack of clear

entree to such public forums may dampen that desire, in a self-perpetuating dynamic. Michael Berube analyzes the different impacts on the
public psyche of popular forums and representations versus academic
ones:

> And where [during the 1992 presidential campaign] the Clinton camp had
> its banks of faxes ready to flood print and TV media with instant rebuttals
> of Bush-Quayle claims, we [left academic intellectuals] had only quarterly
> journals in which we could conduct analyses of the PC wars on our own
> terms long after the specific charges had receded from public memory, long
> after the public image of loony-left humanities professors had been solidi-
> fied in national news media. (7)

It is ironic, of course, that we are writing about these issues in an
academic book, something even slower to publish and to circulate than
a quarterly journal.

Merit and merit alone will not determine whether an English professor's article gets accepted by the editor of a popular periodical. And slim
chances diminish further to the extent that academics neglect to consider how rules for entering nonacademic forums differ from, say, *College
English*. National magazines and periodicals live in a universe of query
letters and agents, of personal connections and packaging, of market-
ability to an audience of individuals who read not out of professional
obligation but because they choose to do so, perhaps in serious leisure.
We may be put off by what appears to be crass marketing rather than
letting the words speak for themselves, but these are not forums we have
created or controlled. Especially those who evaluate faculty publishing
in popular forums have to be willing to suspend their reservations that
behaving like a freelance writer is unbecoming and impure.

A wealth of publishing opportunities beyond national periodicals,
however, can be discovered for our writing, and if it may take some time
and concerted effort for writing teachers and scholars to earn their place
at the podium as public intellectuals, we ought not wait for the millen-
nium. One thing we can do immediately is write for local newspapers
and regional magazines. The easiest way to do this is occasionally to
write responses to issues impinging on the teaching of writing as they
are reported.

For example, at 8:30 on the morning I read Will's "Teach Johnny to
Write" column in my morning newspaper, I telephoned the Bloomington
Pantagraph's editorial page editor to inquire about writing a guest
column in response. I wanted a more visible and capacious forum than
"Letter to the Editor," and once I outlined my credentials and perspective, the editor was quick to agree. I delivered to him a 750-word
piece—and a black-and-white glossy photo—by 4:30 PM that same
afternoon.

Simultaneously, I published my article in a professional forum of sorts, copying it to the WPA listserve (WPA-L), and I suggested that other writing program administrators consider writing locally themselves, if they saw fit. A lively and productive discussion thread developed through July 1995, and at least one other writer, Jim Crosswhite, shared drafts of an article he wrote for an Oregon newspaper. Dennis Baron, another WPA-L user, succeeded in having a letter in response to Will's column published in the *Washington Post* itself.

The opportunities for this kind of responsive publication are endless. However, our profession is not well served by responding and publishing only when we are offended or incredulous. The rhetorical situation of response is one in which, at best, the writer is trying to reshape opinion once it has already been established and, at worst, one in which the writer consistently looks defensive. Probably, then, those pieces that can open up new issues for public discussion should be counted as more ambitious or more original contributions to knowledge. For example, Dennis Baron occasionally publishes *Chicago Sun Times* columns in which he discusses language issues for a broad readership, thus role playing a William Safire-like columnist whose ideas are informed by a particular scholarly and research perspective.

Consider, as well, the professional opening available for nonacademic publication (and, alas, unengaged, as far as we know), when President Clinton tried to draw connections between the Oklahoma City bombing and incendiary rhetoric in talk radio and elsewhere. The prevailing public reaction to the President's claim was that liberal Bill Clinton missed the fact that the bombing was a real event in the world, whereas talk radio was just words. Whether Clinton was justified in his remarks is less our concern here than the fact that, for a moment, there existed a public space in which relationships between words and deeds could be discussed. Rhetoric and composition specialists could have seized this occasion for writing to acquaint (and perhaps no more than acquaint) members of the public with a long tradition, going back to Gorgias, at least, in which language and physical action inhabit the same spheres. Such a piece would be more than merely responsive, if the writer took as his or her aim the articulation of ideas about language, rather than a defense of or an attack on President Clinton.

CONCLUSION

Surely, a scholar able to publish a popular article describing the relevance of Gorgias and Isocrates for modern political debates ought to have that work valued as professional within the academy. For beyond its intellectual substance—something departments and peers can ascertain—such an article could have much impact. "Cultural critique in the classroom," Edward Schiappa said in an address at the Rhetoric Society of America, "reaches a handful of students, whereas a column in the student newspaper reaches thousands, and a column in the hometown newspaper can reach even more" (22). And what of the potential impact of an essay in a magazine like *Atlantic Monthly*?

Recently, in just such a forum—the *New York Times Book Review*—University of Colorado history professor Patricia Nelson Limerick wrote:

> [U]niversities and colleges are currently embattled, distrusted by the public. . . . As distressing as this situation is, it provides the perfect setting and the perfect timing for declaring an end to scholarly publication as a series of guarded conversations between professors.
>
> The redemption of the university, especially in terms of the public's appraisal of the value of research and publication, requires all the writers who have something they want to publish to ask themselves the question: Does this have to be a closed communication, shutting out all but specialists . . . ? Or can this be an open communication, engaging specialists with new information and new thinking, but also offering an invitation to nonspecialists to learn from this study, to grasp its importance and, by extension, to find concrete reasons to see value in the work of the university? (23–24)

Similarly, from his lectern, Schiappa advised his audience of rhetoric and composition specialists: "Institutionally, we need to rethink how we evaluate faculty contributions and how we determine what *counts* as 'scholarship'. . . . Individually, we need to recognize that we do not live apart from the 'real' world 'outside' of academe" (25–26). By participating in that world, inviting nonspecialists to learn from our writing in nonacademic forums, we enact and enhance the value of our scholarship and professional discourse in composition studies.

NOTES

[1]George Will based his column on "Why Johnny Can't Write" by Heather Mac Donald in *The Public Interest*, a magazine the public can buy at the local Barnes and Noble, something we cannot say of *Rhetoric Review*.

[2]You will discover in the next sentence and subsequent paragraphs that we have wrestled with form and authorship during our collaboration on this essay. How can Doug Hesse's *I* speak on the page alone without cowriter (and rewriter) Barbara Gebhardt? Does editing individual voices to blend in *we* and *us* and *our* result in generalizing, homogenizing, or even excluding Doug's recent experience in public discourse (responding to the Will column)? His professional interest and expertise, as a scholar and a practitioner, in nonacademic publication so enlivened Doug's initial draft that rewriting for homogeneity seemed certain to Barbara to lessen the chapter's substance. So Doug's singular *I* remains, speaking individually, sin-

gly—even in passages constructed (or reconstructed) jointly—along with the collective (editorial? authorial?) plural of the profession and our collaborative *we*.

[3]For all the furor the Wyoming Resolution caused, even within writing programs and English departments, that document still preached to the choir. The likelihood of its goals being substantially achieved depends not only on right thinking within the academy, but also on the convictions and actions of parishioners beyond.

[4]One of the achievements of writing across the curriculum has been to create an occasion for compositionists to share theoretical or research knowledge directly with colleagues in other departments. Still, most faculty know about the humanities generally and about writing specifically more through journalists' and popular media representations than through direct professional contacts.

WORKS CITED

Berube, Michael. *Public Access: Literary Theory and American Cultural Politics*. New York: Verso, 1994.

Bloom, Lynn Z. "Why Don't We Write What We Teach? And Publish It?" *Composition Theory for the Postmodern Classroom*. Ed. Gary A. Olson and Sidney I. Dobrin. Albany: State U of New York P, 1994. 143–58.

Hesse, Douglas. "Writing: College Courses Are Driven by Professionalism." *Pantagraph* [Bloomington, IL] 17 July 1995: A7.

Limerick, Patricia Nelson. "Dancing with Professors: The Trouble with Academic Prose." *New York Times Book Review* 31 Oct. 1993: 3, 23–24.

Mac Donald, Heather. "Why Johnny Can't Write." *The Public Interest* No. 120 (Summer 1995): 3–13.

Schiappa, Edward. "Intellectuals and the Place of Cultural Critique." *Rhetoric, Cultural Studies and History: Selected Papers from the 1994 Conference of the Rhetoric Society of America*. Ed. John Frederick Reynolds. Mahwah, NJ: Lawrence Erlbaum Associates, 1995. 21–27.

Schuster, Charles I. Telephone conversation. 20 July 1995.

Will, George F. "Teach Johnny to Write." *Washington Post* 2 July 1995: C7.

4 Writing Administration as Scholarship and Teaching

Duane H. Roen
Arizona State University

Each fall as I peruse the rhetoric and composition advertisements in MLA's *Job-Information List* and the *Chronicle of Higher Education*, I see ads similar to this:

> Assistant professor of English (tenure track) and writing program director. Composition theorist to teach writing and administer freshman writing program. Summer duties for additional pay.

The main problem with such an ad is that it sets the stage for a drama whose main character is likely to become a Joan of Arc of writing administration. Everyone may admire the lead player's lofty goals and perseverance. But very few members of Dr. Arc's promotion and tenure committee—who will be looking for excellence in scholarship and teaching—will find that her significant administrative work warrants tenure.

For this reason, I always advise graduate students and untenured faculty to postpone any commitment to writing program administration. Unfortunately, the realities of the job market force many untenured faculty members into administrative positions—the compromising positions that Charles Schuster describes all too vividly in "The Politics of Promotion." Too frequently, I get phone calls from former graduate students, relatively new assistant professors, who begin conversations something like:

> Duane, I know you always told us not to do administration until after tenure, but they really need me to direct composition. There's no one else to do it. How should I negotiate the position?

I try—and fail—to dissuade the caller. Then we discuss strategies for negotiating assurances that their work will lead to tenure and promotion, as well as annual merit salary increases.

Until composition studies matures enough—or until the politics of the profession Jim Slevin has described so well improve enough—that untenured writing faculty do not have to take on the work of martyrs, we need to help department chairs, personnel committees, and deans understand that being a writing program administrator involves much teaching and scholarship. WPAs constantly teach writing instructors about the nexus of composition theory and practice. On most campuses, they do more than anyone else to prepare the reflective practitioners Donald Schon describes. They do this in weekly group meetings, individual conferences, and even in seemingly casual coffee-room conversation. To do this teaching of other teachers, WPAs must know the scholarship in the field well—well enough to translate it into application. And because WPAs interact with so many other faculty, in the English department and beyond it, they must try to stay current with scholarship in a fairly wide range of disciplines—composition, rhetoric, literature, literary theory, linguistics, psychology, sociology, philosophy, anthropology, education. Their familiarity with scholarship in these fields seldom leads to long lists of refereed articles and books, but it does result in curriculum revisions, course descriptions, and teacher-training outlines, as well as in the hundreds of reports, memos, and letters that they write each year.

Because university faculty members and administrators so often fail to see the teaching and scholarly functions of writing program administration, those of us who consult on program evaluation and write supporting letters must explain those functions. This is my intention for the pages that follow. I describe some of the scholarly and teaching activities in which writing program administrators engage as they perform their normal duties. I try to make careful distinctions between administrators' duties and senior faculty members' duties, although the two are sometimes difficult to distinguish for senior faculty serving as program administrators. I also try to cover a range of administrative positions within writing programs, for in my experience, nearly every writing program faculty member performs some administrative or at least quasi-administrative roles. My vehicle for doing all of this will be a sort of case study of Hanna, whose history of administrative work loosely parallels my own.

HANNA: A CASE STUDY

Second-Year Assistant Professor

During the second year after finishing her degree, Hanna agrees to serve as a mentor to first-year teaching assistants. The mentoring of first-year

TAs can have many different forms, but in Hanna's program, each group of five new TAs works with a mentor, whose responsibilities include planning and participating in a late-summer, week-long workshop preparing assistants to begin teaching the first-semester course; meeting each week with TAs for two hours to discuss composition theory and practice, program practices, and classroom experiences; visiting each assistant's classroom two or more times each semester; reviewing each assistant's written responses to at least two full sets of students' papers; writing end-of-semester evaluations for all mentored TAs.

In response to practical questions during any given weekly meeting, phone call, or office visit, Hanna may need to outline some theory and practice that focuses on engaging students in several of the canons or divisions of rhetoric (invention, arrangement, and style); responding to students' writing; orchestrating small-group discussion; employing ethical, logical, and pathetic proofs; and introducing students to writing-to-learn strategies. To do all of this well, Hanna needs to be familiar with a great body of work, ranging from Aristotle's *Rhetoric* to contemporary works of composition theory and pedagogy.

Hanna is granted released time from teaching to perform what her department considers quasi-administrative duties, although most of the work involves teaching. The work assignment creates some anxiety for Hanna because she discovers that working with five new TAs demands more time than teaching the section from which she had been released. That, she realizes, means less time for what counts most to the department: scholarship. In the eyes of some promotion and tenure committee members, Hanna's work does not count for much because it does not generate lots of credit hours. Someone needs to help these committee members understand that Hanna's work makes it possible for TAs to deliver—with greater confidence and competence—instruction to hundreds of fee-paying students.

Fourth-Year Assistant Professor

In her fourth year out of graduate school, Hanna (who has not yet learned the art of declining invitations to do more work) agrees to direct the second-semester composition course, a course in which students write about texts, typically literary texts. This assignment requires that she orchestrate the mentoring for all TAs, new and experienced. That means that she plans and chairs all meetings for the six mentors of new TAs, as well as the four mentors of experienced TAs. She is responsible for constructing or revising the model syllabus, on which all teachers of the course pattern their own syllabi.

In addition to all that Hanna needed to know to serve as a TA mentor, the work requires her to understand Louise Rosenblatt's version of reader-response theory, the pedagogical underpinning for the course. She needs to be able to discuss with ease *Literature As Exploration* and *The Reader, the Text, the Poem*, and, because some TAs will know other versions of reader response, Hanna needs to be able to explain (i.e., justify) the use of Rosenblatt's version rather than the ones offered by Fish, Bleich, Holland, or Iser. Of course, TAs all will expect her to discuss their questions about other ways, besides reader response, of working with literary texts. And since TAs, being an intellectually curious lot, will have questions about the intellectual traditions that gave rise to reader-response theory, Hanna needs to be prepared to discuss the Sophists, phenomenology, and social constructionism. She will be well equipped for such discussions if she is familiar with work in psychology, sociology, philosophy, anthropology, and the history of science. Clearly, Hanna must be a scholar-teacher just to articulate the goals of the course.

Achieving Tenure

In May of her sixth year, Hanna learns that she has been granted tenure and promotion. The news means that she will fret much less than she has for the past half decade. But the news is tainted by some of what Hanna learns through the campus grapevine.

The happy news is that her department's promotion and tenure committee voted unanimously to recommend tenure. The committee's full professors, all literary scholars, listened to the other committee members, two associate professors in rhetoric and composition, who eloquently argued that Hanna's research was first-rate. They also persuaded the senior committee members that Hanna's administrative responsibilities involved much teaching and much scholarship, most of which led to effective mentoring rather than publishing. So far, so good.

But Hanna learns that the rest of the process was rocky. The college committee, half a dozen textual scholars from the modern languages, voted unanimously to recommend denial of tenure. They noted that Hanna had not been as prolific as other scholars coming up for tenure and that most of her publications have multiple authors. They further noted that her publications deal with composition, sometimes even focusing on students' unbelletristic texts. Not many names of dead males of European descent appear in her lists of works cited. Pretty low-brow stuff. Hardly what one would call real scholarship.

When the university committee received Hanna's materials, it discussed her case at length. It was lucky for Hanna that some of the committee members had read her publications carefully and that some of the members had been responsible for the kind of graduate assistant mentoring that Hanna had done. This committee voted unanimously to recommend a positive decision on tenure.

When the provost received the file, she was baffled, never having seen a file where each committee reversed the decision of the preceding one. She discussed the matter with the university committee, which helped her understand the politics of the case. The provost subsequently granted Hanna tenure. Hanna's future is secure, but she is disturbed that the college committee had so misread her work.

Newly Tenured Associate Professor

During her first year after tenure Hanna hardly has time to catch her breath. The department chair, recognizing Hanna's administrative skills, asks her to direct the graduate program in rhetoric and composition. Before accepting the job, she consults some senior faculty members for guidance. They advise that taking the position would be a good career move. Hanna accepts the job.

Hanna is excited about the work, but she worries that she will not have time to publish enough to earn promotion to full professor in six or seven years. Hanna does not mind all of the paper-pushing that her new job requires, and she loves the many opportunities to mentor graduate students. She regularly advises each of the 60 students in the program about course selection, exams, assistantships, fellowships, and the policies of the program, department, and graduate school. She attends endless workshops to learn all that she needs to know to serve graduate students well. She also develops a series of 26 weekly professional development workshops, treating topics such as writing for publication, the politics of the profession, surviving graduate school, preparing conference proposals, and searching for jobs. Further, she organizes a weekly series in which graduate students present papers that they are preparing for publication. To do this work well, Hanna needs to stay abreast of work in many areas within rhetoric and composition, as well as English studies more broadly.

For this, Hanna is released from teaching one section each semester, but she quickly discovers that the work consumes nearly as much time as teaching two sections. She now needs to be available for advising during the summer. She earns supplementary compensation for the summer commitment, but again she worries that her administrative work is taking time away from publication. She further worries that her frequent scholarly collaborations, which she considers mentoring, will earn the ire of the college committee when she again subjects herself to the promotion process. She fully appreciates Mary Belenky's observation, shared in an interview with Evelyn Ashton-Jones and Dene Kay Thomas, that collaboration requires greater commitments of time and intellectual energy than single authorship does. But she realizes that those who will sit in judgment of her work hold a very different view of scholarly publishing.

Full Professor

After five years as an associate professor, Hanna leaves her institution to direct a major writing program. The new institution promotes her to the rank of full professor as part of the hiring package. Central administrators at her new school wisely understand the need for department and program administrators to work without worrying about promotion.

Hanna finds her new job interesting and challenging. A typical day includes meetings with program teachers, a few students, and a dean or department chair. She is expected to represent the program on numerous college and university committees. She writes an endless stream of letters, memos, reports, and e-mail notes. She participates in some campus event at least one evening each week—sometimes as many as four evenings a week. Time to write for publication has become, for Hanna, one of life's great luxuries.

Here is a facsimile of one day in Hanna's calendar:

9:00–9:45	Discuss teacher portfolio evaluation with committee
10:00–11:00	Help History faculty construct writing assignments
11:15–11:55	Meet with development officer and Director of Summer Sessions to discuss grant proposal
12:00–12:55	Brown-bag discussion of publishing opportunities
1:00–1:25	Meet with coordinator of new TA training
1:30–1:55	Meet with dean to discuss space needs
2:00–2:25	Discuss student's complaint about course
2:30–3:30	Meet with college committee on the writing-intensive course planning
4:00–5:00	Conduct university writing-to-learn workshop
5:30–7:00	Attend Graduate School working dinner (re: mentoring strategies)

At Hanna's 9:00 AM meeting with the committee that evaluates teachers' portfolios, she charges the committee with the task of revising the procedures to make them more formative, supportive, and meaningful for instructors who want to develop professionally. In the course of the discussion, Hanna draws on her knowledge of portfolio construction, portfolio evaluation, and teacher evaluation more generally. Further, she draws on many of her rhetorical skills to persuade the committee to shift its emphasis from mostly summative to mostly formative evaluation. She listens patiently to objections and responds to each. By the end of the meeting, she has convinced the committee to consult widely with other instructors to engage in dissensus to develop consensus for change.

At 10:00 AM, Hanna meets with some History Department professors and graduate assistants to help them develop effective writing assignments for the introductory history course. Hanna works to help these teachers understand some principles that guide the construction of writing assignments. From the outset, the teachers ask what the literature says about writing assignments. Hanna, to raise her logos to the occasion, talks about a range of work, from Aphthonius' *Progymnasmata* to Moffett's theory and sequence of assignments. Some of the history professors, not surprisingly, ask Hanna about bits and pieces of the history of writing instruction. Her responses resemble excerpts from Murphy's collection, *A Short History of Writing Instruction*. She also draws upon her knowledge of learning theory and cognition during the meeting.

At 11:00 AM, Hanna meets with the Director of Summer Sessions and a development officer for two purposes: to refine plans for a proposed summer writing-across-the-curriculum institute for public school students and teachers, and to devise strategies for finding a named donor for the institute. During the course of the discussion, Hanna helps her coplanners understand the diversity that exists in WAC programs across the country. She again draws on her knowledge of the field, in this case citing historical information that David Russell presents in his review of college writing over 120 years. When asked about practical activities that they might use with students and teachers, Hanna describes some of those demonstrated in Ann Gere's collection, activities that focus more on writing to learn than learning to write.

At noon, Hanna hosts one of her weekly brown-bag professional development workshops, this one dealing with publishing opportunities in rhetoric and composition. In attendance are more than a dozen graduate students, several part-time instructors, and a first-year assistant professor. Hanna comes to the session with a list of some 40 journals that publish work in the field, NCTE's list of state affiliates' addresses, some sample calls for manuscripts, and several information-for-authors pages from better known journals such as *Rhetoric Review, College Composition and Communication,* and *Journal of Advanced Composition.* Hanna describes the focus of nearly a fourth of the journals on the long list, explains how to use the affiliate list to find the many state journals in the country, does a close reading of each sample call for manuscripts and each page giving information to authors. As she speaks, participants frequently interrupt her to ask questions. At the end of the session, she invites everyone to sign up for a slot in the weekly series in which authors may share their manuscripts-in-process. She explains how she and everyone who attends reads each manuscript and offers oral feedback during the session and written feedback at the end. She adds that she will always suggest suitable outlets for the manuscripts.

After the lunchtime workshop, Hanna holds a short meeting with the faculty member who coordinates the mentoring activities for new TAs. As the two of them begin planning the schedule for the next year, they list topics for the weekly new-TA workshops, appropriate theoretical and pedagogical readings for those topics, and activities to demonstrate teaching strategies that assistants may use in the two courses that TAs will teach next year. They also assess the strengths of program faculty to begin the process for selecting the mentors for new TAs. Essentially, Hanna and her colleague are beginning to plan a syllabus for the course of study in which the first-year teachers will engage; their planning does not differ substantially from the planning that any teachers do when they construct courses.

During her 1:30 PM meeting with the dean, Hanna argues for additional space for the writing center, which has had inadequate housing since it began operation in the late 1980s. When the dean asks about other writing centers, Hanna is able to sketch functions and floor plans of centers described in a collection Joyce Kinkead and Jeanette Harris edited. In response to other questions, Hanna explains how the writing center, with adequate space, could do more to engage students in discussions of writing, of writerly talk. She also explains how the center could do more to support the WAC work of faculty across campus.

A first-year student is waiting for Hanna when she returns to her office at 2:00 PM. He has come to see her to complain about his writing course. Hanna quickly comes to realize that the student's complaint is not about the course or the teacher, per se. Rather, he considers himself a competent writer, not one in need of further formal training in writing. Hanna engages the student in Socratic dialogue, asking a series of questions, at times offering her own insights as a writer and a scholar of writing, until the student comes to acknowledge that there may be room for him to grow as a writer. When the student mentions that his field is electrical engineering, which he claims does not require any writing, Hanna talks about some of the scholarship that indicates that electrical engineers actually write quite a bit as they do their work.

At 2:30 PM, Hanna attends the weekly meeting of the College of Arts and Sciences' Committee on Writing-Intensive Courses, of which Hanna is a member. At this week's meeting, Hanna argues to keep the focus of each course on the disciplinary content, making writing a tool for learning and communicating about that content. Writing, she convinces her colleagues from six other departments, should support the goals of each course, not become *the* goal of any writing-intensive course. She argues against mechanistic writing requirements in the courses. She also comes to the meeting with a draft of a statement suggesting ways in which the writing program and the writing center can support faculty members as they develop and teach the courses. The statement also includes a section arguing that central administration will need to find funds for this support. During the meeting, Hanna explains principles of writing instruction, writing to learn, peer-group work, responding to students' writing, revising as distinct from editing, and the functions of the writing center. As has been the case so often today, Hanna has to draw on her knowledge of theory and pedagogy to educate her colleagues. At times, they readily accept her insights, but they also offer some refutation.

At 4:00 PM, at the invitation of the Dean of the Graduate School, Hanna conducts a university-wide TA workshop on writing to learn. Although one hour is less time than she would like for such a workshop, Hanna has done enough workshops (more than 80) to know how to introduce some generative activities, ones that effectively demonstrate principles of using writing-to-learn course material. On this occasion, she uses an overhead projector to show a dozen or so examples of student writing that engaged students in course content. As she describes the kinds of learning going on in each example, she encourages members of the audience to suggest how they might modify the activities to fit their own courses and subject matter. Hanna also answers several dozen audience questions, many of which focus on ways of responding to such student writing. Hanna offers suggestions for responding in ways that generate further thinking. At the end of the session, the Dean asks Hanna to use her workshop material to write a chapter for a book that he is editing. The audience will be TAs across the disciplines.

At 5:30 PM, Hanna attends a Graduate School working dinner to discuss strategies for mentoring graduate students. She participates in a 90-minute discussion with graduate students, faculty, and campus administrators. Hanna's contributions include descriptions of her weekly professional development workshops and the weekly sessions in which drafts of graduate students' scholarly manuscripts are discussed.

PRINCIPLES FOR PROMOTION AND TENURE

Hanna's case illustrates the need for principles establishing fair working conditions for WPAs, as well as guidelines for evaluating their work for annual merit review and, especially, promotion and tenure. But as Edward White wrote in a Writing Program Administration online conversation, developing such principles and guidelines is not easy:

> We don't have a guideline for evaluating WPAs because we lack a common definition of what a WPA does. At many campuses, the WPA is a temporary

casual position, filled by a literature person slumming, who does relatively little and is less informed about composition than many of the part-timers. At the other end of the spectrum, we have WPAs who are full-time administrators, with assistants and staffs, running a major program that includes TA training, faculty development, writing across the curriculum, portfolio assessments, and the like. Perhaps the only aspect of the job that everyone has in common is that the WPA "speaks" for writing on campus and has some responsibility for writing instruction and standards. How could a single document, of whatever scope, reflect such a diverse reality?

David Schwalm, former Director of Composition at Arizona State University, indicates in the same WPA online conversation that his dean asked him to write his own job description because he—as is the case with many WPAs—had recreated the job. Schwalm argues that "WPAs should define their jobs, set goals in each area (research, teaching service, administration), and identify measures of success." Of particular relevance to the discussion here is the way in which Schwalm and his institution defined his research:

> I had a special provision in my research/scholarship section: in addition to articles and conference papers, I stipulated that internal research reports, research manifested in the curriculum, placement, or assessment, preparation of the annual composition guide—scholarship manifested in the program rather than in typical publication—should be credited.

Hanna's case demonstrates the wisdom of adopting Schwalm's provision. In addition to all of the face-to-face meetings in which Hanna's synthesis of scholarship plays a role, her hundreds of pages of memos, letters, reports, plans, and proposals represent the same sort of scholarly activity. (For me, such activity results in 400 to 600 pages a year—equivalent in length, if not in coherence, to a book manuscript.) With so many written products growing out of their administrative duties, Christine Hult is right in suggesting in "The Scholarship of Administration," that WPAs save and organize their work in administrative portfolios. Beyond such written products, Richard Bullock has argued eloquently, the work of writing program administrators should be treated as scholarship, broadly defined:

> [I]f the WPA's role is to innovate, to erect and maintain a program that embodies and tests theoretical principles and monitors the results over several years, that activity is scholarly and should be recognized as such, and the traditional disciplinary view restricting scholarship to written publication must broaden to include performance in the artistic or theatrical sense. (17–18)

Those interested in fair evaluation standards and working conditions for writing administrators can turn to "The Portland Resolution," drafted in 1990 by Christine Hult, David Jolliffe, Kathleen Kelly, Dana Mead, and Charles Schuster. The document (a revision of which was accepted by the Executive Committee of the Council of Writing Program Administrators in 1992) offers sensible guidelines that focus on conditions conducive to "Quality Writing Program Administration" (89), as well as good suggestions about creating job descriptions for WPAs and evaluating writing administrators.

Written promotion and tenure guidelines should echo job descriptions for those performing administrative duties. At Syracuse University, for example, the Writing Program's "Promotion and Tenure Guidelines" clearly acknowledge that most writing faculty perform such duties: "Every faculty member is therefore provided with some released time for administrative duties, and all candidates for tenure and promotion are evaluated in this category for the quality of intellectual work and for academic/professional citizenship" (6). The key words here are "the quality of intellectual work," for they point to an important criterion for evaluating administrative efforts. The quality of administrative work mirrors the quality of its intellectual underpinnings.

Treating administrative work as teaching and as scholarship is consistent with Ernest Boyer's call in *Scholarship Reconsidered* to blur the boundaries that have for too long occupied the academy and preoccupied those who call themselves academicians. Rather than view scholarship as something distinct from service, teaching, and administration, Boyer argues convincingly that scholarship must be defined broadly enough to encompass the full range of academic work as it serves not only the academy but also society more generally.

In Boyer's scheme, the scholarly work of the professoriate has four interrelated functions: discovery, integration, application, and teaching. The scholarship of discovery is essentially what academics traditionally consider research to be—investigation for its own sake. Hanna, like other writing program administrators, has done plenty of this work, but as she performs administrative duties, she does more scholarship of integration, application, and teaching.

Boyer defines the scholarship of integration as "making connections across the disciplines, placing the specialties in larger context, illuminating data in a revealing way, often educating nonspecialists, too" (18). Hanna's work with faculty on writing across the curriculum probably best represents the scholarship of integration, but many of her other projects also embody this kind of "connectedness" and "multidisciplinary work" (Boyer 19).

Boyer's third category, the scholarship of application, best captures the essence of Hanna's administrative work—and that of writing directors at large. Here the scholar asks, "How can knowledge be responsibly applied to consequential problems?" and "Can social problems *themselves* define an agenda for scholarly investigation?" (21). We need not define *social* that broadly, because writing administrators usually are thinking about literacy, a social concern. What may be most important to consider, though, is Boyer's observation that "[n]ew intellectual understandings can arise out of the very act of application. . . . In such activities as these, theory and practice vitally interact, and one renews the other" (23).

Promotion and tenure guidelines would better serve students, institutions, and society if they contained language like that. Stressing the interaction of theory and practice within application would make the evaluation of writing administrators more accurate and fair, and it would make administrative work more attractive to those who are best qualified to do it.

ACKNOWLEDGMENTS

I thank Richard Gebhardt, Barbara Genelle Smith Gebhardt, and Maureen Roen for helpful comments on earlier versions of this chapter.

WORKS CITED

Aphthonius. *Progymnasmata*. Trans. Ray Nadeau. *Speech Monographs* 19 (1952): 264–85. Rpt. in *Readings from Classical Rhetoric*. Ed. Patricia P. Matsen, Philip Rollinson, and Marion Sousa. Carbondale: Southern Illinois U P, 1990. 267–88.

Ashton-Jones, Evelyn, and Dene Kay Thomas. "Composition, Collaboration, and Women's Ways of Knowing: A Conversation with Mary Belenky." *Journal of Advanced Composition* 10 (1990): 275–92.

Bleich, David. *Subjective Criticism*. Baltimore: Johns Hopkins U P, 1978.

Boyer, Ernest L. *Scholarship Reconsidered: Priorities of the Professoriate*. Princeton: Carnegie Foundation for the Advancement of Teaching, 1990.

Bullock, Richard H. "When Administration Becomes Scholarship: The Future of Writing Program Administration." *Writing Program Administration* 11 (1987): 13–18.

Fish, Stanley. *Is There a Text in This Class?* Cambridge: Harvard U P, 1980.

Gere, Ann Ruggles, ed. *Roots in the Sawdust: Writing to Learn Across the Disciplines*. Urbana: NCTE, 1985.

Holland, Norman. *The Dynamics of Literary Response*. New York: Norton, 1975.

Hult, Christine A. "The Scholarship of Administration." *Resituating Writing: Constructing and Administering Writing Programs*. Eds. Joseph Janangelo and Kristine Hansen. Portsmouth: Boynton/Cook-Heinemann, 1995. 119–31.

Hult, Christine, David Jolliffe, Kathleen Kelly, Dana Mead, and Charles Schuster. "The Portland Resolution." *Writing Program Administration* 16 (1992): 88–94.

Iser, Wolfgang. *The Act of Reading: A Theory of Aesthetic Response*. Baltimore: Johns Hopkins UP, 1978.

———. *The Implied Reader*. Baltimore: Johns Hopkins U P, 1974.

Kinkead, Joyce A., and Jeanette G. Harris, eds. *Writing Centers in Context: Twelve Case Studies*. Urbana: NCTE, 1993.

Moffett, James. *Active Voice: A Writing Program Across the Curriculum*. Portsmouth: Boynton-Cook, 1981.

——. *Teaching the Universe of Discourse*. Boston: Houghton Mifflin, 1968.

Murphy, James J., ed. *A Short History of Writing Instruction fromAncient Greece to Twentieth-Century America*. Davis: Hermagoras, 1990.

Rosenblatt, Louise. *Literature As Exploration*. New York: D. Appleton-Century, 1938. Rpt. New York: MLA, 1983.

——. *The Reader, the Text, the Poem: The Transactional Theory of the Literary Work*. Carbondale: Southern Illinois U P, 1978.

Russell, David. *Writing in the Academic Disciplines, 1870–1990*. Carbondale: Southern Illinois UP, 1991.

Schon, Donald A. *Educating the Reflective Practitioner: Toward a New Design for Teaching and Learning in the Professions*. San Francisco: Jossey-Bass, 1991.

Schuster, Charles I. "The Politics of Promotion." *The Politics of Writing Instruction: Postsecondary*. Ed. Richard Bullock and John Trimbur. Portsmouth: Boynton/Cook-Heinemann, 1991. 85–95.

Schwalm, David E. Writing Program Administration electronic dialogue contribution. 6 July 1994.

Slevin, James F. "The Politics of the Profession." *An Introduction to Composition Studies*. Ed. Erika Lindemann and Gary Tate. New York: Oxford UP, 1991. 135–59.

White, Edward. Writing Program Administration electronic dialogue contribution. 6 July 1994.

Writing Program. *Promotion and Tenure Guidelines*. Syracuse: Syracuse University, 1989.

5 Scholarship, Tenure, and Composition Studies in the Two-Year College

Keith Kroll
Kalamazoo Valley Community College

Barry Alford
Mid Michigan Community College

The issues of scholarship, promotion, and tenure within composition studies have very different meanings for two-year college writing faculties than for writing faculties at four-year institutions. To be sure, some two-year college faculty, particularly those teaching at two-year branch campuses of four-year institutions, face similar issues with respect to scholarship, promotion, and tenure as those discussed in other chapters in this book. But as we hope this chapter makes clear, most two-year college writing faculty members work in departments—typically not English departments—and at institutions where composition occupies a very different social and pedagogical space than it does in four-year institutions.

Given these circumstances, tenure and promotion review in the two-year colleges presents a different constellation of issues. Even when the terms sound familiar—research, publication, teaching, scholarship—the focus in the two-year colleges is different from that in senior institutions. Two-year colleges have to produce standards for tenure and review that reinforce their commitment to teaching without succumbing to the lore of their institutions. They must begin to construct a professional discourse that recognizes the locality of their practice without severing all ties to a broader sense of theory and practice in composition studies. In short, two-year college faculty members must reinvent and reimagine their own place in both their institution and their profession.

ENGLISH, COMPOSITION STUDIES, AND THE TWO-YEAR COLLEGE

Most two-year college writing faculty do not teach composition in what would traditionally be considered an English department. In her study of two-year college writing programs, Helon Raines found that "seventy-five percent of schools . . . indicated that English . . . is a part of a larger department or division" (154). It is more likely that writing faculty spend their careers teaching in Humanities, Communications Arts, Liberal Arts, and Arts and Sciences departments. What's in a name? For two-year college writing faculty, the answer is quite a lot. For example, one of the more visible and important issues in the English profession, particularly for composition teachers, concerns the relationship between composition and literature, what Peter Elbow describes at one point in *What Is English?* as "the damaging warfare between literature and writing at the college level" (95). Two-year college writing faculties would be hard-pressed to locate themselves within this debate, except perhaps as outsiders looking in. The debate between composition and literature in this form has rarely, if ever, been considered at two-year colleges, and for one simple reason: literature has never had central status in the two-year college English department as it has in the four-year college and university English department.

Teaching writing has historically been the main work—for some faculty it has been the only work—of two-year college English faculty. In the period before 1960, the *Junior College Journal* (perhaps the best source for studying the early history of the junior college movement) published a number of essays concerning the teaching of writing, particularly as it related to terminal versus transfer writing courses. Only an occasional essay concerned literature. In describing the rapid expansion of two-year colleges after 1960, one faculty member noted: "We knew, most of us, that we were probably going to teach composition, and very little but composition, for the rest of our professional lives" (McPherson 93).

Although two-year college faculties who teach writing continue to be trained primarily in literary studies (Kroll 40–41)—a prime example of literature's dominant position in university and four-year college English departments—they teach mostly writing courses. In one study of English faculty, 84% of full-time faculty and 92% of part-time faculty reported that their teaching responsibilities were "leaning toward or very heavy in writing" (Kroll 40). This is not to suggest that two-year colleges do not offer literature courses—a vast majority do (VanderKelen 35)—or that two-year college English faculty are not interested in teaching literature courses beyond those associated with a second-semester composition course (e.g., introduction to literature or writing about literature)—they are. Literature courses rarely, if ever, go unassigned in class schedules, and it is not uncommon for English faculty to teach a literature course as overload beyond a typical four-or-five-writing-courses-per-term teaching schedule. In many ways, literature courses have become somewhat of a luxury for two-year college English faculty. Ultimately, however, teaching writing has always been, and probably will always be, the primary work of two-year college English faculty.

Despite this almost exclusive focus on composition, the fact that two-year colleges enrolled over 50% of all first-year college students and over 45% of all undergraduates in 1993 (National, "Fall"), and the fact that in 1991 over 1.3 million students were enrolled in two-year college writing courses (Cohen and Ignash 54), two-year college writing faculty members have remained all but invisible in the histories and studies of composition and rhetoric, including recent works like Berlin's *Rhetoric and Reality*, North's *The Making of Knowledge in Composition*, Elbow's *What Is English?* and Miller's *Textual Carnivals*. This is not to suggest that the histories and issues discussed in these books are irrelevant to two-year college writing faculty members, because they are—or should be.[1] It is to suggest, however, that composition theory has been largely site neutral.

As composition theorists begin to move away from the process model of writing and toward theories that can variously be referred to as *rhetorical, pragmatic,* or *semiotic,* the uneasy sense that composition is an intensely local construction calls a big-tent definition of the field into question. In this climate, the differences between both the practitioners and the institutions that constitute composition and composition studies are more important. With the exception of Ira Shor's work, for example, *Critical Teaching and Everyday Life,* little important work in composition has considered the differences between two- and four-year institutions. What Shor calls the "budget colleges" (3) have been staffed by faculties who, when they have had any training in composition, were trained to replicate, without thinking, both the structure and assumptions of freshmen courses at four-year colleges. These books have had little to say about adult learners, the social fragmentation of the two-year college, or the culture shock that many writing teachers find when they leave the safe haven of graduate school for teaching positions in the two-year college. Even work in basic writing has failed to shed much light on the textbook-centered and exercise-driven practices of most basic writing programs. This is not to lay blame only on the doorstep of four-year college composition faculty and scholars. The two-year college and its faculty are culpable in this invisibility and need to take an active role in reflecting on, and redirecting, their practices.

The Culture of the Community College

Various reasons can be given for the comparative invisibility of two-year college faculty in academia, but the primary reason is the two-year college's original connection to high schools, where the emphasis—at least in theory—has always been on teaching. From the outset, junior colleges were connected both physically and philosophically to high schools. In describing the very early years of the junior college, a recent book noted that:

> [m]any junior colleges had started as high school extensions, and their representative leaders felt very strongly that the junior college should not separate in its funding and administration from the parent high school. In effect, they regarded junior college education as secondary, not higher education. (Witt et al. 79)

Furthermore, as Cohen and Brawer write in *The American Community College,* "beginning with the earliest two-year colleges and continuing well into the 1960s, instructors tended to have prior teaching experience in the secondary schools" (69). Only in more recent years have two-year college faculty members come directly from graduate programs or teaching positions at two- or four-year institutions. And, in many respects, secondary schools and secondary school teachers remain the reference group for both two-year college administrators and faculty.

Regardless of one's beliefs concerning the growth and development of two-year colleges, one fact is indisputable: Two-year colleges were established as teaching institutions to the virtual exclusion of faculty research and scholarship as they are viewed at the four-year college and university. As an early prominent leader of the two-year college movement described it:

> It is very doubtful whether pure research of the university type should be strongly encouraged on the part of junior college instructors. Such is likely to consume time, thought, and nerve energy which is better expended on teaching and student contacts. (Eells 334)

Caught between an academic culture rooted in a high school model and a traditional model of research and scholarship defined by four-year colleges and universities, two-year college faculty members never have been given sufficient time for engaging in research and scholarship, nor have they ever developed their own model of research and scholarship appropriate for their own situation. As a consequence of the two-year college's overwhelming emphasis on teaching, two-year college faculties have rarely played an active role in their respective disciplines as knowledge-makers. This is not surprising since, according to Stephen North, "the whole thrust of the academic reform movement was to remove authority over knowledge from the hands of those whose main source of such authority was their practice" (21).

The separation of teaching and scholarship has also influenced the tenure and promotion process within the two-year college. Both two-and four-year institutions consider teaching ability important with respect to granting tenure and promotion. As a National Center for Education Statistics report puts it: "Quality of teaching was considered very important in granting tenure to full-time instructional faculty by 84 percent of department chairs in four-year schools and 99 percent of department chairs in two-year schools" (*Faculty* 12). There were, however, as would be expected, differences in how each type of institution views the role of scholarship in the tenure process:

> Three factors that were held to be very important in tenure decision by sizable minorities of department chairs in four-year schools were rarely mentioned by department chairs in two-year schools: quality of research (45 percent vs. 2 percent), quality of publications (40 percent vs. 5 percent), and number of publications (28 percent vs. less than 1 percent) (National, *Faculty* 13).

A more recent study of two-year college English supports these findings (see Kroll 37–54). When asked, "What do you feel are the principal criteria used to determine promotion in rank at your institutions?" 82% of those responding reported that length of service was somewhat or very important, and 76% reported teaching ability as somewhat or very important, but 71% reported that publications were somewhat or very unimportant. In addition, 42% reported that the community college where they taught had no academic rank, and 23% reported that their college had no tenure system. Kroll's findings suggest that based on some type of assessment of teaching ability and, even more importantly, on length of service, two-year college faculty members receive tenure (39). Once tenured, promotion—usually in the form of salary advances alone—appears contingent on length of service more than any other factor (39).

Faculty in Higher Education Institutions, 1988 suggests that two-year college departments have little control—certainly far less control than departments at four-year institutions—over hiring, tenure, and promotion decisions: "In contrast to the four-year schools, only 41% of departments in two-year schools exercised control over the hiring of full-time teaching faculty" (9) and "only 8 percent . . . reported control over most decisions to promote full-time faculty" (National, *Faculty* 10). Only 30% of two-year college English faculty members reported that they had a great deal of influence on institutional policies. Two-year college faculty members (both full- and part-time) appear to be disempowered and silent not only within their respective professions but also within their respective institutions.

Scholarship and Faculty Productivity

In the traditional model of research and scholarship, professional identity is established most often through presentations at professional conferences and through publication in academic journals and books. According to the Carnegie Foundation's *National Survey of Faculty, 1984*, community college faculties do little of either. The survey found that 75% of community college faculty members had attended none or one national professional meeting, 75% were not engaged in any scholarly work that might lead to publication, 82% had not published nor had accepted for publication any professional writing in the last two years, and 65% had never published in an academic or professional journal (Carnegie 104). For English faculty members, the picture is not much brighter.

Few English community college faculty members present at conferences or contribute to professional journals. One study of English faculty members found that only 32% had presented at one or more conference in the past three years, only 38% of faculty were engaged in scholarly activities that might lead toward publication, and 40% had published an article during their career (Kroll 46); "[m]oreover, 87% reported that their interests were leaning toward or very heavy in teaching rather than scholarship" (Kroll 45). Work by community college English faculty rarely appears in *College English* (*CE*) and *College Composition and Communication* (*CCC*), and only in recent years have two-year college faculty members begun to publish regularly in *Teaching English in the Two-Year College* (*TETYC*).

With this history, it is not surprising that two-year college faculties are rarely mentioned in calls for the re-examination of faculty workloads and of the productivity of American higher education. Two-year colleges, it seems, are widely known as teaching institutions and therefore not in need of re-examination. (Or it may be that two-year colleges still are not considered part of higher education; in many states, community colleges are legislated as part of K through 14 education.) When two-year colleges are mentioned in critiques of higher education's emphasis on faculty scholarship, it is typically in a positive light. For example, in *Higher Education in America: Killing the Spirit*, Page Smith says that:

These institutions, with close ties to their parent communities, free for the most part of the snobbish pursuit of the latest academic fads that so warp their university counterparts, and free of the unremitting pressure to publish or perish, are, I believe, the hope of higher education in America. Unheralded and scorned by "the big boys," they carry out their mission with spirit and élan. (19–20)

On the one hand, as Smith's quote suggests, two-year colleges are praised because they are teaching institutions and because changing enrollment patterns will mean that "the quality and scope of instruction at community colleges . . . will assume growing importance" in the future (Jacobson A1). On the other hand, a growing number of writers are questioning the academic culture and teaching effectiveness of two-year colleges.

These writers, some of whom are two-year college faculty, argue that for various reasons—including the two-year college's growing emphasis on career education and its lack of faculty scholarship—the academic culture of the two-year college continues to suffer. For example, Kevin Dougherty argues that:

[a]s the community college has steadily increased its interest in and spending on vocational education over the last three decades, it has also stopped mentioning transfer as an important option. Students have not been strongly introduced to the idea and given adequate preparation. The liberal arts curriculum has steadily shriveled, with many fields abandoned and sophomore or postintroductory courses becoming rare. (96)

With respect to the teaching of writing, a 3-year case study of an open-access community college found that:

[c]onsistent with information available about community colleges nation-wide . . . we saw little evidence at Oakwood that extensive reading or writing demands were placed on students. Obviously absent were forms and genres of written language earlier considered typical of college work: term papers, essay exams, and required reading lists were rare. (Richardson et al. xii)

And *The Academic Crisis of the Community College* states that "[c]omposition teachers are as despairing as their disciplinary colleagues, as lost as everybody else in the face of the continuing deep erosion of the academic culture" (McGrath and Spear 108).

If any conclusion can be drawn from these reports and arguments, it is that two-year colleges are not as effective as they could be in promoting critical literacy skills among their students. That is, just as advocates of the two-year college applaud those colleges and their faculty for emphasizing teaching, critics of the two-year college question the quality and kind of teaching they provide. Although it is clear that two-year college faculty members spend more time in the classroom, simply claiming that two-year colleges emphasize teaching does not necessarily make them effective teaching institutions.

Others argue that the lack of scholarship by two-year college faculty members has contributed to the decline in the collegiate function of the two-year college and to the invisibility of two-year faculties in academia. As for the former, they argue that "the split between teaching and research is a false dichotomy that serves to undermine the intellectual fabric of the community college" (Seidman 280–81); as for the latter, they argue that two-year college faculty "are pushed toward a marginality that virtually cuts them out of the academic profession" (Clark 266). And while it is true that the connection between scholarship and effective teaching remains unclear—although it seems hard to argue with the notion that writing teachers should themselves be writers—Cohen and Brawer discovered that two-year college humanities "instructors with a high orientation toward research tend also to show a high concern for students" and that

> [t]he instructors who are oriented to research are an involved group. They participate in activities related to the humanities on their own time and attend classes, lectures, and seminars for their own benefit. . . . There is no support for the contention that an instructor's orientation toward research interferes with his teaching. On the contrary, the two may be mutually supportive. (*Two-Year* 55)

Finally, even the very notion of two-year colleges as teaching institutions is open to question. A National Center for Education Statistics study of faculty members found that, with respect to total time spent per week at their respective institutions, "those in two-year colleges averaged 40 hours per week, less than [faculty] at any of the four-year schools" (*Faculty* vi). And as for actual teaching practices, Alexander Astin, William Korn, and Eric Dey concluded that "the faculty in different types of institutions use very similar pedagogical approaches" (15). Both of these findings lend support to the notion that although two-year college faculty may spend more time in the classroom, they are not necessarily teaching any differently than their four-year college and university colleagues, and that they certainly have less attachment to their respective institutions than do four-year faculty: they come on campus, teach their classes, hold office hours, and leave.

COMPOSITION STUDIES
AND TWO-YEAR COLLEGE FACULTY MEMBERS

It may be, as several sources we have cited suggest, that greater commitment to research would enhance the involvement and teaching of two-year college writing teachers. We certainly believe that and, also, that the published insights and experiences of two-year college faculty members are needed within composition studies.

There have been positive indications that input from two-year college faculty is needed—and wanted—within the professional conversation in composition studies. In 1982, for instance, the editor of *College English*, observed that:

> among the 8000+ members of the [NCTE] College Section there are many women, and yet *many more teachers in two-year colleges,* whose voices are needed as complement and counterpoint to those voices which, varied though they certainly are, nevertheless more than half the time come from men teaching in universities. (Gray 385, our emphasis)

In 1984, the National Council of Teachers of English (NCTE) acquired *TETYC* and has published it since as a refereed journal whose editor and editorial board are two-year college faculty. In 1994 through 1995, NCTE restructured its College Section to better recognize the importance and membership of two-year college writing teachers. The results of such efforts, however, have not been encouraging. Practice in the two-year college has not become much of a concern in the national focus on composition studies—two-year college writing instructors have yet to claim a place in the national conversation equal to the role they play in teaching writing to undergraduates.

As North has argued, "[f]or an autonomous composition to survive," the dependency of practitioners on other methodological communities "has to change, and at both ends. Practitioners will have to make the same efforts as other communities to become methodologically aware and egalitarian, while other communities must treat practice with much greater respect" (372). Two-year college faculty members should be part of this transforming process. But in joining the conversation, they need to develop professional standards that reflect their local and specific circumstances. They cannot simply imitate the research and scholarship model of the four-year college and university, and they cannot simply maintain a model of classroom acumen based more on unreflective acceptance of traditional pedagogical practice and "lore" (North 22) than on research.[2] Instead, two-year college faculty members need to develop standards that show that teaching is an intellectual endeavor in which knowledge-making plays an important part. If community college teachers are to gain the intellectual vitality that fosters effective teaching—and if community colleges are to become attractive institutions for teachers—then the binary opposition between teaching and scholarship must end.

Transforming composition studies in the two-year college will require a different set of reforms than those focused on extricating composition studies from the tyranny of literary criticism. In the two-year college, the operative tyranny is the "what-can-I-do-in-class-Monday" mentality. In most two-year colleges, the sole grounds for receiving tenure, or a continuing appointment, is something called *teaching effectiveness*. More often than not, teaching effectiveness translates into whatever system is already in place, including grading schemes that require mandatory reductions for mechanical errors, 50-minute writing placement exams, five-paragraph essays, and course syllabi that are excessively textbook or workbook driven (Haight). Teaching becomes a means of enforcing both a conservative and service-driven agenda in composition. That is, composition instruction in the two-year college has little to do with knowledge-making or research and everything to do with shop-worn pedagogies and unexamined notions of good writing. Teachers (many of them part-time staff) who enter this system with a background in composition studies often are frustrated and neutralized by it. For full-time faculty in this system, tenure means going along to get along, and the dialogical and intellectual energy that new faculty could bring to the system is squandered.

If composition studies is going to be transformed at the two-year college level, the tenure and promotion review system must change, and it must change in a way that values new training and new skills. The exclusive emphasis on teaching effectiveness blinds the review process to the research agenda of composition studies. As an antidote, we propose a system of tenure and promotion review that emphasizes local research by faculty. This would be a logical first step in making the real work of composition studies—and not just the lore of teaching composition—the basis for tenure and promotion.

By *local research*, we mean research focused on a teacher's institution, its students, and the needs of its students and faculty. Local research projects might include such things as surveys of the concerns of students and faculty members served by the basic composition course, longitudinal tracking of students from the developmental course through the rest of their curriculum, or work norming the expectations of the composition faculty to open a dialogue about staff expectations of the writing courses.

The local nature of this research should also be reflected in the way the studies are reported and the articles based on them are published. While it is unrealistic, and probably counter-productive, to expect most two-year college teachers to publish nationally, it would be highly productive for them to publish in local periodicals or in technical-report series published by departments or colleges. Such publications would help provide colleges with the necessary data to meet growing demands (from both inside and outside the college) for good-faith efforts to assess student learning, teacher performance, and program and institutional effectiveness.[3]

It would also be possible—and desirable—for findings of local research projects to be published by a consortium of two-year colleges with similar students and missions. And state or regional associations, perhaps operating as assessment clearinghouses, could publish the findings of local teacher-researchers as a way to promote both the teaching and research agendas of two-year colleges. These publishing arrangements could serve as a springboard for two-year faculty members who want to join national conversations about the future and direction of composition studies, but who have had little incentive to participate and little hope of being heard.

Whether published locally, regionally by consortia of two-year colleges, or nationally in journals like *TETYC*, *CCC*, *CE*, and *College Teaching*, locally-centered scholarship could help two-year college teachers develop as professionals and let them participate more actively within composition studies. And it also would provide evidence—during review for reappointment, merit pay, tenure, and promotion—of the reflective and scholarly efforts of two-year college teachers.

CONCLUSION

We think that emphasizing local standards and local research in tenure and promotion review would enhance the time-honored commitment to teaching at two-year colleges without lapsing into a system petrified by its commitment to outmoded and invalid theories of teaching, composition, and language. This sort of tenure and review system at two-year colleges might also help spur an accelerated rate of change in graduate programs in composition studies.

Currently, few English instructors at two-year colleges have extensive training in composition studies (Kroll 40–41), let alone in how to conduct research in composition. Few of these faculty, then, have the skills needed in the tenure system we propose. To fill the increasing demand for writing instructors at two-year colleges (Banach 12), graduate programs in composition studies should be encouraged to promote skills necessary for tenure and advancement at these institutions. This arrangement could also prompt two-year colleges and graduate programs in composition studies to develop cooperative arrangements that give doctoral candidates background in two-year college teaching and assessment systems at the same time as they bring new energy and initiatives into the two-year college. It even might be possible to elevate the perception of two-year college teaching to the level of meaningful intellectual work by creating a market for serious practitioners who would help alleviate what Miller calls the "sad women in the basement" status of composition (121) at both two- and four-year institutions.

For anyone who has ever taught in a community college, our proposal must include one final clarification. It probably is easier for practitioners at four-year institutions to imagine the local research and publication efforts we have sketched than it is for two-year college faculty. Too often, at community colleges, tenure and promotion reviews have been administrative activities closed to meaningful input from one's colleagues. We envision something very different, something that connects each two-year college faculty member to a community of teacher-scholars.

Our proposal for a new role of research and publication in the tenure and promotion review of two-year college faculty members could apply, as well, at many four-year institutions. The current approach—overemphasizing scholarship and publication at some kinds of institutions while giving it inadequate emphasis at others—contributes to a widening gap between writing faculty at two- and four-year institutions that cannot be bridged merely by efforts to include more two-year authors in scholarly journals or to create two-year college sections in professional organizations. What could help, we believe, would be a reform initiative at two-year colleges to develop personnel review standards that see teaching as a reflective and intellectual endeavor in which research and publication play important parts. This would help community college teachers gain the intellectual vitality that fosters effective teaching. And it would allow them to participate more actively in professional discussions about the nature and future of composition studies.

NOTES

[1]Berlin's theories of rhetoric are as relevant for writing teachers at two-year colleges as they are for writing faculties at four-year colleges and universities: The tension between expressivist tendencies and students' own writing and thinking is, if anything, even greater in two-year colleges. Two-year college writing teachers can locate themselves within North's discussion of "Practitioners" (22). Elbow notes the presence of five two-year college teachers at the 1987 English Coalition Conference and includes the voices of two-year college teachers in this book's "interludes." And Miller's reconceptualization of composition studies offers much to two-year college writing faculty.

[2]By *research*, we prefer the definitions offered by Ernest Boyer in *Scholarship Reconsidered*. Rather than the traditional institutional definition of *scholarship*, meaning research as solely the production of new knowledge, Boyer argues that scholarship be extended beyond discovery to include integration, application, and the scholarship of teaching (15). Also, we make a distinction between unreflective acceptance of pedagogical methods and *lore*, which North defines as "the accumulated body of traditions, practices, and beliefs in terms of which Practitioners understand how writing is done, learned, and taught" (22).

[3]Although community colleges face mounting pressure from outside groups (including accrediting associations and governmental bodies) for assessment of student performance, many two-year colleges are not well-prepared to meet these demands

(Alfred and Linder 7–10). Carefully researched and professionally published articles and technical reports on instructional effectiveness, retention, and so forth could prove valuable evidence of the institution's efforts at assessment—at the same time that they provide faculty with valuable opportunities for research and publication.

WORKS CITED

Alfred, Richard L., and Vincent P. Linder. *Rhetoric to Reality: Effectiveness in Community Colleges.* Ann Arbor: Community College Consortium, 1990.

Astin, Alexander W., William S. Korn, and Eric L. Dey. *The American College Teacher: National Norms for the 1989–90 HERI Faculty Survey.* Los Angeles: U of California Higher Education Institute, 1991.

Banach, William J., ed. *Critical Issues Facing America's Community Colleges.* Warren: Strategic Alternative Series, 1992.

Berlin, James. *Rhetoric and Reality: Writing Instruction in American Colleges, 1900–1985.* Carbondale: Southern Illinois UP, 1987.

Boyer, Ernest L. *Scholarship Reconsidered: Priorities of the Professoriate.* Princeton: Carnegie Foundation for the Advancement of Teaching, 1990.

Carnegie Foundation for the Advancement of Teaching. *National Survey of Faculty, 1984.* Princeton: Carnegie Foundation for the Advancement of Teaching, 1985.

Clark, Burton R. *The Academic Life: Small Worlds, Different Worlds.* Princeton: Carnegie Foundation for the Advancement of Teaching, 1987.

Cohen, Arthur M., and Florence B. Brawer. *The American Community College.* 2nd ed. San Francisco: Jossey-Bass, 1989.

—-. *The Two-Year College Instructor Today.* New York: Praeger, 1977.

Cohen, Arthur M., and Jan M. Ignash. "Trends in the Liberal Arts Curriculum." *Community College Review* 20.2 (1992). 50–56.

Dougherty, Kevin J. *The Contradictory College: The Conflicting Origins, Impacts, and Futures of the Community College.* Albany: State U of New York P, 1994.

Eells, Walter C. *The Junior College.* Boston: Houghton, 1931.

Elbow, Peter. *What Is English?* New York: MLA, 1990.

Gray, Donald. "Another Year with *College English*." *College English* 44 (1982): 385–89.

Haight, Robert. "Glencoe 17." Conf. on Coll. Composition and Communication Convention. Grand Hyatt Washington Hotel, Washington, D.C. 23 Mar. 1995.

Jacobson, Robert L. "Academic Leaders Predict Major Changes for Higher Education in Recession's Wake." *Chronicle of Higher Education* 20 Nov. 1991: A1, A35–A36.

Kroll, Keith. "A Profile of Community College English Faculty and Curriculum." *Community College Review* 22.3 (1994): 37–54.

McGrath, Dennis, and Martin B. Spear. *The Academic Crisis of the Community College.* Albany: State U of New York P, 1991.

McPherson, Elisabeth. "Where Were We, Where Are We As Community College English Teachers?" *Teaching English in the Two-Year College* 17 (1990): 92–99.

Miller, Susan. *Textual Carnivals: The Politics of Composition.* Carbondale: Southern Illinois UP, 1991.

National Center for Education Statistics. *Faculty in Higher Education Institutions, 1988.* Contractor Report. Data Series DR-NSOPF-87/88-1.27. Washington: U.S. Department of Education, 1990.

—––. "Fall Enrollment Surveys, 1993." *Education Statistics on Disk.* Washington: U.S. Department of Education, 1995.

North, Stephen M. *The Making of Knowledge in Composition: Portrait of an Emerging Field.* Upper Montclair: Boynton, 1987.

Raines, Helon. "Is There a Writing Program in This College?" *College Composition and Communication* 41 (1990): 151–65.

Richardson, Richard C., Elizabeth C. Fisk, and Morris A. Okum. *Literacy in the Open-Access College.* San Francisco: Jossey-Bass, 1983.

Seidman, Earl. *In the Words of the Faculty: Perspective on Improving Teaching and Educational Quality in Community Colleges.* San Francisco: Jossey-Bass, 1985.

Shor, Ira. *Critical Teaching and Everyday Life.* 1980. Chicago: U of Chicago P, 1987.

Smith, Page. *Higher Education in America: Killing the Spirit.* 1990. New York: Penguin, 1991.

VanderKelen, Barry. "Stability and Change in the Liberal Arts Curriculum." *New Directions for Community Colleges.* Ed. Arthur M. Cohen. San Francisco: Jossey-Bass, 1994. 31–41.

Witt, Allen A., et al. *America's Community Colleges: The First Century.* Washington: Community College Press, 1994.

6 Scholarship, Tenure, and Promotion in Professional Communication

Nancy Roundy Blyler
Margaret Baker Graham
Charlotte Thralls
Iowa State University

When thinking about scholarship, tenure, and promotion in professional communication, we must remember that the field has come into its own only in the last decade. Called by different names—technical writing, technical and scientific writing, business communication, or the more inclusive term we use—professional communication has now moved from a nearly invisible position in the service ranks of academic departments to recognition as a discipline with its own scholarly agenda.

This recognition has brought corresponding growth in the outlets for research in professional communication. Journals that specifically address professional communication include such well-established publications as *Journal of Technical Writing and Communication*, *Journal of Business Communication*, and *Technical Communication*, as well as the newer publications, *Journal of Business and Technical Communication*, *Technical Communication Quarterly*, and *Management Communication Quarterly*. In addition, broader journals—for example, *Written Communication* and *Journal of Advanced Composition*—occasionally publish work in professional communication.

This recognition and the growth in outlets for scholarly productivity are certainly positive signs, and they accompany another positive sign: the growing success professional communication faculty members appear to be experiencing in the tenure and promotion process. One example is provided by Iowa State University's rhetoric and professional communication (RPC) program, which currently includes 18 tenured or tenure-line faculty. During a recent 14-year period, nine people in RPC went up for tenure, and all nine cases were successful. However, at that time there were no full professors in RPC, and three cases for promotion to full professor had been turned down at the college level (Haggard 87–88). Since then, two more RPC faculty members have received tenure, and, more important perhaps, two have been promoted to full professor.

This generally favorable trend in tenure and promotion is also supported by an informal survey we conducted in preparation for writing this chapter.[1] A number of our respondents spoke of their positive experiences with tenure and promotion, remarking that "I have had no problems with committees evaluating my work," "My tenure committee was supportive and sprung no nasty surprises," and "I have been treated fairly and well." One respondent in particular addressed this current favorable trend:

> When I went up for promotion to associate professor about fifteen years ago, the college committee needed additional background on my work before they would recommend my promotion to the provost. . . . I'd say from my own four years as a member of this committee that my junior colleagues will have no difficulty in this area.

As our opening remarks suggest, the existing tenure and promotion process appears to be serving faculty in professional communication well, so we do not intend to begin this chapter on a negative note. We do contend, however, that, despite these successes, tenure and promotion in professional communication can be problematic, especially because the process may not yet be fully understood.

Only recently has scholarship addressing tenure and promotion in professional communication begun to appear. For example, the Association of Teachers of Technical Writing (ATTW) recently produced an anthology designed to "provide guidance to those involved in tenure and promotion decisions" by "describ[ing] an effective process for both evaluators and those evaluated" (Tebeaux 1). The authors included in this useful volume offer advice to faculty preparing for tenure and promotion (e.g., Harris, "Getting Promoted"; Killingsworth, "What Counts As Quality in a Publication Record?"; Rude, "Standards versus Standardization: Constructing Criteria for Tenure and Promotion in Technical Communication"; and Warren, "Tenure and Promotion at Oklahoma State University: Difficult But Not Impossible"). And they draw on their own experiences and the experiences of others to contextualize their discussions (e.g., Sanders, "Tenure, Promotion, and the Department of English at the State University"; and Haggard, "Gaining Acceptance of Rhetoric Research Within an English Department").

Although such practical perspectives are important, we believe that the discipline would benefit from yet another perspective: the theoretical. More specifically, we contend that articulation theory, as developed by neo-Marxist social critic Stuart Hall, provides an important critical lens for examining tenure and promotion as a set of ideological practices. These practices, although open to change, nonetheless circumscribe how professional communication faculty members make sense of and direct their academic lives.

We begin this chapter, then, by discussing articulation theory in relation to tenure and promotion. Next, we use this theoretical discussion to examine tenure and promotion within particular settings important to faculty in professional communication. Finally, we address the implications of this theoretical view of tenure and promotion.

ARTICULATION THEORY
AND TENURE AND PROMOTION

Originally conceived by Ernesto Laclau and Chantal Mouffe, and then developed into a more coherent position by Stuart Hall, articulation theory attempts to account for the way social practices—such as tenure and promotion—are invested with meaning, forming ideological fields within which individuals are positioned. Because articulation theory is complex, we cannot hope to explore it fully here. Nevertheless, we believe it helps illuminate the tenure and promotion process to understand a few key concepts: *articulation, valorization, positioning*, and *rearticulation*.

According to Hall, there is no necessary or fixed relationship between social practices and the meanings associated with them. Instead, meanings must be assigned—constructed and reconstructed—through a network of linkages that yoke social practices with particular connotations. These linkages are what Hall calls *articulations*: "the connection[s] that *can* make a unity of two different elements, under certain conditions" (Grossberg, "On Postmodernism" 53; italics in original). To illustrate this concept of articulation—and the nonnecessary linkage between two elements—Hall offers the analogy of a "lorry [truck] where the front (cab) and back (trailer) can, but need not necessarily, be connected to one another. The two parts are connected to each other, but through a specific linkage, that can be broken" (Grossberg, "On Postmodernism" 53).

Like the parts of the lorry, social practices can be linked or unlinked to various structures of meaning. Social practices such as tenure and promotion, however, are often more complex than the simple linking of two elements like a trailer to a cab. According to Hall, social practices typically link together with other social practices, creating complex clusters of associations in different sites at different historical moments. Depending thus on the place of a social practice "within a formation" (Grossberg, "On Postmodernism" 54) or social structure, a practice can have "quite different connotations because it operate[s] within different 'systems of differences and equivalencies.' " (Hall, "Signification" 108). As an example, Hall draws on his own experience with blackness as a racial category. For him, the meaning of the term *Black* has varied greatly, depending on how it has been linked with other social practices. In his native Jamaica, Hall found *Black* linked to hierarchical and "finely-graded classificatory systems" that differentiated among shades of skin tone, allowing differing levels of status to be assigned people of color ("Signification" 108). Conversely, in England, he found *Black* linked to a binary "white/not-white" dichotomy where, despite his light skin color, he was considered " 'black' for all practical purposes" (Hall, "Signification" 108).

As Hall's example demonstrates, articulations derive their meanings from the place of a particular social practice within a social setting, and articulations help shape human identities by positioning individuals within hierarchical relations of power. When social practices become linked with certain structures of meaning, they construct ideological fields of dominant and subordinate discourses. Within these fields, certain meanings are thus valorized—that is, "positively marked" or foregrounded "in relation to what is absent, unmarked, the unspoken, the unsayable" (Hall, "Signification" 109). Articulations can thus privilege or, alternatively, exclude or silence certain experiences and possibilities. As a result, individuals become positioned within ideological structures where their "relations to a social identity, political interests, etc. have already been defined" (Grossberg, "History" 67).

Although articulations within a given ideological formation or structure can be particularly "tenacious" (Slack, Miller, and Doak 37)—that is, deeply ingrained in their ideological field and thus resistant to change—articulations can be altered, or rearticulated. As Hall explains, an ideological field is "never fully closed or 'sutured' " (Grossberg, "On Postmodernism" 56), and hence individuals can "rupture or contest it by supplementing it with some wholly new alternative set of terms or transfer its meaning by changing or rearticulating its association, for example, from the negative to the positive" (Hall, "Signification" 112).

We believe that articulation theory offers a powerful heuristic for examining tenure and promotion. Specifically, the theory allows us to understand how faculty members are positioned in various ways, as the tenure and promotion process is inserted into different ideological formations where different meanings are marked for valorization. In the next section, we discuss positioning in relation to two academic formations important to faculty in professional communication: institutional and disciplinary sites.

TENURE AND PROMOTION: INSTITUTIONAL AND DISCIPLINARY SITES

In studying institutional sites, we focus on the insertion of particular tenure and promotion practices into universities and colleges as academic units; with disciplinary sites, we examine tenure and promotion practices in relation to the fields with which various professional communication faculty identify.

Institutional Sites

The triad of research, teaching, and service is a widely used set of tenure and promotion practices that varies in meaning, in part, because of the institutional sites in which the practices are located. In his discussion of discursive formations, Hall claims that ideological chains are not "mutually exclusive." Rather, says Hall, these chains "contest one another, often drawing on a common, shared repertoire of concepts, rearticulating and disarticulating them within systems of difference or equivalence" ("Signification" 104). This tendency for a shared repertoire of concepts or practices to be relinked or rearticulated provides a rich context for understanding the different meanings accorded to research, teaching, and service.

Our survey of faculty in professional communication suggests another rich context for understanding these different meanings of research, teaching, and service. In particular, our survey indicates that the variations may depend, in part, on whether the chain of promotion and tenure practices is inserted into an institution that is oriented primarily toward research, or into one primarily oriented toward teaching.

Research-Oriented Institutions.   Responses to our survey suggest that research-oriented institutions tend to link (or articulate) research, teaching, and service in a hierarchy that valorizes scholarship over teaching, with service often mentioned as a distant third. For example, when asked to describe the requirements for earning tenure and the rank of full professor at his (primarily research) institution, one respondent mentioned only requirements having to do with scholarship:

Tenure—major book at a major university press; and

Full—another major book and strong national reputation.

Indeed, when asked to discuss the role that teaching would play in tenure and promotion, this same respondent replied as follows, concerning the institutions where he had received tenure:

> At all three institutions, [teaching] has played only a disqualifying role, although at my current one the standards are higher, so you have to be a good teacher not to be disqualified, whereas at previous institutions you only had to be not-awful.

Finally, when asked whether consulting, an important activity in professional communication, could play any role in tenure and promotion, this respondent answered with one word: "No."

The following respondent summarizes this hierarchy at research-oriented institutions, stressing as well the value accorded to research:

> Bad teaching can get you fired if you don't publish enough; good teaching won't get you retained if you don't publish enough; service is used as an excuse to fire someone if the service record is slight and the committee needs such an excuse. Teaching in itself never plays much of a role. An exemplary teaching record would buoy a marginal publication record, extending a bit what would be acceptable. But publication remains the yardstick for all decisions. Service in itself never plays a role worth mentioning.

Although service appears at the bottom of the hierarchy, an exception seems to occur when material from consulting and from other professional activities can be funneled into research, or, to a lesser extent, into teaching. As one respondent put it, concerning research:

> Consulting is like working at the 7-11: It gets you money but no credit towards tenure/promotion. Now if you do your consulting in such a way that it generates new knowledge that you can turn into publications, that's something different; if you consult on a unique or significant problem, the products of that work should be there to show. But the main thing is generating refereed publications. Consulting itself has no value.

And as another respondent said concerning both research and teaching:

> Consulting can count if you publish or present new methods or new knowledge or integrate such insights into curriculum. In other words, the value is that you bring it to the university or to other professionals some way, not merely that you have been hired by an external organization.

These three practices—research, teaching, and service—are also linked within the tenure and promotion process at teaching-oriented institutions. However, the particular hierarchy and the value accorded to the practices appear to differ.

Teaching-Oriented Institutions. Responses to our survey suggest that teaching-oriented institutions tend to link the three practices in a hierarchy that valorizes classroom performance over scholarship. As one respondent, who identified her site as primarily a teaching institution, remarked: "[Teaching is] very important. We have to submit evidence of good teaching, including student evaluations. The only instances of which I'm aware that people have been denied tenure were because of poor student evaluations."

Another respondent echoed this point, saying that the role teaching plays is "a big one. No one gets tenured or promoted if teaching is demonstrably weak." Finally, a respondent at what she called a "teaching college" indicated that, because teaching is so important to her institution, she had to "do double duty in order to be allowed to conduct research." "The university's administration," she said, "is pleased at the results of my work, but they have a policy of encouraging only teaching in the classroom." Hence, she continued:

> I've been warned that I have to "do everything"—be available on campus, have good evaluations from students, participate in additional committees, teach more courses—if I'm going to be allowed to continue participating on the board of professional societies, publishing papers and books, attending and making presentations at conferences, and working as a consultant. So far I've been able to do it all, but I often find I'm working 90-hour weeks.

Despite the different values given to teaching and research, teaching-oriented institutions—like research-oriented ones—still appear to rank service third. Our survey suggests, however, that this third-place ranking may not be quite so distant as it is at research-oriented institutions. One respondent, for example, addressed the issue of administration, an important service activity for faculty in professional communication: "Actually, I would say that my institution likes administrative stuff. They call it service, and it can make up for a mediocre publishing record." Teaching-oriented institutions, then, may be more willing than research-oriented ones to see the value in service activities and to reward those activities during tenure and promotion reviews. Although our survey does not allow us to determine why this difference may occur, we speculate that service may be more easily and comfortably linked with teaching. For example, some service activities, such as administration, are already closely tied to teaching. In addition, both teaching and service tend to focus on the interpersonal and on what might be considered outreach.

The fact that the practices of research, teaching, and service are so variously ordered and valued at different institutions affects the way professional communication faculties are positioned within the tenure and promotion process: Faculty members are "situated differently in relation to a different range of social sites" (Hall, "Signification" 106), with their social identities already circumscribed. Hence, these faculty members must package their work accordingly, taking care to fit it into the hierarchies privileged at their particular institutions. As an example of the difficulties that can arise with this packaging, one of our respondents mentioned a "category problem at [his] previous institution" regarding whether his scholarship should be viewed as a research or a teaching practice:

> There was some discussion about whether or not my research was "pedagogical publications" vs. research or scholarship, but I managed to win that argument because my research was considered "theoretical" enough. People doing classroom or teacher research (or workplace studies) could not have counted that as research/scholarship at that time.

The fact that an argument had to be made indicates the pressure this respondent felt to fit his work into his institution's value-laden hierarchy.

For faculty in professional communication—particularly for those at research-oriented institutions—the most problematic linkages may concern research and teaching, on the one hand, and that distant third, service, on the other. We have already mentioned the difficulties involved with consulting. Problems, however, also may arise with other professional activities, such as editing scholarly collections or journals, training teachers, or administering writing programs. Concerning editing, for example, few would want to claim that a person can be a good editor without also being proficient at scholarship and teaching. Yet, despite obvious connections, faculty members who wish their editing to count may have to link it to other, more valued practices: for scholarly collections, through writing either a major introduction or a chapter; for journal editing, through additional scholarship that draws on the editing experience, or through teaching courses in editing.

A similar dilemma may exist for those involved in teacher training or administration. Concerning teacher training, for example, our survey suggests that such work may not be given as much weight as teaching or perhaps may not be recognized at all. Concerning administration, our survey also suggests that, as important and time-consuming as it is, administration may have to be repackaged as research—that is, faculty members may have to structure their research programs around administrative issues—if it is to be of use for tenure and promotion.

Clearly, then, the triumvirate of research, teaching, and service is strongly linked within the tenure and promotion process at many institutions, although the hierarchical ordering of these practices and the values accruing to them vary greatly with the institutional site in which they occur. The tenure and promotion process, however, is also articulated or linked to other systems of representation within institutional settings. One important system of representation is the notion of academic discipline. In the next section, then, we examine disciplinary sites.

Disciplinary Sites

Disciplinary sites can be especially problematic for professional communication faculty members because they may be housed in a number of different academic disciplines—including English, engineering, and business—and these differences, in turn, can critically affect the status granted professional communication faculties. For example, in some business programs, faculty members in professional communication cannot earn tenure because, as one respondent—an award-winning scholar—wrote, her field "is not recognized." Another respondent wrote about the problems she faced when caught between two disciplines, neither valuing her field: "The difficulties I went through were enormous. I started out on a tenure track in an English department, but teaching in a business school. That arrangement broke down after a few years, and I spent years on a lecturer track in the business school."

Even when professional communication faculty members are in tenure-track positions, their research is judged by the dominant ideology of the academic discipline within which they work. Hall defines ideology as "the mental frameworks—the languages, the concepts, categories, imagery of thought, and the systems of representations—which different classes and social groups deploy in order to make sense of, define, figure out and render intelligible the way society works" ("Problem" 59). Hall is discussing economic and political systems, but his concept of ideology can also be applied to disciplines.

The disciplinary-driven, ideological nature of research is revealed in published statements by two professors on the nature of the topics and methodologies they valorize. Larry Smeltzer, a faculty member of a college of business, offers five recommendations for research (192–93). Three of his recommendations ("Test hypotheses," "Conduct the research within the business context," and "Use creative tests and analyses of hypotheses") clearly indicate empirical research, both quantitative and qualitative. The other two ("Understand and 'feel' the needs of business practitioners" and "Relate current theoretical perspectives and the literature to the problems business faces") suggest that the purpose of research is to serve the business world (Smeltzer 192–93). On the other hand, Carl Herndl, a member of an English department, objects to methodologies associated with the social sciences; he specifically addresses professional communication's recent move to employ descriptive ethnography. Herndl finds problematic "the fact that [such] research describes the production of meaning but not the social, political and economic sources of power which authorize this production or the cultural work such discourse performs" (351).

Smeltzer's approach suggests that research should support existing business values, whereas Herndl's view of research invites analyses that critique and possibly subvert business values. These different ideological notions of research have recently played themselves out in volatile exchanges between English and business faculty at Association for Business Communication conferences.

The disciplinary-specific nature of research, in which certain topics and methodologies are valorized—and the tension this valorization creates—are suggested by the following three responses to our survey:

> I got tenure [in an English department] on history of education stuff, very humanities-like, really, so no problem. But now that I'm doing stuff that has more a social science flavor, using numbers, too (God forbid!), I'm not so sure. I think some of my colleagues may have trouble understanding and valuing stuff that's not mainline humanities-sounding. But I have no evidence of this so far. Just suspicions.

> I work in an engineering college and the college-level promotion and tenure committee consists of engineering faculty. These individuals do not understand my work well (or the work of my technical communication colleagues). In some cases, the P&T committee has shown certain biases (e.g., a tendency [to] undervalue research without numbers). All things considered, however, the P&T reviews of technical communication faculty are reasonably fair.

> The administration was not the problem—the faculty of the business school was. They had a great deal of trouble, even though I changed fields to do work that I thought would be valued more highly by them. In general, the faculty rejected management communication, business communication, communication, English, etc., as fields in which I could get tenure. Thus my research and its methodology had to stand up to reviewers from other disciplines recognized by the business school. . . .

All three respondents recognize that their research, which is at odds with a dominant approach in their respective departments, puts them at some risk. Although quibbling over methodology may seem pedestrian, it can be of paramount importance because valorizing a particular methodology determines, in large part, what is studied. And, ultimately, methodology and subject matter reflect and limit how a discipline defines the nature of knowledge and reality.

Although these responses on methodology and subject matter reflect different ideologies concerning what knowledge is and how it is created, sometimes disciplinary differences concern how knowledge is packaged. That is, where research is published can be as important as or even more important than subject or methodology. Does the work appear in a book or journal? Is the book published with a university press? Is the journal refereed? With what discipline is the journal allied? All of these questions affect how a work is judged. One respondent, a member of an English department, noted:

> The NATURE of the research isn't important. The important thing is to place your research, whether it's interdisciplinary or not, such that it has an impact on the profession. You've got to establish a scholarly reputation, and so WHERE you publish is far more important than WHAT.

The decision of whether to package research in a book or in a journal can also be discipline-driven. English departments, which traditionally have been dominated by literature faculty, may honor individuals who have published books or written chapters in books. But, as one response to our survey indicates, books and book chapters are not highly regarded in business schools:

> I would like to note that business schools don't think much of book chapters. I have to fight constantly to get them to "count" book chapters; they tend to believe that only journal articles are truly refereed. They won't count book chapters as equivalent—no matter how insignificant the journal. This is clearly a disciplinary distinction separating the humanities and the social sciences, I would think.

Packaging research in journals can raise similar concerns. For example, several of our respondents indicated that the assessment of the research itself matters less than the reputation of the journal in which the research is published. Elucidating this quality, one person who teaches in an engineering college observed that her essay in *College Composition and Communication* was valued less by her colleagues than her publication in *IEEE* (a journal sponsored by the Institute of Electrical and Electronic Engineers). If she were a member of an English department, the judgment would undoubtedly have been reversed.

Although clear disciplinary differences exist in defining valuable research, none of these responses suggests that research is unimportant. One person responding to our survey pointed out that this valuing of research is ultimately more important than the nature of the research. She observed that she "like[s] being 'on the edge.' " She then continued, "The margin works for me because I have accepted the main rule of the center—publish." Hall writes that "ideological structures" are most tenacious when they become "common sense, the regime of the 'taken for granted'" ("Signification" 105). Even though, as disciplinary sites, business, engineering, and English may value different kinds of research and package it differently, the importance of research is taken for granted in all disciplines. Indeed, at many institutions, research appears to be valorized above all other aspects of the profession.

Thus far our discussion has centered on the institutional and disciplinary sites within which tenure or promotion in professional communication occurs. These sites, we have suggested, place different values on the research, teaching, and service activities of faculty in professional communication; thus the meaning of tenure and promotion—the requirements and opportunities that define faculty success—can vary greatly. We turn in the next section to the implications of this variability for professional communication faculty involved in tenure and promotion.

IMPLICATIONS FOR TENURE AND PROMOTION

The variability of the tenure and promotion process means that professional communication faculty can expect some inconsistencies in the way their work is assessed from institution to institution. Sometimes these inconsistencies concern the interpretation of scholarship in professional communication. For example, one of our respondents—a person who has been tenured in three different English departments—reported vastly different interpretations of his scholarship at each site:

> At my first, I had to struggle to get the comp stuff recognized as relevant. At the second it was fully accepted, but in part reinterpreted as cultural history. In the third, it was entirely reinterpreted as cultural history and discourse theory.

These inconsistencies, although striking, did not negatively affect the tenurability of this faculty member.

Faculty members may find, however, that some inconsistencies do affect tenure status because institutions vary in the value they assign to professional communication as a field. These differences were most dramatically illustrated in our survey through the experiences of two respondents we mentioned earlier. Both have impressive research records and are employed by business schools, although at different institutions. One, despite job offers from other top-level universities, remains in an untenured position at her preferred institution where business communication is not recognized as a tenurable discipline. The other, after more than a decade of struggle, eventually saw her position converted to tenure line and was recently tenured, developments she attributed to her institution's "finally learning to evaluate interdisciplinary work."

If the variability of tenure and promotion practices can produce such inconsistencies across institutions, this variability can also create different levels of resistance or, alternatively, openness to change—what Hall called *rearticulation*. Some institutions, like the one unwilling to recognize professional communication as a tenurable field, may be highly resistant to rearticulating the values traditionally attached to tenure-line positions or to tenure and promotion categories, whereas other institutions may be more open to rearticulation. In fact, according to our surveys, faculty may expect to find an increase in the number of institutions willing to entertain changes that favor professional communication activities. Even more important, faculty may find that, under certain conditions, they can influence these rearticulations—gaining recognition for work that falls outside the established hierarchy of values in effect at a particular institution.

This increased openness to change was most apparent in our survey respondents' comments on research and service. Regarding research, for example, one respondent reported that "the college formerly objected to qualitative research, but that is changing." Regarding service, two others remarked on their institutions' willingness to value consulting:

> If consulting brings in contract dollars that provide overhead support and jobs for students, it seems to meet with approval.

> My university is glad I do consulting and training and encourages work with economic development and workplace literacy.

In mentioning a connection between consulting and the economic interests of their institutions, these two respondents reveal an important condition for effecting change: Activities not normally counted toward tenure and promotion in professional communication must be positively linked with existing values of the institution. Given this condition, faculty members wishing to alter institutional attitudes toward service—for example, consulting that does not result in publication—may meet with greatest success if their work directly supports the institution's economic mission, bringing resources or accolades to programs especially important to the institution. In scholarship, faculty seeking to overcome negative biases—either toward experimental research or toward professional communication research in general—may find greatest receptivity when linking their work to whatever institutional expectations for research are already in place—for example, expectations about quantity of publications, book versus article formats, and the status of the journal or publishing house.

Although effecting such linkages means that faculty members at some sites can influence changes favorable to professional communication, at other sites faculty may find themselves subject to changes or rearticulations outside of their control. Our surveys suggest that in professional communication one of these changes may be higher performance standards for gaining tenure and promotion. At some teaching institutions, for example, faculty may find a movement toward requiring more research, as indicated by one of our survey respondents:

> We are primarily a teaching institution, so good teaching is considered requisite for anything else. Teaching is supposed to be rated more important than research. However, if you don't have a good research record, it doesn't matter how good your teaching is, you won't get promoted or tenured.

At certain research institutions, where we would anticipate such research demands, faculty may find that higher performance standards center on teaching. In one respondent's words, "You are expected to show evidence of good or excellent teaching, even to support a case based on research. Good teaching is *sine qua non*."

Accompanying these higher performance standards, professional communication faculty members at some sites may also find increased demands for documenting their work via teaching portfolios and external letters. Many institutions, for example, are beginning to require external letters from individuals who hold a rank higher than the candidate's at a college or university with stature equal or superior to the candidate's. At least in the short term, this requirement may pose special difficulties for faculty in professional communication—particularly with promotions to full professor, as one of our survey respondents points out:

> It's often difficult because we want TEN letters—five from people suggested by the candidate and five to be anonymous, chosen by the department. In the first place, when coming up for full professor, there are probably no more than two dozen (if that) full professors of technical communication out there to choose from.

For new faculty members in professional communication, however, this problem may gradually diminish if the current favorable trend regarding promotions to full professor continues.

CONCLUSION

Because tenure and promotion practices vary with institutional and disciplinary sites, faculty members in professional communication can expect to be positioned within a process that both constrains and defines possibilities for their work. In terms of constraints, faculty members will find that tenure and promotion practices at some sites limit options, exerting a measure of control over how faculty direct careers, set priorities for their work, and ultimately, prepare for the tenure and promotion process. In terms of possibilities, faculty members will find some institutions more open than others to valuing the range of research, teaching, and service activities particular to professional communication.

For faculty members in professional communication, then, we believe the key to success in tenure and promotion lies in anticipating the ways in which research, teaching, and service activities are linked at particular institutions and within particular disciplinary units. Such anticipation, we feel, will enable faculty members to understand how they are positioned and how their work is to be packaged—the connections, that is, that must be forged between their work and the activities valorized in tenure and promotion practices. Such anticipation may also enable faculty members to rearticulate research, teaching, or service activities that they believe are not sufficiently valued at their institutional or disciplinary sites. In these ways, we believe, faculty in professional communication will be able to participate in—even alter—a process that, despite its tenacity and its power to position, is never fully closed.

NOTE

[1]We sent out, largely over e-mail, an open-ended survey that asked faculty members in professional communication to recount their experiences with tenure and promotion. We sent these surveys to individuals who belong to the Association for Business Communication (ABC) and the Association of Teachers of Technical Writing (ATTW), as well as to members of the Council for Programs in Technical and Scientific Communication. We also sent the survey to the bulletin boards for ABC and ATTW, making it impossible to count how many people may have received the survey. Thirty-five completed surveys were returned.

Having both an e-mail address and membership in a professional organization suggests that our respondents have achieved a measure of success in the academy, and indeed, all but a few of our respondents had already been tenured. Because having such an e-mail address was a prerequisite for receiving the survey, it is difficult to determine how using e-mail affected our data collection.

WORKS CITED

Grossberg, Lawrence. "History, Politics and Postmodernism: Stuart Hall and Cultural Studies." *Journal of Communication Inquiry* 10.2 (1986): 61–77.
——, ed. "On Postmodernism and Articulation: An Interview with Stuart Hall." *Journal of Communication Inquiry* 10.2 (1986): 45–60.

Haggard, Frank E. "Gaining Acceptance of Rhetoric Research Within an English Department." Tebeaux, 87–90.

Hall, Stuart. "The Problem of Ideology—Marxism without Guarantees." *Marx: A Hundred Years On.* Ed. Betty Matthews. London: Lawrence and Wishart, 1983. 57–85.

——. "Signification, Representation, Ideology: Althusser and the Post-Structuralist Debates." *Critical Studies in Mass Communication* 2 (1985): 91–114.

Harris, John S. "Getting Promoted." Tebeaux, 9–20.

Herndl, Carl G. "Teaching Discourse and Reproducing Culture: A Critique of Research and Pedagogy in Professional and Non-Academic Writing." *College Composition and Communication* 44 (1993): 349–63.

Killingsworth, M. Jimmie. "What Counts As Quality in a Publication Record?" Tebeaux, 43–49.

Rude, Carolyn. "Standards versus Standardization: Constructing Criteria for Tenure and Promotion in Technical Communication." Tebeaux, 117–28.

Sanders, Scott P. "Tenure, Promotion, and the Department of English at the State University." Tebeaux, 21–31.

Slack, Jennifer Daryl, David James Miller, and Jeffrey Doak. "The Technical Communicator As Author: Meaning, Power, Authority." *Journal of Business and Technical Communication* 7 (1993): 12–36.

Smeltzer, Larry. "Emerging Questions and Research Paradigms in Business Communication Research." *Journal of Business Communication* 30 (1993): 181–98.

Tebeaux, Elizabeth, ed. *Issues in Promotion and Tenure for Faculty in Technical Communication: Guidelines and Perspectives.* N.p.: Association of Teachers of Technical Writing, [1995].

Warren, Thomas L. "Tenure and Promotion at Oklahoma State University: Difficult But Not Impossible." Tebeaux, 99–108.

7 Presenting Writing Center Scholarship: Issues for Faculty and Personnel Committees

Muriel Harris
Purdue University

As in other areas of composition studies, writing center scholarship is a tightly woven blend of theory and practice with the same goal: to help writers achieve greater insight into, and control over, their writing abilities. Although writing center scholarship draws on current theory and practice in composition, it is also a specialized subfield with unique, defining characteristics that influence the way writing center specialists should be reviewed by their departments.

One characteristic that sets writing center studies off from the broader field is its ever-present need to contextualize, to use a framework that recognizes the importance of the physical environment within which writing center theory turns into writing center practice. That is, a writing center is a particular place that must be created and given shape, and the very shaping of the place is a working out of the theory. In a very real sense, a writing center is the result of someone's research—it is the publication of the writing center director who sets it in motion, and it is revised or updated regularly by that person and by every new director who takes over later. A second characteristic feature of writing center studies is that all theory and practice must consistently and carefully shift the focus of learning from *the student* or *the writer* (as general concepts) to each particular student in a tutorial, with all the emphasis on individualized instruction and messy reality this implies. A third characteristic derives from the need for writing centers to reinforce and be closely tied to their particular institutions. Because of this, writing center scholarship includes a great quantity of localized, site-specific research.

Because of such characteristics of writing centers, scholarship in this area looks different—in the topics discussed and the methods used to make knowledge—from much composition studies scholarship. So the materials in the tenure or promotion file of a writing center specialist may not look familiar to administrators and faculty members versed in reviewing traditional evidence of scholarship. To address this situation so that writing center scholars can be evaluated appropriately, this chapter examines briefly the nature of writing center theory and practice, along with its central concerns, and considers how and where writing center scholarship appears. Such a discussion leads to suggestions for the kinds of evidence that accurately indicate the quality of a writing center specialist's work. All of this, I hope, will be useful for evaluation committees as well as writing center scholars preparing their review documents. Such a discussion can also provide search committees with suggestions for how to define a writing center position that they are seeking to fill and can, as well, offer job applicants suggestions for materials to put in their dossiers that will present them effectively and appropriately to others. In addition, graduate students will find among the lists that follow suggestions for the kinds of evidence they can be accumulating as they work in writing centers during their graduate days.

TWO NOTES ABOUT PREPARING FILES FOR REVIEW

Before turning to the nature of writing center scholarship, I need to stress that writing center specialists should not put off preparation for tenure or promotion until the year of review. Rather, evidence should be accumulated beginning years before promotion or tenure is imminent. The same advice to start early is also relevant to graduate students preparing for careers in writing center work. The humble statements of some graduate students on the market—that they did some tutoring—usually understates a great deal of knowledge and experience they acquired in their centers. They too can offer an impressive paper trail if they start collecting evidence in advance.

Another cautionary word is necessary because presenting evidence is itself an art form. As I explain, the need to present materials that represent the various facets of writing center work is likely to result in a large, overstuffed dossier. The outcome can be a pile of materials so daunting that it is in danger of being overwhelming and inaccessible to its readers. Accessibility is all. Providing too much material, as Donald K. Jarvis reminded us in his book on faculty development, is likely to have a negative effect. Instead, anyone preparing a dossier should think of presentation in terms of preparing a portfolio. Portfolio evaluation, which is becoming a nationally recommended approach for teacher evaluation in addition to student evaluation (Edgerton, et al., Seldin), stresses the need for clearly indicated sections and personal statements or narratives written by the candidate, statements that introduce and provide a perspective on the contents of that section. Offering advice from a technical writing text, Jarvis noted that "the more likely the reader is to need a piece of information, the more accessible it should be" (37). A cover letter for the portfolio explains how the portfolio is organized and what to look for, a table of contents lists the sections and subsections, tabs or separators demarcate the sections, and an appendix or two can contain low-impact supporting data. The materials in each section should be arranged in descending order of importance with the most important categories placed first.

SCHOLARSHIP OF DISCOVERY, APPLICATION, AND INTEGRATION

Composition specialists who explore the nature of the writing tutorial and the place of writing centers in writing instruction have, as a core challenge, the need to define the special niche that writing centers occupy. From there, writing center scholarship moves on to investigate the necessary theories and practices that shape the functioning of the center.

One way to view all of this scholarship is through the lens of Ernest Boyer's *Scholarship Reconsidered*. This widely read call to define more creatively what it means to be a scholar implicitly accuses academia of being content to follow an outmoded and constraining view of scholarship as the discovery of new knowledge (see Boyer 14–25). This first kind of scholarship is, of course, needed, and it is evident in writing center studies which contribute to the formulation of the fundamentals of writing center theory and practice. But scholarship of discovery defines neither scholarship in its broadest, most inclusive sense—nor the rest of writing center scholarship.

Two other forms of valuable scholarship that Boyer calls to our attention, scholarship of application and scholarship of integration, are apt descriptions of a great body of writing center studies. Scholarship of application, applying knowledge to problems, is where theory and practice most notably interact. And it is here that so many writing center specialists have contributed their abilities, both in structuring actual writing centers and in applying what is known to contexts such as training tutors (by means of creating tutor training manuals, writing training textbooks, and writing about tutor training), creating instructional materials, introducing much-needed knowledge from other fields, and tackling a broad range of administrative concerns. Scholarship of integration, Boyer's third form of scholarship, gives meaning to isolated facts, puts them in perspective, and makes connections across disciplines, and it is equally vital to knowledge-making. It is here that Boyer places participation in curricular innovations, an endeavor that has moved writing centers forward in new and challenging ways, from instituting online writing environments for tutorial interaction to joining tutor training and faculty development programs with writing-across-the-curriculum reforms to intersecting with the training of future high school teachers.

Whereas application and integration are lenses through which to view various kinds of knowledge-making as scholarship, it is also important to consider the particular kinds of scholarship needed in the field of writing centers and why such knowledge is needed. To do so requires a bit of history to appreciate why certain kinds of writing center knowledge-making are so vitally important to the field.

Writing centers are not an entirely new phenomenon but, in fact, have a venerable history (Carino). Still, the vast majority opened their doors within the last two decades, a time when composition studies was also developing as a discipline with graduate programs, rapidly proliferating lists of journals and books, and expanding subsets of specialties within the field. Graduate programs are beginning to include studies in writing center scholarship and administration in order to prepare graduate students to move knowledgeably into writing center work. But this is not yet a widespread condition, and many new directors gain their knowledge in some apprentice position, perhaps as a graduate student tutoring in a writing center. Other new directors are people who find themselves thrust into a new position in response to a local need or an administrative request. They become the director of a writing center without ever having worked in (or perhaps even stepped into) one—a condition some have likened to constructing a violin while playing it. Moving from the classroom instructional setting to the tutorial one, with its many novel administrative concerns and different theoretical emphases and pedagogies, is a larger step than is generally realized and creates a great need for scholarship that presents in immediately accessible terms useful information on writing center theory, pedagogy, and administration. Doing this is very much in the spirit of Boyer's scholarship of integration (see 18–21).

WRITING CENTER SCHOLARSHIP

Against the previous section's overview of how writing center scholarship can be described from Boyer's perspective, I offer a more concrete discussion of some important topics in writing center research and of the vehicles through which writing center scholarship is distributed.

Scholarship Disseminated in Publications

Published writing center scholarship can be generally (although not completely) described as defining, exploring, and expanding our knowledge of six broad topics: theories and practices, models and local practices, tutorial methods and training, materials, administration, and professional development concerns.

Theories and Practices. Among its most fundamental tenets, writing center theory posits the primacy of nonevaluative, collaborative interaction in which the role of the tutor is to help the writer learn to find his or her own solutions. Drawing on an extensive body of composition scholarship that explores knowledge as socially constructed (Ede, Lunsford), the emphasis here is on working individually with each writer, moving the student from group instruction in the classroom to the nonhierarchical and individualized setting where the writer, not a teacher, has a major role in controlling the agenda of learning. Learning becomes an interactive, collaborative process where talk is the primary mode of communication and learning. In this collaborative setting, which both resembles and is distinct from collaboration in the classroom (Harris, "Collaboration"), tutors occupy a different conceptual space in working with writers than classroom teachers do and provide a unique context for writing development (Harris, "Talking").

Scholarship that investigates writing center theory and practice addresses questions such as:

- how to move writers to an active role in tutorial collaboration and why this results in learning;
- how talk promotes learning and what the most effective modes of tutorial conversation are;
- what the center's instructional role is within a composition program;
- how the center can work with students writing in various disciplines;
- what the appropriate interaction is between center and classroom teacher;
- what the nature of tutorial collaboration really is;
- how writers and their contexts differ and what effects these differences have on tutorial instruction;
- how theory and practice intersect and reinforce—or conflict with—each other, and how composition theories influence writing center studies;

- how tutorial learning can be evaluated; and

- what research models are appropriate for studying writing centers and writing center instruction.

An excellent introduction to the scholarship of theory and practice is *Intersections: Theory-Practice in the Writing Center*, a collection of essays edited by Joan Mullin and Ray Wallace.

Models and Local Practices.   Like textbooks that contextualize and operationalize composition theory, every writing center is itself an application of theory to reality, an instantiation of theory. Setting up and running a writing center, like writing a textbook or structuring a composition curriculum, requires knowledge of a rather forbiddingly long list of matters that must be considered: the students to be served; the types of tutorial help they will need; instructional materials that will be needed; approaches that will be used to select, train, and evaluate tutors; faculty development needed for appropriate use of the writing center; the placement of the center within the institution and its mission; and administrative matters such as budget, space, public relations, paperwork, and assessment. Books, articles, and conference papers that address these issues are scholarship—scholarship that is vitally needed (usually yesterday) by center directors. A good example of such scholarship is a recent collection of essays, *Writing Centers in Context: Twelve Case Studies*, edited by Joyce Kinkead and Jeanette Harris.

Writing center publications often include studies of local practices, or descriptions of specific programs or special services, and how they serve the particular missions of different institutions. These articles focus on how specific centers work with writing-across-the-curriculum programs, with credit-bearing courses, with faculty development workshops, with online tutoring and grammar hotlines, with group tutoring, with programs for special student populations, with outreach services, and with efforts to promote institutional missions such as retention or diversity or multicultural awareness.

Tutorial Methods and Training.   Because the tutorial is a defining context of writing center instruction, much scholarship is devoted to studying tutorial methods and their effectiveness. The nature of tutorial interaction is examined in case studies, assessed in a variety of ways, and explored in terms of how people can be trained to be effective tutors. Some scholarship looks at current practices and how these reflect underlying theories of composition. Other scholarship deals with how to diagnose and work with individual differences and with how to respond to the concerns of various groups (ESL students, basic writers, learning-disabled students, nontraditional students, physically disabled learners, etc.). As tutoring moves into new environments, such as online interaction or other forms of distance learning, other studies focus on how such environments affect tutoring and student learning, and how they contribute to writing center theory and practice.

Materials. Although tutorial conversation is central to writing center instruction, writing centers also provide materials and resources that can be incorporated into tutorials or be made available for writers and teachers. It is thus important that some writing center scholarship be devoted to examinations of the creation and use of instructional and reference materials, the role of computers, the creation of nonprint media such as computer programs and audio and video recordings, and the use of personality and cognitive preference tests that can illuminate tutorial collaboration.

Administration. Scholarship devoted to writing center administration considers, for example, how the director and staff interact with faculty; how future directions and goals are determined and implemented; how budgeting, scheduling, recordkeeping, and assessment are handled; how to publicize and promote the center; what kinds of outreach are possible; how local needs are identified; how the physical surroundings of the center impinge on its mission and goals; and what problem-solving techniques can be used to find answers to troublesome administrative questions.

Professional Development Concerns. As in any field, professional development of writing center specialists needs to be thoughtfully considered, and some scholarship is devoted to how and where professional development occurs. In addition, writing center scholars study the needs and the structures of their professional organizations, their own forms of collaborative interaction, and their professional status within their institutions and the composition profession at large.

Where is scholarship on these six topics published? There are, of course, the general composition journals (some of which are described in the Appendix to Richard Gebhardt's chapter "Mentor and Evaluator"). For writing center specialists, however, the most immediately useful venues—the journals read regularly by writing center directors and their staffs—are the *Writing Center Journal* and the *Writing Lab Newsletter*, the two publications of the National Writing Centers Association, an affiliate of the National Council of Teachers of English (NCTE). Both publications have been in existence for almost 20 years; together, they

have published more than 1,000 articles and they have readerships
wider even than their combined subscription figure of 1,600 would
suggest. (A reader survey of the *Writing Lab Newsletter* indicated that
each copy was read, on average, by more than 10 people. Some
respondents said the director either copied relevant material for the
tutoring staff or circulated issues among the staff before forwarding
them to departmental administrators and, in some cases, to administrators elsewhere on campus.) Some commercial publishers have
produced tutor training manuals, and a few collections of essays on
writing centers have appeared from other publishers. But NCTE is
the major outlet for books on writing center scholarship and has
published both essay collections and books focusing on tutorial interaction, tutor-training, models for writing centers, and high school
writing centers.

Scholarship Disseminated at Conferences

Much writing center scholarship is presented, beyond print, at professional conferences—a particularly important and appropriate venue for
writing center specialists, given the field's emphasis on collaboration
and interaction. There are writing center sessions at the annual meetings of CCCC and the NCTE. And conference papers, panels, and
workshops on writing center issues are offered at the annual meeting of
the National Writing Centers Association and at the dozen yearly
regional writing center association meetings.

Regional writing center conferences are generally very well attended,
and the exchange of ideas is energetic and vigorous. In addition, regional
conferences are important because they permit networking with nearby
writing centers. Staff training through conference attendance is an
important responsibility of a writing center director and tends to influence the director's choice of whether to use limited funds to attend a
national meeting alone or to drive to a nearby regional meeting in a van
filled with tutors about to have their first exposure to other methods,
approaches, and settings for writing center tutorials. Thus, although
review committees for other fields of study may not regard regional
conference presentations as highly as papers presented at national
meetings, writing center scholarship presented at regional conferences
should be recognized as especially useful contributions for a variety of
audiences, some of whom would not have come in contact with that
scholarship through print. Moreover, chairs of writing center conferences are increasingly discouraging the reading of papers, turning
instead to workshops, poster sessions, and think tank discussions,
formats in which the scholarship presented transfers less well to print
media.

Scholarship As Institutional Inquiry

The six topics outlined in the section on scholarship disseminated in publications identify what might be called research in the field of writing center practice, but writing center directors must also do local, institutional research. This is necessary because writing center specialists work in a variety of contexts to accomplish a range of tasks different from classroom instruction in writing. For example, they may have responsibilities to integrate their work with institution-wide writing-across-the-curriculum programs, or to handle testing and placement, or to serve as the institutional support system (perhaps the only one) for nontraditional students, students whose first language is not English, students with learning and physical disabilities, and other segments of the student population.

Such responsibilities can spread the work of a writing center across the whole university even when it is housed in a particular department or college. Where a writing center is integrated within a departmental or college writing program, programmatic research is especially important, resulting in "curriculum development as a form of knowledge-making" (867), as Louise Phelps describes such work. Phelps characterizes such efforts as practical inquiry, "a semi-autonomous activity producing propositional knowledge that is bound to the interests and purposes of a concrete teaching community" (875, 877).

Because of the variety of responsibilities and contexts within which writing centers function, writing centers have to develop a good fit with the needs of their particular institutions, so that the primary emphasis and major goals of the writing center respond to those of the institution. Because inquiry is a local matter, writing center directors achieve a better understanding of the needs the writing center should serve when they meet with faculty, offer faculty development workshops, do statistical analysis of student populations, participate in campus committees, visit classes around campus, or work on campus mandates such as heightening multicultural awareness or preparing for proficiency tests.

Institutional research—or (from another perspective) inquiry that reads the institution as a text—is a critical part of writing center scholarship. For no matter how many conferences a writing center specialist attends or how many articles she publishes, lack of local inquiry weakens the writing center, the particular theories that inform its operation, and its value to the institution.

Documentation of such institutional research takes many forms, such as internal documents and position papers, assessments of workshops and in-service sessions, grants and funding proposals, and statistical reports prepared by the computing center at the director's request. In fact, the writing center's yearly report—which documents accomplishments, analyzes problems, and defines the center's goals and future directions—is an important document of local research.

The sort of work I have been describing in this section often is characterized as institutional service or perhaps as teaching (as in the case, for example, of offering faculty development workshops or of producing campus newsletters on writing instruction). But if research provides the researcher and others with needed information, it is a form of research when writing center directors meet with people around their campuses in order to understand the needs, interests, and emphases of their institutions, and it is a form of research when they prepare reports, proposals, and other documents based on what they have learned. Understanding local needs, interests, and emphases is necessary if, as some writing center theorists hope, writing centers are to serve as sites of institutional change (Grimm, Simpson). For that can only happen when the influence of the writing center is felt programmatically and institutionally within the context of an institution's goals.

EVALUATING WRITING CENTER ADMINISTRATION

Because writing center directors typically have released time for administrative responsibilities, evaluation of their administrative competence is an important issue. As the CCCC's pamphlet *Scholarship in Composition* puts it, "administrative contributions should be given significant weight during tenure and salary reviews." Moreover, administrative work should be part of any review process because of the evidence it can provide of both scholarly inquiry and teaching effectiveness.

A primary source of such evidence of administrative work is the writing center's mission statement, which typically includes not only the goals of the center but also an indication of how the center works to promote institutional goals. The yearly report that most directors write is another major source of information about the administrative work of the writing center—and of the director's administrative abilities. Other important documents include annual performance reviews and other assessments made by administrators; statements from tutors about the director's administrative abilities; student feedback forms; letters and other evidence of faculty attitudes toward the center; and samples of publicity releases, budgets, recruitment procedures for new tutors, and evaluation forms used in the center.

Whereas university administrators know how time consuming and labor intensive administrative work is, reviewers in academic departments may need help understanding the nature and extent of administrative efforts. So directors may also choose to present logs they have kept, indicating time spent in activities such as faculty consultations, staff meetings, campus workshops, committee meetings, preparing materials, writing reports, collecting data, budgeting, and scheduling.

Yet another approach to consider when documenting administrative competence, especially in institutions where accountability is an important issue, is to establish a list of specific outcomes the director is expected to accomplish. This results-oriented approach has many problems, but it does permit the director to talk in language other administrators will easily recognize.

Effective writing center administrators, however, must have other qualities more elusive than those captured in management-by-objectives language. A writing center, to be truly effective, must have a collegiality that permits students and tutors to work collaboratively in an atmosphere of trust and friendship. It is of prime importance that the director be a leader who brings a unifying vision to the whole center, who handles the stresses and strains of its work with good will and humor, who promotes equality and free flow of communication in an unstructured setting, and who knows how to create a harmonious, pleasant working environment. Because most writing centers exist with inadequate space, inadequate resources, and inadequate staff, the director must be able to ward off a siege mentality among the staff while dealing with students and teachers unhappy that the center cannot meet all their needs.

One way to assess writing center directors is to use Warren Bennis's list of eight skills of prime importance for academic leaders:

> Resource allocation skills: the ability to decide among alternative uses of time and other scarce organizational resources.

> Conflict resolution skills: the ability to mediate conflict, to handle disturbances under psychological stress.

> Information processing skills: the ability to build networks, extract and validate information, and disseminate information effectively.

> Skills in unstructured decision-making: the ability to find problems and solutions when alternative information and objectives are ambiguous.

> Peer skills: the ability to establish and maintain a network of contacts with equals.

> Leadership skills: the ability to deal with subordinates and the kinds of complications that are created by power, authority, and dependence.

> Entrepreneurial skills: the ability to take sensible risks and implement innovations.

Skills of introspection: the ability to understand the position of a leader and his or her impact on the organization. (See Farmer 15.)

Anyone who has had more than two days' experience in directing a writing center will recognize in this list many of the daily activities that define a director's life—from creating a tutoring schedule that permits the center to be open enough hours without having enough tutors (resource allocation skills) to talking with an irate student who demands to see a tutor immediately (conflict resolution skills). The outside reviewer who enters the writing center with the skills list may need some help in realizing which skills are operating at any given moment. Here, a director's self-assessment statement would be particularly valuable in making connections between observable conditions and the director's use of such skills to keep the center operating smoothly and effectively.

EVALUATING WRITING CENTER TEACHING

Although the evaluation of any faculty member's teaching is still more of an art than a science (despite quantitative evaluation forms), the evaluation of teaching abilities in a writing center is particularly difficult. Writing center theory promotes an approach to learning that turns responsibility for learning over to the learner, that promotes nonevaluative interaction, that proceeds by conversational collaboration, and that has alternative modes of finding out how much the student has learned.

Thus, in setting out to evaluate the teaching abilities of a writing center specialist, review committee members will enter a world very unfamiliar to them, one where the usual guideposts have been removed. They may even find themselves groping for some familiar paper trails that do not—and should not—exist in writing center teaching. There are no syllabi for tutorials, no tests, no grades, no lecture notes, no papers to grade (although tutor-training classes produce a great deal of student writing that is read and commented on but may not be graded in a traditional manner). Rarely does a director position herself in front of a group in a lecturing stance, even when meeting with groups. So a review committee may find itself sitting in on what looks like very informal conversational interaction, even in collaborative group work.

Instead of conventional classroom performance, reviewers should be concerned with how tutors are trained—one of the best tests of a director's abilities to teach. Reviewers should also consider how the director interacts with his or her staff for ongoing, inservice training; how writing center pedagogies are operationalised in instructional materials the director has created for use in the center; how effective the director is as a tutor; and how effective the director is in helping students and their teachers learn how to use the center appropriately. The director's teaching effectiveness can also be observed during faculty workshops. Educating the institutional community about the center's work is an integral component of the director's teaching responsibilities. Writing center directors thus spend a great deal of time helping others learn, but not in familiar teaching postures or modes.[1]

Among the sources of evidence for the director's teaching effectiveness is the effectiveness of the writing center itself. Evaluations of the tutors are evidence of the director's abilities in that the tutors' abilities are the result of the training program and ongoing or inservice training at staff meetings and conversations. Similarly, evidence of the effectiveness of the writing center throughout the campus is proof of a director's ability to construct a successful learning environment. Documentation for this can include evaluations by both students and their teachers. Faculty across campus can be invited to submit comments about what they and their students have learned from the writing center. For example, in addition to workshops, campus newsletters, and personal assistance a faculty member may have had from the director, there are also the reports sent by tutors to teachers whose students have visited the writing center. By working closely with tutors in writing such reports, as Joan Mullin observed in an e-mail message, the director can help educate faculty members about writing center theory and practice and about how to assess their own assignments and classroom practices.

Outside reviews of the director's teaching can be done by a group of peers on campus. Most reviewers will need assistance in understanding the unique nature of writing center teaching—issues discussed in the past several paragraphs, for instance. Such a review would be based on a wide range of evidence, including objectives for the center and for the tutor training course; instructional materials prepared for use in the center; syllabi, readings, and assignments for tutor training courses; and such evaluation documents as self-evaluation statements, evaluations by former student users, tutors, and former tutors.[2]

WRITING CENTER
PROFESSIONAL SERVICE AND ACTIVITY

For writing center directors who present evidence of their professional involvement and activity, that portion of their portfolio can include activities similar to those listed by other faculty and staff. These include attending conferences and presenting papers and workshops, participating in electronic discussion groups relevant to their profession,

reviewing for publishers and journals, writing letters of recommendation, serving in regional and national professional organizations, writing tenure and promotion reviews for others, assisting tutors who
prepare for their own conference participation, and mentoring undergraduate or graduate students who are acquiring their own professional
expertise, as well as mentoring new writing center directors who come
to visit, borrow materials, phone, or write for help.

ADVICE TO WRITING CENTER SPECIALISTS
PREPARING FOR REVIEW

It should be evident from the previous discussion that there are large
quantities of materials to gather and that such collecting should begin
at the time a director starts the job. Jeanne Simpson, a former writing
center director who moved up and on into university administration, is
particularly emphatic about the need to start early, and she offers some
useful advice in an e-mail message:

- Know the evaluation process at your institution.

- Find out if the evaluation process is governed by collective bargain-
  ing agreements.

- Read the college mission statement.

- Write a mission statement for the writing center if none exists yet.

- Be sure there is a job description for the writing center director,
  and write one if none yet exists.

- Read the institution's criteria for promotion and tenure.

- Carefully read the fine print in all of the above documents.

In addition to the readings on Simpson's list, following are five other
important sources of information:

> Russell Edgerton, Patricia Hutchings, and Kathleen Quin-
> lan's book *The Teaching Portfolio: Capturing the Scholarship
> in Teaching.*

> Peter Seldin's *The Teaching Portfolio.*

> Kathleen Yancey's article "Dialogue, Interplay, and Discov-
> ery: Mapping the Role and the Rhetoric of Reflection in
> Portfolio Assessment."

> Two CCCC pamphlets, *Scholarship in Composition: Guide-
> lines for Faculty, Deans, and Department Chairs* and *State-
> ment of Professional Guidance* (available from NCTE).

Preparing extensively for personnel review brings a number of benefits. Of course, it allows you to present your work in an appropriate way. It will also help you to clarify your own goals and to set an agenda for future personal growth and professional development. In addition, such extensive preparation will let you educate others about your work, goals, and achievements and help them understand better what writing centers are and why writing centers are important to the field of composition studies.

NOTES

[1]This is a problem shared by all those in composition studies who use collaborative, conference, or workshop classes. Anyone peering into such a classroom will see the composition teacher walking between groups of students or sitting off to one side, chatting with one student. The careful and extensive work that went into, for example, setting up a successful dynamic for peer response groups or students collaborating on linked computer terminals may be missed entirely.

[2]A basic principle for all academic evaluation is that the data sources be appropriately diverse and representative (see Jarvis 21). Diversity here means the collection of evidence from a number of sources. Writing center specialists interact with such a variety of people that diversity in data sources can easily be achieved. The second characteristic of a sound body of data sources is representativeness, which "requires that enough data be collected over a broad enough period of time and in sufficiently varied situations to give a fair picture of the candidate's teaching" (Jarvis, 21). Representativeness, then, takes planning and preparation far in advance of any review.

WORKS CITED

Boyer, Ernest L. *Scholarship Reconsidered: Priorities of the Professoriate*. Princeton: Carnegie Foundation for the Advancement of Teaching, 1990.

Carino, Peter. "Early Writing Centers: Toward a History." *Writing Center Journal* 15.2 (Spring 1995): 103–15.

CCCC Executive Committee. *Scholarship in Composition: Guidelines for Faculty, Deans, and Department Chairs*. Urbana: NCTE, n.d. N. pag.

——. *Statement of Professional Guidance*. Urbana: NCTE, n.d. N. pag.

Ede, Lisa. "Writing As a Social Process: A Theoretical Foundation for Writing Centers?" *Writing Center Journal* 9.2 (Spring 1989): 3–14.

Edgerton, Russell, Patricia Hutchings, and Kathleen Quinlan. *The Teaching Portfolio: Capturing the Scholarship in Teaching*. Washington: American Association for Higher Education, 1991.

Farmer, Charles H. *Administrator Evaluation: Concepts, Methods, Cases in Higher Education*. Richmond: Higher Education Leadership and Management Society, 1979.

Gebhardt, Richard C. "Article Publication in Composition Studies—Notes for Evaluation Committee Members." Appendix to "Mentor and Evaluator: The Chair's Role in Promotion and Tenure Review." *Academic Advancement in Composition Studies* . Ed. Richard C. Gebhardt and Barbara Genelle Smith Gebhardt. Mahwah, NJ: Lawrence Erlbaum Associates, 1997.

Grimm, Nancy. "Contesting 'The Idea of a Writing Center': The Politics of Writing Center Research." *Writing Lab Newsletter* 17.1 (Sep. 1992): 5–7.

Harris, Muriel. "Collaboration Is Not Collaboration Is Not Collaboration: Writing Center Tutorials vs. Peer-Response Groups." *College Composition and Communication* 43 (Oct. 1992): 369–83.

———. "Talking in the Middle: Why Writers Need Writing Tutors." *College English* 57 (Jan. 1995): 23–38.

Jarvis, Donald K. *Junior Faculty Development: A Handbook.* New York: MLA, 1991.

Lunsford, Andrea. "Collaboration, Control, and the Idea of a Writing Center." *Writing Center Journal* 12.1 (Fall 1991): 3–10.

Kinkead, Joyce A., and Jeanette G. Harris, eds. *Writing Centers in Context: Twelve Case Studies.* Urbana: NCTE, 1993.

Mullin, Joan. E-mail communication. 19 December 1994.

Mullin, Joan A., and Ray Wallace, eds. *Intersections: Theory-Practice in the Writing Center.* Urbana: NCTE, 1994.

Phelps, Louise Wetherbee. "Practical Wisdom and the Geography of Knowledge in Composition." *College English* 53 (Dec. 1991): 863–85.

Seldin, Peter. *The Teaching Portfolio.* Bolton: Ankor Publishing Co., 1991.

Simpson, Jeanne. "The Challenge of Innovation: Putting New Approaches into Practice." *Writing Lab Newsletter* 18.1 (Sept. 1993): 1–3.

———. E-mail communication. 18 December 1994.

Yancey, Kathleen Blake. "Dialogue, Interplay, and Discovery: Mapping the Role and a Rhetoric of Reflection in Portfolio Assessment." *Writing Portfolios in the Classroom: Policy and Practice, Promise and Peril.* Ed. Robert Calfee and Pam Perfumo. Mahwah, NJ: Lawrence Erlbaum Associates, 1996. 83–102.

8   Promotion and Tenure Review of ESL and Basic-Skills Faculty

Nancy Duke S. Lay
City College of New York

Over the past 30 years, American higher education has seen a large influx of students who need what once might have been called non-traditional instruction in ESL or in basic skills of writing, reading, speaking, and studying. To provide this instruction, universities have hired faculty members, many of whom are not trained in traditional English specialties nor committed to doing the research and publication traditionally required for tenure and promotion. Traditional criteria for professional advancement fit these faculty members badly, but students need ESL and basic-skills instruction; it is only fitting, then, that we find ways to evaluate these teachers so that they can continue, as tenured faculty, to contribute to student access and student learning.

Helping us move in that direction is the reason I am writing this chapter. As a former chair of an ESL department and a former chair of a promotion committee, I hope to help ESL and basic-skills teachers to understand the difficulties they face in tenure and promotion review and to learn strategies that will increase their success during personnel review. At the same time, I hope to convince personnel committees and administrators that tenure and promotion criteria should be applied flexibly—although still rigorously—to ESL and basic-skills faculty members.

UNDERSTANDING
THE INSTITUTIONAL ENVIRONMENT

In discussing tenure and promotion for ESL and basic-skills faculty, it is important to understand where these faculty members belong in the university structure, as opposed to where they are located. These non-traditional faculties usually are located either within discrete departments or within another department, often the English department. In any case, personnel policies and procedures are determined by the department where the ESL or basic-skills program is housed.

Departments or Programs

Many special programs and departments were created when open admissions started several decades ago. Reading programs, for instance, were housed in different nontraditional departments, such as Compensatory Programs, Academic Skills, or SEEK (Search for Excellence, Education, Knowledge). Many teachers for these special departments were hired without the doctorates that most institutions required for tenure and promotion, and they were told that their only job was to make their students more able to cope with college.

Basic writing faculties, on the other hand, usually were located in English departments. Sometimes they have been viewed differently from faculties who teach literature or creative writing. But in many institutions, most of their department colleagues also teach basic writing or other composition classes. Also, many basic writing teachers have literature degrees and, depending on rank and influence, they may teach some upper-level courses. In this way, basic writing faculty may end up being seen as having dual interests, in teaching basic writing as well as literature or humanities courses.

In the few ESL departments across the country, ESL faculties have set up their own evaluation criteria in conjunction with institutional criteria, and they are evaluated by peers in their discipline. (Sometimes, when an ESL faculty member comes up for promotion to full professor, faculty members from related departments are sought to comprise the committee; ideally, the candidate is consulted and comes to a mutual agreement with the administration about these faculty representatives.)

Status as a separate department is an issue among ESL teachers in some institutions without ESL departments. Some ESL programs, however, are not interested in attaining departmental status because they are satisfied in an academic department and have representation on department committees, or because the program does not have enough faculty and students to warrant a separate department.

Many ESL programs are housed in departments such as English, Foreign Languages, Linguistics, and sometimes Speech. In some cases, this arrangement may be an injustice to ESL teachers. Very often, however, departments realize the importance of having ESL faculties to help students in their programs. Clearly, these teachers are a minority in such departments. However, they are respected and consulted because of their expertise, which helps the department respond to issues pertaining to some nontraditional students. Thus, these faculty members become assets for the department and their positions are enhanced, even though the primary concerns of these departments lie elsewhere than in the teaching English to individuals for whom it is not a native language.

The Importance of Teaching

Recently, many universities have put more emphasis on teaching, especially undergraduate teaching. The importance of teaching in four-year colleges may be somewhat different than in two-year colleges, where faculties have heavier teaching loads. Good classroom observations by peers and faculty services to students and the college are extremely crucial in these schools. And there is much less pressure for scholarship in two-year colleges than in those universities and four-year colleges where a "publish or perish" tenet still prevails. (For related ideas see Keith Kroll's and Barry Alford's chapter "Scholarship, Tenure, and Composition Studies in the Two-Year College.")

Although it is difficult to evaluate, teaching is an important determinant of promotion and tenure for ESL and basic-skills faculties. It might be a good idea for faculty members to have their ESL and basic-skills students write anonymous evaluations of their courses, rather than just use official department questionnaires. Students could be encouraged to answer such questions as "Does the teacher often come to class late?" and "Does the teacher return papers in a timely fashion and with constructive feedback?" In fact, instead of looking just at instructors, we need to look at students more. Are they learning? Are they expressing themselves effectively? Such evaluations would be very useful to document teaching in tenure and promotion files.

Class observations also provide useful documentation. To prepare, the teacher should give the observer a copy of the course outline before the visit and explain the day's lesson and how it relates to the goals of the course and program. The more information provided, the better will the observer understand the lesson and the course. If a bad observation occurs, the teacher should try to get another senior faculty member to observe the class.

The Doctoral Degree

Getting a college teaching job does not necessarily require a doctorate, but a terminal degree often is necessary for an assistant professor position, as well as for tenure and promotion to higher ranks. This difference in degree expectations presents a problem for some teachers who had been hired without terminal degrees a long time ago but are not eligible for tenure.[1] As some universities created ESL and basic-skills programs over the last 20 years, many men and women with MA degrees were hired as lecturers or instructors. They were told that excellent teaching was the sole important criterion: "Help your students and be an excellent teacher." Today, this is a much less common approach to hiring, especially in four-year institutions, and a doctorate is usually necessary. In my college, the doctorate may be in TESOL or a related discipline, such as linguistics, bilingual education, or rhetoric and composition.

Benefits of Being the Only Expert

Many ESL and basic-skills programs start with as few as one full-time specialist. As the only expert in the department, this teacher can do a lot to build credibility by developing many facets of the skills program—such as placement, curriculum development, and faculty development workshops. The hard work sometimes pays off, provided one does not become merely a full-time adjunct (doing very little for the department besides teaching classes). The person who builds a program from scratch usually gets recognized eventually. Thus, being the only ESL or basic-skils expert in a department may turn out to be an opportunity to demonstrate professionalism, expertise, and sound pedagogy.

Expectations for Scholarship

Some institutions require scholarship for tenure and promotion of ESL and basic-skills faculty; at others, professional activity—which includes attending conferences—will suffice. In some community colleges, scholarship is not needed for tenure, although it is for promotion. A few short articles may be sufficient for tenure at some schools, but promotion may require more substantial publications dealing with subjects that are more serious, more theoretical, and of wider implications. Some institutions allow scholarship and publication on a wide range of topics, and some encourage ESL and basic-skills teachers to pursue classroom-related research that can lead to improvements in the the classroom instruction which is at the heart of the institution's mission. But some expect traditional literary scholarship of their ESL and basic-skills faculty.

New faculty members should be clear about such institutional expectations so that they can work to meet them. They should keep in mind that a paper given at a conference can be turned into an article that counts more as scholarship. They should understand that one strong publication probably is better than several insignificant articles. Most important, perhaps, they should understand how—for ESL and basic-skills specialists—classroom-related research and good textbook authorship can provide credible evidence for tenure and promotion.

RESEARCH AND PUBLICATION

The application of theory and research to pedagogy is essential to professional practice in ESL and basic-skills instruction. I concur with Andrew Kerek, a linguist and a dean, that: "[r]esearch should be relevant to the field and shown to be significant and of high quality. External evidence is critical. Whether the work is theoretical or experimental or applied should not make a difference" (qtd. in Gebhardt, "Editor's" 440).

For ESL and basic-skills teachers, valid measures of scholarship include whether they conduct classroom research to try out instructional techniques and approaches, how well they keep abreast of relevant research by others how effectively they share with other specialists promising ways of using theory and research, and whether they share their work with others in reputable publications and conferences.

"Reputable" publications include refereed journals and books—which in my experience are preferred by promotion committees—but many other outlets for scholarship are important for ESL and basic-skills faculty. Among these are non-refereed journals (of varying degrees of professionalism), published textbooks, self- or custom-published texts, conference papers and workshops, professional influence and leadership, and grants.

Textbooks

In some respects, a good textbook in ESL or basic skills of composition, reading, or speech requires authors to demonstrate command over a broader range of research than is required for the writing of an article or a monograph on some limited segment of the field. Nor is breadth of scholarship the only requirement. Because information must be thoroughly learned before it can be applied, the preparation of a publishable text in this dynamic, competitive field calls for really close acquaintance with scholarly issues and trends. And as Gerald Alred and Erik Thelen have written:

When we teach writing, we create theory; when we communicate theory, we inform composition pedagogy; and when we enrich pedagogy, we affect the practice of writing for both our students and ourselves. A scholar who understands that relationship is up-to-date; a textbook which embodies that relationship is scholarly. (472)

Eventually, universities must establish policies about textbooks as scholarly work. For instance, a textbook might be acceptable as scholarship if its selection of texts and its instructional activities are based on sound pedagogical theory and if it shows awareness of recent research and scholarship (in psycholinguistics, sociolinguistics, discourse analysis, generative grammar, communicative competence, or other areas). But a textbook that cuts and pastes readings with little originality and creativity should not be considered a meaningful publication. To make such determinations, it is extremely important to have evaluation by experts in the field. This is especially true, perhaps, in helping a department evaluate the contributions of a faculty member to a co-authored book.[2] (For a detailed discussion of the importance of external review, see Lynn Bloom's chapter "The Importance of External Reviews in Composition Studies.")

Custom-Published Books

More and more publishers are asking classroom teachers to publish their own materials if they can guarantee a sale of 250 copies. Many of these custom-published books are really examples of curriculum development masking as academic publications. They may also be financial boons for an author because a program administrator may be able to insist that all sections of a course purchase the book. For both reasons—and because there is a difference between having one's manuscript reviewed by peers and having it published without review—external evaluations are crucial in deciding the scholarly merit of a custom-published book.

Conference Presentations

ESL and basic-skills faculties attend quite a number of meetings and make a lot of conference presentations. These activities signal that the instructor is active in the field and a part of professional circles. So ESL and basic-skills faculty members under review for tenure and promotion should be able to show a series of presentations at professional conferences.

At the same time, they should be aware that conference presentations may have little to do with scholarship, and that they usually are so short that they may be considered just an early stage of publication. It makes sense, then, to try to build publications out of conference presentations. (This is a good way to head off questions, like these that a personnel committee member once asked: "If he's presented on this subject at several conferences, how come he's not been published? If this subject is so significant, why haven't any journals accepted an article?") Even if conference presentations do not lead to publications, professionals in the field can review and evaluate them for scholarly and professional significance during promotion or tenure review.

Professional Contributions

During tenure and promotion review, it is important to demonstrate one's contributions to the field and the characteristics expected of a professional. The issue is not the number of committees, for it is easy to spread oneself too thin, both within the college and outside; what is significant is making a real contribution in service to the college and professional associations. The fact that one has held several elective and appointed offices in professional organizations, for instance, or served as a consultant to commercial publishing houses testifies to an individual's standing in the profession.

Grants

Some institutions and departments view grants as substitutes for scholarship, with their weight during tenure and promotion review depending on the size and type of the grant. If a grant relates to innovative teaching approaches, it could lead to publication. But the grant itself speaks to the faculty member's productivity and indicates that the faculty member has done something significant in the field, and both things are relevant to receiving tenure or getting promoted.

Faculty members working toward promotion or tenure should be aware, however, that grant-attaining sometimes can create tensions with colleagues. In some instances, faculty members who get grants do not teach, they have clerical and secretarial staff, and they can purchase all kinds of equipment; meanwhile others struggle with the minimum resources available. Such things can complicate the personnel-review process.

PERSONAL STRATEGIES
FOR SUCCESSFUL TENURE REVIEW

Participate in Departmental Mentoring

In institutions where new faculty members are given an orientation to the policies and criteria for appointment and reappointment, they are being guided from the outset as to what is needed to survive in the system. One colleague said that a mentor assigned to her explained the annual evaluation procedures, gave her an outline, reviewed with her what she had to do, and made available a copy of his own portfolio.

Policies and criteria have to be repeated clearly again and again. Although new faculty members may benefit from going through a dry-run reappointment, promotion, or tenure review, they need not be overwhelmed at first with too much information. In the first term, probably what is most crucial is classroom performance and peer observations. But junior faculty members should know that, before they submit their portfolios for review, they should ask themselves questions like these: Have I published in the last year? How is my teaching performance? Did I volunteer for any college committee?

Educate Your Colleagues

ESL and basic-skills faculties need to educate department chairs and other faculty members about the research that is going on in the field—theory as well as practice. Many senior faculty and non-basic-skills faculty members think that ESL and basic-skills faculties are only equipped to teach practical things. They may even believe that anyone who speaks English can teach the language. Because they are not familiar with the field, they are mystified and do not understand what is going on in the ESL classroom. One senior faculty member could not imagine how one could teach a class consisting of students with 15 different language backgrounds; he asked if one needed to speak all 15 languages!

Traditional faculty members sometimes do not see that the practical side of ESL and basic-skills teaching is actually grounded in theory. Basic-skills instructors need to show the importance of theory in their own work. They should express their enthusiasm and have conversations with colleagues about the strengths, problems, and needs of their students. ESL and basic-skills faculties should get senior faculty members in the department who understand what they are doing to be their allies and supporters. Since the voice of the novice may not be heard or respected, junior faculty members should try to get senior faculty members on their side. (For ideas about orienting other faculty members to your research and teaching, see Richard Gebhardt's chapter "Preparing Yourself for Successful Personnel Review.")

Junior faculty members will have to take the initiative to engage in dialogue with respected senior faculty members in the department. They should get involved in departmental meetings and activities. They should be visible. Although mentoring does not have an evaluative role, it may not be a bad idea to get advice from senior faculty members and even ask them to evaluate some classroom teaching, publications, success stories of students, and professional activities. When the time for tenure comes, these senior faculty members will have a good understanding of the work and will be able to speak up for the junior faculty.

Understand the Hard-Work-No-Reward Problem

ESL and basic-skills faculties have always been asked to oversee basic-skills activities in their departments. Some become coordinators, directors, and supervisors. The work in ESL and basic-skills programs is endless. Every time one finishes a project, another one pops up. And placement, testing, curriculum, training of adjuncts, faculty development workshops, tutoring, support services, and the use of technology all need to be looked at and modified at least every year.

Such activities—curriculum development, tutor training, and all the rest—are the backbone of a basic-skills program. A good administrator has to manage the day-to-day details of the program and also conceptualize the needs of the students and the curriculum. What are the language-learning principles underlying the program? What changes should be made to help students progress? If such leadership is important, the department and institution should have clear policies to reward faculty members who work in program administration. (For a discussion of related issues see Duane Roen's chapter "Writing Administration As Scholarship and Teaching.")

Policies about the work and reward of ESL and basic-skills faculties vary widely. In one program I know, a faculty member coordinated courses without released time because he thought it served important department needs. In another program, a faculty member was hired to work on the sort of program leadership activities I mentioned earlier, but when he came up for promotion, that work carried no weight with a review committee that was looking for scholarship and publication. On the other hand, another assistant professor I know was granted promotion to associate because of the innovative implementations of significant curricular changes—requiring many hours of hard work, experimentation, and follow-up—that were part of the job description.

Don't Rely on the Longevity Myth

There is a myth that if you have been in a certain rank for a long time you will get a promotion simply by applying for it again and again. Unfortunately, this has happened in some cases. But you should not rely solely on the number of years you have been serving the department. Remember that the application forms for tenure and promotion ask "What have you done in the last five years?" When the record shows that there has not been any significant movement since the last application, the question always raised is, "Why not?"

Beware of Unmentioned Criteria

Earlier, I wrote about the importance of following the criteria of teaching, service, and scholarship as measures of professional evaluation. However, to be realistic, there is another category that comes into play—the unmentioned criteria.

It is clear that faculties need to acknowledge that politics sometimes plays a part in the tenure and promotion process. It is also true that the faculty member's ability to work with a larger community is an important factor. Have I acquired conventional standards of sociability, one might ask. Am I able to work with my colleagues? Am I a loud-mouth? Do I complain a lot? Do I have good rapport with students? Can I deliver to the department, program, or college what I am supposed to do?

Sometimes there are personality conflicts or cultural conflicts that a candidate discovers through the grapevine. It sometimes happens that culture-bound behaviors have turned people off. That is one of the reasons institutions have procedures for appealing tenure and promotion decisions. It protects faculty members who have done everything they could according to the process but find, because of personality differences and unmentioned criteria, that problems still arise.

Develop a Professional Portfolio

How can ESL and basic-skills faculties best present themselves to tenure and promotion committees? Using portfolios, a practice already followed in some colleges and departments, gives faculty members a chance to prove themselves by writing up their own presentation and showing evidence of their work. Perhaps a portfolio will prove to be more meaningful and real to review committees than a mass of letters and memos without the candidate's own input. To make this possible, the faculty member should update and add materials to the portfolio without waiting for invitations from the chair or review committee.

FAIRNESS IN PERSONNEL REVIEW POLICIES[3]

Every department has its own criteria for tenure and promotion and, although they have to be revised every now and then, these standards should not be too different from general university criteria. For example, in a department where teaching and counseling are important, scholarship or publication expectations have to be flexible. Similarly, there needs to be a balance between scholarship and the administration of a skills program. In each case, scholarship, teaching, and service all remain important; the proportional weight of each may vary, however, in the department's criteria.

ESL and basic-skills faculties in English departments may find it difficult to attain tenure and promotion unless the department and review committee make an effort to understand the field and the work done by these candidates.[4] It is not surprising if literary scholars are not sympathetic to ESL activities. But it is unfortunate and unfair if they are placed in the position of judging those activities without using consistent criteria that every member of the department is expected to meet.

We all can tolerate certain ambiguities within our own departments. However, when these become too extreme, faculty members begin to lose faith in the department, they become unfriendly, collegiality is gone, and, worst of all, faculty members feel alienated from the department and distance themselves from any service or contributions they may make.

New faculty members usually have little idea of the review process followed at their new institution. Tenure and promotion criteria may not be what most occupies their minds in the first year, and young faculty members may be afraid to ask too many questions. Left on their own, then, new faculty members may not find out what is required for tenure and promotion until the fourth or fifth year of probation—when there is not much time to fill in the gaps. To avoid this unfortunate situation, each department should have a Faculty Advisement Committee (or similar support system) to help new faculty members with the complicated process of tenure and promotion review. Such a committee could share information about expectations for tenure and promotion and offer guidelines about how to prepare for tenure and promotion, when to apply for promotion, and how to appeal negative tenure and promotion decisions.

CONCLUSIONS

Requirements for scholarship and publication in ESL and basic skills are generally ambiguous, with good reason, because of the emphasis on teaching and the need for change inherent in these fields. Many departments still find it difficult to evaluate ESL and basic-skills instructors without reverting to the mindset of the traditional faculty.

I am not suggesting that basic-skills and ESL instructors should be evaluated by standards different from those by which the rest of the faculty is evaluated. They should be evaluated on their scholarship, teaching, and service, but different weights may be assigned to each criterion. I am advocating that the evaluation of ESL and basic-skills faculty members should involve broader and more flexible concepts of scholarship, of the importance of teaching, and of meaningful service to the students and the institution.

Department chairs should make sure that requirements for tenure and promotion are clearly stated in writing, that criteria are adhered to in tenure and promotion review, and that favoritism is avoided. They also need to assure that external evaluations from experts in the ESL and basic-skills teaching carry sufficient weight in promotion and tenure review. They also should set up orientation activities and advisement committees for junior faculty members.

Junior faculty members in ESL and basic skills should make use of their dissertations by trying to publish articles based on them. Update your file frequently in line with institutional procedures and criteria. Network with colleagues in the department and, most important of all, acquire department mentors who can support your work and speak for you during tenure and promotion review. Educate and re-educate them on what you do professionally.

ACKNOWLEDGMENT

I want to thank my CUNY colleagues (who will remain anonymous) for sharing their experiences.

NOTES

[1]In the past, applicants for full-time ESL positions had at least a master's degree in TESOL or a related discipline, and sometimes a PhD. Recently, there has been pressure for the doctorate, because without one it is hard to move to professorial rank.

[2]A co-authored book of high significance and visibility and with excellent evaluations by external peers can be as strong as a significant piece of individual research. Although our field encourages collaborative work, the single-authored textbook still carries more weight than co-authorship. There are instances where full-time faculty members co-author with part-time faculty or graduate students, and the full-time faculty member tries to get all the credit because the part-time teacher is not especially concerned with the value of publication for tenure or promotion. It is important for an evaluator to get an account of each individual contribution to a collaborative work and to evaluate each section accordingly. The other co-authors can be consulted to ensure that the process is fair. And it is crucial that experts in the field be consulted before making a judgment on the scholarship presented in a co-authored textbook.

[3]For a fair assessment of ESL and basic-skills faculty, one point needs particularly to be kept in mind: the nature of TESOL and composition studies as professional fields today. They have become highly competitive disciplines, as indicated by membership growth (TESOL has 6,000 at its annual conventions, and CCCC attracts around 3,000 participants). The scope of influence of ESL now extends around the world. In the United States alone, there are more than 2 million people who know no English at all, in addition to millions more whose inadequate grasp of the language requires special instruction. In almost every institution, increasing numbers of students need the services and expertise of ESL and basic-skills teachers to help them succeed in mainstream courses.

[4]The complexities involved in teaching English in disparate circumstances, in various countries, to students of widely differing ages and language backgrounds, have generated much research. A TESOL specialist today is obliged to keep abreast of research not only in linguistics, but in several related disciplines as well. Publishers are aware of this. It is quite likely, in fact, that publishers are more fully aware of the scholarly dimensions of TESOL today than are most university faculties.

WORKS CITED

Alred, Gerald J., and Erik A. Thelen. "Are Textbooks Contributions to Scholarship?" *College Composition and Communication* 44 (Dec. 1993): 466–77.

Bloom, Lynn Z. "The Importance of External Reviews in Composition Studies." Gebhardt and Gebhardt 167–76.

Gebhardt, Richard C. "Editor's Column: Scholarship, Promotion, and Tenure in Composition Studies." *College Composition and Communication* 44 (Dec. 1993): 439–42.

———. "Preparing Yourself for Successful Personnel Review." Gebhardt and Gebhardt 117–27.

Gebhardt, Richard C., and Barbara Genelle Smith Gebhardt, eds. *Academic Advancement in Composition Studies*. Mahwah, NJ: Lawrence Erlbaum Associates, 1997.

Kroll Keith, and Barry Alford. "Scholarship, Tenure, and Composition Studies in the Two-Year College." Gebhardt and Gebhardt 57–70.

Roen, Duane H. "Writing Administration as Scholarship and Teaching." Gebhardt and Gebhardt 43–55.

9 Preparing Yourself for Successful Personnel Review

Richard C. Gebhardt
Bowling Green State University

I am regretful but not troubled when the work of a candidate for tenure is just not good enough to support a positive decision; the system is intended to produce such outcomes. But gifted persons who are denied tenure because they made bad choices haunt me long after they are gone.

—Williamson (52)

There's a great deal of sense in those words by Marilyn Williamson, a former English department chair at Wayne State University. The substance of tenure review (evaluating accomplishments and predicting future potential on the basis of five-year records in teaching, scholarship, and service) and its process (the chair's work, personnel committee deliberations, a tenured-faculty vote, collegiate and university review of department recommendations) are complex and difficult enough. Probationary faculty members hardly need to complicate them with bad choices like these:

> Beginning so many publishing projects that all are delayed, or committing to one major project so fully that, unless it is completed on time, there is no scholarly record to support tenure.

> Giving substantial scholarly papers but never finding the time to revise them toward publication.

Assuming that high ratings on student course evaluations are the only mark of good teaching, and trying to curry high student ratings by lowering expectations.

Assuming that low ratings and critical student comments are always uninformed, malicious, or otherwise unworthy of serious attention.

Accepting so many committee assignments that research suffers, or so few that you look like a malingerer to senior faculty members with strong service orientations.

Failing to include an informative self-appraisal statement if one is invited as part of the reappointment review process.

Not taking the time to update your curriculum vitae before the chair does your end-of-year evaluation.

Not keeping faculty generally aware of your work by sending items about your publications and other activities to the department newsletter.

Assuming, as you prepare materials for personnel review, that you do not need to spell out abbreviations familiar to specialists (ATTW, CCCC, *JAC*, *JBW*, RSA, *RTE*, STC, *TETYC*, WPA, etc.) but alien to many readers of tenure applications.

Forgetting to mention in personnel reports the circulation and acceptance rates of journals, the very competitive and blind-refereed nature of the annual CCCC program, or that certain conference proceedings are refereed and selective.

Failing to pay careful attention to written guidelines about the criteria for tenure, the nature and time line of tenure review, and the contents and format of tenure applications.

"All that's just common sense," you are probably thinking, and I agree. Still, I have seen bright, motivated assistant professors make all of those mistakes, as well as these: treating the preparation of reports for personnel review as petty red tape; and thinking of tenure review as something done to a candidate rather than as an active process in which the probationary faculty member has important responsibilities.

All of those bad choices complicate personnel review and make the path toward tenure more difficult than it has to be. So, logic and, better yet, common sense suggest that you should try to avoid such mistakes over the five years or so you are building the record in teaching, scholarship, and service upon which the department will decide if you merit tenure and the promotion that usually accompanies it. And I hope this chapter—and this book, for that matter—provides information on which you will make good choices as you begin developing your professional record.

INFORMATION ON WHICH TO BASE
YOUR APPROACH TO TENURE

Aden Ross of the Utah State University English Department wrote that it is the responsibility of the faculty member seeking tenure "to determine the relative importance of teaching and publication across your institution" and to "learn how [you] are evaluated, allocating [your] energies proportionately and asking the right questions at the right time" (54–55). That advice—self-reliance in understanding the expectations for tenure and promotion—is sound, even though AAUP guidelines make it the institution's responsibility to advise probationary faculty "early in their appointment, of the substantive and procedural standards generally accepted in decisions affecting renewal and tenure" (48) and even though it is official policy, at most colleges and universities, to put personnel handbooks into the hands of new faculty members. The stakes involved in your work toward tenure are high, and the time available to build a strong tenure file is short. For both reasons, you should heed this advice from the CCCC Committee on Professional Guidance to Departments and Faculty:

> After accepting a position, the candidate should discover and become familiar with any faculty handbooks, union contracts, and similar personnel policy materials. The new faculty member should know the practice, policy and philosophy on such issues as released time, rewards for grant seeking, summer school teaching, consulting with industry or other schools, and the relative weight given to teaching, service, publication, and professional involvement in evaluations for reappointment, raises, promotion, and tenure. Candidates should know, for example, if there is a systematic review process, and if so what criteria and procedures are used. In any such review process, both individual faculty members and the responsible administrators have specific responsibilities; the new faculty member should understand these clearly. (494)

Part of what the CCCC committee recommends here is understanding procedures (how the review process works and the responsibilities of committees, administrators, and probationers) and part of it is understanding expectations—for instance, how teaching, scholarship, and service are valued in your department and your institution. Clearly, understanding the expectations by which you will be judged—in annual evaluations for reappointment and merit pay, as well as in future tenure review—is important so that you can focus your energy and attention on professional activities that will be acknowledged and rewarded. (It is important in another way, too. It may help you realize, early on, that your professional values and priorities match your department's so poorly that you should seek a position elsewhere.)

Because understanding expectations is so important, it is too bad that the documents most likely to be sent to new faculty members seldom give full descriptions of how teaching, scholarship, and service are valued and evaluated. Consider my university's criteria for tenure and promotion to associate professor:

> Demonstrated ability as a teacher;
>
> Demonstrated ability to do research, scholarship or creative work, ability that is demonstrated by "publications, significant research, or presentation of refereed papers at regional or national meetings;" and
>
> Evidence of active involvement in service to the University community and the profession. (see *Governance* B.I.D.1)

Those statements are typical of institutional criteria in teaching, research, and service. By design, they give only the roughest sort of outline of what actually may be required for tenure in a particular department, and for this reason, they may cause dangerous misconceptions. Will strong conference papers really count, as the statement on research implies, as much as articles? Will unpublished research, no matter how significant, carry as much weight as a research project yielding a refereed article or two? Maybe, but probably not. So it would be risky for a new faculty member to start building a scholarly agenda around the high-level generalizations in most official statements on tenure and promotion. Instead, as the CCCC Committee on Professional Guidance puts it, you should try to develop

> a clear understanding, in writing, of what activities will be considered important in evaluation for reappointment, raises, promotion, and tenure. Some institutions base such evaluations solely on teaching and other locally assigned activities. Some institutions consider service to the profession and/or scholarship as well. Where service to the profession is a factor, a junior faculty member needs to know which activities (e.g., workshops, committee assignments, offices) and which professional organizations are deemed important by the institution. Where scholarship is a factor, the junior faculty member needs to know which journals and types of publication will "count." (495)

Toward this end, you should seek out—if they are not given to you routinely—detailed department guidelines for tenure and promotion, as well as materials used by the chair and the personnel committee in reappointment evaluations, merit pay review, and other pretenure evaluations by which you will build a tenure track record. Almost certainly, you will find in such documents gaps, ambiguities, and contradictions that you should discuss with your chair. And these discussions will give you a chance to ask about the unformalized customs and practices in the way the department evaluates faculty.

Discussions with your chair also can be a good way for you to explore the department's attitudes toward fields, like composition studies, in which a faculty member's educational impact on students may come through administration and advising as much as through classroom activity, her research often is applied and pedagogical rather than theoretical, and a scholar's work comes out in a variety of forms besides scholarly articles and books (textbooks, curriculum development and materials, software, etc.).

In most English departments, the majority of tenured faculty members view teaching and scholarship from their perspectives as literature professors. These faculty members probably have not given much thought to the idea, put forward by the MLA Commission on Professional Service, that "scholarship/research" is but one site of a faculty member's "intellectual work" (10–11) or to the Commission's view that scholarship "need not be published or disseminated in traditional forms" (17). They probably are unfamiliar with the MLA Commission on Writing and Literature's 1988 statement that research in composition studies "is often disseminated in the form of textbooks" as well as in "workshops" and other unpublished means, and that for writing directors and others whose job involves "an unnaturally heavy dose of administration," such leadership "should be given significant weight during tenure and salary reviews" (Report 73–74). And they are likely to be unaware of a 1993 position statement from the Association of Departments of English: "In evaluations of scholarship, different kinds of activities and products should be given credit. Suitable measures of excellence should be developed for nontraditional as well as for traditional forms of scholarship" ("ADE" 44). Almost certainly, however, the tenured faculty members who will vote on your tenure have opinions and feelings about the issues addressed in these reports. And it is important to know something about these attitudes, if you are likely to do applied research, to write pedagogical articles and books, or to put significant time and energy into staff workshops or administrative activities.

If you would like additional background, longer quotes from the MLA and ADE statements appear with some other relevant materials, in my chapter "Mentor and Evaluator." Susan McLeod's chapter "A View from the Dean's Office" discusses another useful resource, the book *Scholarship Reconsidered*, which proposes expanding the idea of research to make a place for "scholarship of integration," "scholarship of application" and "scholarship of teaching." And Duane Roen, in his chapter

"Writing Administration As Scholarship and Teaching," discusses that book's relevance to the work of writing program administrators.

WORKING TOWARD TENURE AND PROMOTION

The past few pages have emphasized broad tenure criteria and more specific department expectations because these will form the basis of your tenure review, as well as various important pretenure evaluations (annual reappointments, year-end evaluations, or whatever they are called in your department). The CCCC Committee on Professional Guidance was correct in saying that "[t]he best way . . . to prepare for the decision of reappointment, promotion, and/or tenure is to discharge professional responsibilities to the best of one's ability . . . " (497). But "professional responsibilities" vary a good bit from institution to institution. So following the CCCC committee's advice means that you must understand how your department defines the professional responsibilities of faculty.

In the chapter "Mentor and Evaluator: The Chair's Role in Promotion and Tenure Review," I discuss the value of developing descriptive tenure and promotion profiles. You might find it useful to read that section as background for the conversations you have with your chair about the expectations the department has of you. If your department has not developed clear, written statements of expectation for tenure and promotion, these conversations may help the department start working on them; at the least, the conversations should result in a statement of expectations about your work.

Knowing department expectations does not make it easy to prepare for tenure, but *not* knowing the expectations makes it harder. If you know from the first semester that the minimal research expectation for tenure and promotion to associate professor is a single-author university press book and four refereed articles, you can work at those publications on a four- or five-year schedule—perhaps writing a conference paper and revising it into an article each year—while taking several years to develop your dissertation into a book. But what if you began your publishing efforts thinking that the expectation was a single-author university press book *or* four articles, or what if you thought *any* book would suffice and spent most of your probationary period collaborating on a writing textbook? If you knew that the minimum scholarly requirement for tenure may be satisfied by publishing several refereed articles (or a book) backed up by a record of scholarly papers and workshop presentations, you still would be able to pursue a more ambitious publishing agenda—in the interest of merit pay, early tenure, job mobility, or personal satisfaction. But you would know that your professional agenda could include more time and energy for meeting the department's teaching and service expectations.

In the previous paragraph, I mentioned a multiple-year publishing schedule and a professional agenda of research, teaching, and service activities. Thinking with such metaphors of time management and systematic work on complex tasks may be one of the best things you can do to prepare for the tenure review. In the first place, it encourages you to analyze and organize the task of pursuing tenure and promotion—by understanding department expectations in your first months on campus. It also gives you as much time as possible to develop a record—to document improvement in teaching effectiveness after a rocky first semester, no less than to build an adequate list of refereed publications—that will justify a positive tenure vote.

Besides understanding the expectations and working to satisfy them, there is a good deal you can do during the probationary years leading to your review for tenure and promotion. Let me mention three of these approaches.

Do Not Think of Tenure As a Solo Activity

I have emphasized the importance of close work with your department chair because chairs have a professional obligation—and in my experience, most have the personal desire—to help in the development of faculty members. But there are many other human resources you may be able to draw on.

Even when they are in different specialties, probationary faculty members in your department share problems and perspectives in a way that can make them a natural source of information and support. Look, too, for senior faculty members with whom to discuss the expectations the department has of you, as well as how you can work effectively with the students at your university, how you can tap university research and faculty development funds, and other inside information they have to offer. Senior composition studies faculty members, of course, can be particularly valuable mentors. But so may those in applied linguistics, English education, and other areas in which faculty members often have applied or pedagogic research programs and heavy administrative demands.

Many literature professors, of course, will probably vote on your tenure. So it can be helpful to forge relationships with these faculty members—for instance, by asking the author of numerous books about how to interest a university press in a project, or by inviting a senior literature professor to visit a class and discuss your teaching. John Schilb's chapter "Scholarship in Composition and Literature: Some Comparisons" may help you prepare for such discussions, and you might find it useful to review Edward White's discussions in *Teaching and Assessing Writing* of how poststructural reading theory operates in the teaching of writing (92–102) and of how college writing instruction differs from much other teaching with regard to authority, responsibility, and control (110–13).

Conversations with senior faculty colleagues give you helpful information and insights, and they can help your efforts toward tenure in other ways, too. They let people who will vote on your tenure get to know you as a human being. And they help faculty members in other specialties understand more fully the nature and expectations of scholarship in your field and the special demands of teaching writing.

And do not forget support and resources available to you beyond your institution. Among these are graduate school friends working toward tenure and promotion in other departments, women and men with whom you share sessions at professional conferences or with whom you work on state or national committees, and senior scholars (potential external reviewers of your tenure application) who hear your conference papers or discuss common professional interests with you at conventions or by e-mail.

Use Personnel Reports to Educate the Department

It is easy to think of tenure review and various pretenure evaluations (year-end chair reviews, reappointment evaluations, merit-pay reviews, and the like) as one-way transactions in which personnel committees, faculty members, chairs, and deans judge the work you describe and document in various required reports. But while they are studying the report you submitted (updated CV, compact self-appraisal statement, selected course materials, recent articles, etc.) these women and men are learning things about your work and your field. (How else could a personnel committee made up of a medievalist, a theorist, an American-ist, and a poet even try to do the merit review for a diverse department?) And you can enhance what faculty members and administrators learn about your work and the field of composition studies by making sure that your personnel reports include information nonspecialist readers probably do not have about our field.

For instance, how might you mention a recent *CCC* acceptance in a reappointment-review report? For readers inside composition studies, brief mention of the fact—even using cryptic initials rather than the name of the journal—would be significant. But in a personnel report for nonspecialists you should give more detail. For example:

> In the past year, my article on the "History of Collaborative Narrative" was accepted for future publication in the refereed journal *College Composition and Communication*—the oldest and largest periodical in my field

and, with an acceptance rate under 10%, one of the most competitive. (The editor's acceptance and the referee's reports are attached to the typescript in my file.)

Similarly, composition studies specialists would find significance in brief mention of papers given at the Penn State conference and CCCC. But a personnel report should make it clear that the Penn State Conference on Rhetoric is a well-regarded national meeting, not the local affair its title may suggest, and that the Annual Meeting of the Conference on College Composition and Communication has a highly competitive, blind-refereed program. Specialists would understand without explanation why a rhetoric faculty member and writing director was taking time to work with faculty members in other departments or with teachers in area schools. But a merit-review report might need to elaborate on relevant issues of writing across the disciplines and cooperative approaches to literacy. Specialists would know immediately why a writing director listed program development and staff training activities in her annual self-report, but included few summaries of student course evaluations. However, other readers would need discussion of the significance that curricular and supervisory work has for the teaching mission of the department and college.

Providing such information adds substance to the accomplishments you report, and it helps the faculty members, chairs, and deans who read your various personnel reports understand the nature and professional standards of composition studies. And because several different committees will evaluate your reappointment and merit-review reports during your probationary years before tenure review, this information can have a cumulative effect on what the faculty knows about your work and your field.

Pay Attention to Deadlines and Directions

To have positive impact, of course, your various personnel reports need to be submitted on time and in a form that commands credibility. I hope this point is obvious. But because I have known faculty for whom it was not, I illustrate it here with a few examples.

1. What is a chair to think when a probationary faculty member does not file required reports about her professional accomplishments? Perhaps, that there is nothing to report. Possibly, that she has found another job and is about to resign. At the least, that she cannot be counted on to complete projects on schedule.

2. What does a dean conclude when a probationer's vita does not follow prescribed format by indicating parenthetically each publi-

cation that is refereed? That the probationer has no refereed publications.

3. What does a careless, error-filled annual report say to the personnel committee? Maybe nothing—if the probationer has a very strong record in teaching and publication. But if a person is having difficulty with his classes or research agenda, such carelessness may well intensify the suspicion that he "doesn't have what it takes" for tenure and promotion.

Clearly, you do not want such impressions to undercut your efforts in teaching, scholarship, and service. So it is important to pay attention to the deadlines and to the directions of various kinds that are part of personnel review at your institution.

Submitting timely, well-written reports to the personnel committee may help your case for tenure, if they include worthy accomplishments in teaching, research and service. Inviting senior faculty members to visit your classes can help establish your record as a teacher, if your course outlines are imaginative and current, your lectures are clear and substantive, and your class discussions are animated and productive. Understanding the scholarly expectations of the department and building your publishing agenda around them can strengthen your case for tenure and promotion, if your writing projects result in the required books and refereed articles.

Your accomplishments in teaching, research, and service are critical to the way you will be evaluated, and so are your department's awareness and understanding of your accomplishments. So, as the CCCC Committee on Professional Guidance advises: "The best way, finally, to prepare for the decision of reappointment, promotion, and/or tenure is to discharge professional responsibilities to the best of one's ability, and ensure that these efforts are fully recognized by the department . . . " (497).

WORKS CITED

AAUP Council. "Statement on Procedural Standards in the Renewal or Nonrenewal of Faculty Appointments." *Academe* 76 (Jan./Feb. 1990): 48–51.

"ADE Statement of Good Practice: Teaching, Evaluation, and Scholarship." *ADE Bulletin* No. 105 (Fall 1993): 43–45.

CCCC Committee on Professional Guidance to Departments and Faculty. "Draft Statement of Professional Guidance to Junior Faculty and Department Chairs." *College Composition and Communication* 38 (Dec. 1987): 493–97.

Gebhardt, Richard C. "Mentor and Evaluator: The Chair's Role in Promotion and Tenure Review." Gebhardt and Gebhardt 145–165.

Gebhardt, Richard C., and Barbara Genelle Smith Gebhardt, eds. *Academic Advancement in Composition Studies.* Mahwah, NJ: Lawrence Erlbaum Associates, 1997.

Governance Documents. Bowling Green: Bowling Green State University, 1994.

McLeod, Susan H. "Scholarship Reconsidered: A View from the Dean's Office." Gebhardt and Gebhardt 177–189.

MLA Commission on Professional Service. "Making Faculty Work Visible: Reinterpreting Professional Service, Teaching, and Research in the Fields of Language and Literature." 1995; accepted by the MLA Executive Council 1996.

"Report on the Commission on Writing and Literature." *Profession 88.* New York: MLA, 1988. 70–76.

Roen, Duane. "Writing Administration As Scholarship and Teaching." Gebhardt and Gebhardt 43–55.

Ross, Aden. "Tenure, or the Great Chain of Being." *Change* Jul./Aug. 1987: 54–55.

Schilb, John. "Scholarship in Composition and Literature: Some Comparisons." Gebhardt and Gebhardt 21–30.

White, Edward M. *Teaching and Assessing Writing.* San Francisco: Jossey–Bass, 1994.

Williamson, Marilyn. Rev. of *The Academic's Handbook*, ed. A. Leigh DeNeef, Craufurd D. Goodwin, and Ellen Stern McCrate. *ADE Bulletin* No. 99 (Fall 1991): 51–53.

10 Special Challenges Facing Women in Personnel Reviews

Janice Neuleib
Illinois State University

Recently, I was invited to dinner with three women faculty members from the College of Business. These colleagues, two professors and one associate professor, are suing the university because their salaries are lower than those of the men in their college, even the salaries of the assistant professors. They had taken their case through the appropriate internal channels, but were thwarted at every turn. Their only recourse was the courts. They told me that they had talked to other women faculty on campus, asking whether any had equally specific evidence of personnel inequities. They found that most women faculty members had responded to evaluation outcomes with a kind of codependent selective blindness. Several women said they had suspected a problem, but most said they did not want to know what the really bad news might be.

It is important, however, for us to discover what we already know. In *Women, Girls, and Psychotherapy,* Carol Gilligan, explained that when a girl says "I don't know," she means she knows all too well and that what she knows is unspeakable (8). Past treatment of women faculty has been unspeakable, yet we are still afraid to speak for fear that our few privileges will be taken away if we cause trouble.

The messages are clear.

Women cannot talk about their children in the faculty coffee room, or in the classroom, or even in the hallway. Men can, of course. Women cannot talk about shopping trips, make-up, or cooking in any professional setting. Men can, if they want to. If women break these rules (and other equally subtle understandings), they suffer at evaluation time. Certainly, departmental and university cultures ought not restrict women's social and professional behavior in these and other far more damaging ways, but the unspoken rules control, although laws forbid that control. The rules are unwritten, unacknowledged, and therefore powerful beyond any written codes. Those rules tell women that they must meet different and more demanding professional standards, sometimes while simultaneously being accused of special privilege under the law.

In the last 20 years (approximately the length of time I have been a tenured faculty member), I have served on personnel committees at departmental, college, and university levels. I have also served on or chaired dozens of candidate search committees at every level. As a graduate thesis and dissertation director, I have coped with feminist issues in graduate personnel decisions in a variety of complex circumstances. My experience reflects, in general, many of the personal stories already recounted by others in the profession: Try not to act like a woman.

Judith Pascoe, for example, describes the personal horrors of attending MLA job interviews while pregnant, noting parallel studies of psychotherapists who had to deal with hostile client reactions to a pregnant therapist (72). As a longtime mother and personnel committee member, I cannot stress too strongly the subtle prejudice against motherhood. (Sociological studies confirm a cultural bias against mothers; see Hite 140). I blanch as I write this, but it is true that if women have to try harder, mothers have to disguise their state of being. Motherhood makes clear the otherness of a woman professional.

In *Exiles and Communities*, Jo Anne Pagano posits a Lacanian explanation for this otherness. She argues that because of the maleness of the academic patriarchy, "in the Lacanian story, a woman teacher is an odd creature—one who represents as an actor represents. She is like one of Shakespeare's boys dressed up as a girl masquerading as a boy" (8). A woman researcher may be even odder because she speaks in the language of the patriarchy not only in her words but also in her research. We in composition continue to find ourselves defending research that sometimes ends up being classified as women's work. In *Women Writing the Academy*, one of Gesa Kirsch's testifying writers, Ms. Dannon, says: "One of my scientific friends discounted writing ethnographies as women's stories" (47).

A colleague of mine once said that a woman could not succeed unless she was single and post-menopausal. But that role does not quite work either. The other half of the "Try not to act like a woman" message is, "but for goodness sake, don't act like a man." In "Becoming a Warrior:

Lessons of the Feminist Workplace," Louise Wetherbee Phelps asked "How can we accept and develop our own strength? How stop concealing it, fearing that we will be characterized as bossy, egotistical, or ruthlessly ambitious—or that we are? How become warriors unafraid of our own power?" (332). My acquaintances, colleagues, and friends have struggled with this image at all levels of personnel decisions. We have learned to avoid mention of our children, no matter how talented, in nearly every professional context. At the same time, we avoid mentioning our own successes. The required trick, which one of my young probationary friends seems to be carrying off, is to speak boldly but with reserve, walk the halls unobtrusively although she is eight months pregnant, and publish madly with a two-year-old helping out at the computer.

We have taught our graduate students to avoid mention of family in job interviews, indeed armed them with the knowledge that it is illegal for interviewers to mention personal life. A survival handbook for young women faculty, and older women faculty as well, would have to list all these items as unpleasant realities. Even so, like the old silent selectivity in the sciences that effectively excluded women, personnel committees often psychologically expect women to produce less if they have family responsibilities—and then penalize them at tenure time. In the name of gentleness, kindness, or just neglect, women, especially women with families, get less pressure and fewer rewards. When they then do not perform, they are nudged out or left in lower ranks, given less prestigious assignments, asked to do work with students such as advising, or are just not elected to power committees.

The results of faculty attitudes towards women can be documented in a variety of ways. Last year, a sociology professor in our department sent out the word via our faculty newsletter that she would be spending her spring sabbatical interviewing faculty members about the subject of sexual harassment on campus and asked that faculty who wished to be interviewed call her to make an appointment. I called but told her that my concerns really were not about sexual harassment. She said she would like to talk anyway. As we talked, I told her that I was not the least concerned about politically incorrect conversation in the faculty coffee room. I have always known that some male faculty members could and would make sexist remarks, or just senseless remarks, and that they were the ones who would not vote for me for any important committee. I learned to be thick-skinned early, knowing there was no point in replying to some folk. These behaviors do have serious repercussions, however. My sense of outrage comes to the fore when I see a rank-ordering of salaries in my department and in the university; the women all too often sit at the bottom of each rank. Each spring and fall when I read the lists of distinguished professors or College of Arts and Sciences lecturers, I notice that all but three or four (of 50 or so) are men.

I also feel outraged when I walk into a room where the newly elected members of sensitive faculty personnel committees are gathered and find that I am the only woman, or I note the lists of these committee members and see no women's names at all.

I was frustrated recently when, during a college council meeting, I pointed to a ballot for a major research awards committee, trying to indicate to a young woman faculty member (the only other woman in the room) that she should notice that only one woman appeared on this vital ballot, a ballot voted only in that college council meeting. This committee, which awards the internal summer research grant money, has consistently been all male, until of course we elected a woman. Later the young woman told me she had never before noticed who served on such committees. She asked me if I thought that gender mattered when electing faculty for high-powered committees. It does.

A few years ago I decided that I had to become politically active to insure that women would be elected to sensitive committees on my campus. I started gently reminding colleagues that a woman was on the ballot for this or that committee. Usually, the faculty members, both male and female, were glad to notice and vote for the woman, all other things being equal. I am surprised at how little energy it takes to make a change if one wants change, and how tenaciously inertia will exert its force to avoid change if no one cares. Women must be proactive in all personnel issues, and university administrators, especially chairs, must be on the lookout for insensitivity or outright maneuvering.

Let me illustrate the kinds of problems women face today with a few nods to the past for contrast. I follow with specific suggestions for action. The central problems are archetypal and therefore difficult to attack. The maleness of certain positions and certain behaviors in the minds of the university community is hard to overcome. Several years ago, a chair told me that he would not be offering me a regular line contract because I was a woman with a husband to support me whereas my competitors had families to support (one of those competitors was a confirmed bachelor; I had two children and a teacher husband). Recently, I competed with my good (male) friend for the position of chair in our department. My friend was acting chair already, and I was certain that he would get the job (he did), but I wanted to find out how it felt to be in the applicant's position. Also, friends and colleagues had asked me to run in case my friend was suddenly made acting "goodness-knows-what" somewhere else on campus.

I learned several things. If you are a woman, you really do have to try harder. Foolishly, I had thought that because I had lived so many years as a tenured professor, I would be impervious to the subtle pressures of gender politics. I learned that a woman has to walk a fine line between being confident and being cocky. The line is different than the same line for men, and it can shift under one's feet, usually without warning. I sometimes think that I may be imagining the subtle hints that tell me to mind my place as a woman, but some of the questions in the chair interviews were outright hostile for reasons I could only attribute to my presuming that I could compete with such a fine man for the job. I, of course, have no proof that a man in my position would have been asked different questions. No one else from the department applied; I secretly wondered whether I had made it so far in the search because I expanded the affirmative action file so nicely.

These issues have separate elements, certainly, but the numbers do not lie. More men than women are tenured in my department. More women than men have left for other jobs. More women have recently entered the department at the lower ranks. More men do serve and have nearly always served on our faculty personnel committee and on our departmental council. More men receive summer research funding. More men become exceptional teachers, researchers, and even ordinary and extraordinary chairs. The signals abound that women must try harder. And the following list of guidelines may help with this goal:

> Understand that nothing matters as much as an impeccable vita.

> Find out early what is expected, and then meet those expectations. Remember, however, that the expectations can change from year to year, so keep in touch with the decision makers.

> Document every step of professional progress. Whatever channels are available must be used. Report all professional activities to departmental personnel committees and to university publicity when appropriate. Never be modest, although sometimes tactically it may be a good idea to have a friend mention one's achievements. Send copies of publications, awards, and grant letters to appropriate line administrators.

> Try to serve on sensitive and powerful committees, especially before tenure. Leave the time-wasters like the social committee and the library committee to a tenured professor.

> Vote for other women. The more women who serve in important personnel positions, the more quickly the male image as power figure will fade from the minds of the university community.

> Speak up in faculty meetings, not loudly or harshly but firmly. (I attended an all-faculty university forum this past year that lasted four hours and had over 30 voluntary faculty speakers. Three speakers were women; I was the first woman to speak after an hour of all-male commentary.)

Do not be thick-skinned. Tell the department chair and the personnel committee when you suspect unfair treatment. Silence cooperates with a system that already privileges men.

Never appeal to your family situation to explain anything you do. It may be the reason for whatever impedes your progress, but you are fighting years of built-up prejudice against women with small children, demanding life partners, pets, or ailing parents. Tell your best friend or your counselor but never the personnel committee.

Despite women's best efforts at self-advocacy, they need the proactive support of leaders who can change the basic nature of any system. Administrators, especially chairs, will find the following list of guidelines useful.

Explain exactly what the faculty member must do to achieve in the department. (Richard Gebhardt's chapter "Mentor and Evaluator" provides a number of suggestions). Assume naivete even in the face of bravado.

Watch for signs of impending trouble before any can happen. A woman will be accustomed to being silenced in class from childhood on, so her silence may not indicate contentment.

Encourage faculty members to support women's candidacy for important committees. Appoint women to these committees whenever the opportunity arises, especially when the committees have to do with salary allocations and research awards.

Support senior women faculty members who mentor and champion junior women. Reward this cooperation when appropriate. Role models and mentors are vital. Women want men's approval, but they need women's guidance.

Notice when women faculty and graduate students achieve. Women tend to undervalue their own work and to have it either undervalued by the system or valued only when men assign their imprimaturs (Henry James credentialed Edith Wharton by approving her novels). Women must note and affirm other women.

Assign women faculty members to courses concomitant with their rank and publications. A male junior faculty member should not consistently teach a graduate course while a female junior faculty member teaches a senior course, or worse while a female senior faculty member teaches a sophomore course.

Assume that a woman who has small children (or several children) wants as much challenge and responsibility as a man with small children (or several children).

Resistance causes change, not compliance. Women faculty and the administrators and colleagues on personnel committees responsible for their welfare must continue to resist entrenched cultural expectations. The resistance can be tactful, tactical, and even tasteful, but it must be strategic and strong-willed. Change almost never comes when one is cheerful and long-suffering.

Perhaps a brief telling of Chaucer's "Knight's Tale" is in order. Patient Griselda is tested by her husband to discover the depth of her good humor and loyalty. The husband takes away her status and tells her that her children are dead (although he has only hidden them away). After many years of indignities, she is rewarded for her long suffering by the return of her status and of her grown children. I can remember in graduate school, 20 or so years ago, that this story was interpreted to be about the nature of Christian charity. I was expected to accept that interpretation in the bad old days of guided literary interpretation.

Today I have my own reading of *"Griselda's* Tale": I think it is about women teaching in colleges and universities. We have been in academe far too long to conduct our professional lives like Griseldas any more. We have to admit what we know about the system. It is high time for patience to give way to tactical and strategic action.

WORKS CITED

Gebhardt, Richard C. "Mentor and Evaluator: The Chair's Role in Promotion and Tenure Review." *Academic Advancement in Composition Studies.* Ed. Richard C. Gebhardt and Barbara Genelle Smith Gebhardt. Mahwah, NJ: Lawrence Erlbaum Associates, 1997. 147–65.

Gilligan, Carol, Annie Rogers, and Deborah Tolman, eds. *Women, Girls, and Psychotherapy: Reframing Resistance.* New York: Haworth, 1991.

Hite, Shere. *The Hite Report on the Family: Growing Up Under Patriarchy.* New York: Grove, 1994.

Kirsch, Gesa. *Women Writing the Academy: Audience, Authority, and Transformation.* Carbondale: Southern Illinois UP, 1993.

Pagano, Jo Anne. *Exiles and Communities.* Albany: State U of New York P, 1990.

Pascoe, Judith. "What to Expect When You're Expecting." *Profession 94.* New York: MLA, 1994. 70–74.

Phelps, Louise W. "Becoming a Warrior: Lessons of the Feminist Workplace." *Feminine Principles and Women's Experience in American Composition and Rhetoric.* Ed. Louise W. Phelps and Janet Emig. Pittsburgh: U of Pittsburgh P, 1995. 289–339.

11 Mentoring— and (Wo)mentoring— in Composition Studies

Theresa Enos
The University of Arizona

I am a woman who began graduate school in the early 1970s with no place in or access to the master-apprentice model of mentoring. And I have been, at various points in my career, more of a maverick than a model of traditional practice in academe. So it is ironic to find myself now a role model for female (and male) students and probationary faculty in my department's graduate program in rhetoric and composition and the author of this chapter on mentoring in composition studies. What I would like to do here, though, is suggest some ways we can put the roles of maverick and mentor in apposition, rather than opposition, in order to bring about change in the ideology of power that underlies typical mentoring relationships.

To begin, I want to consciously examine the words *maverick* and *mentor* through the lenses of personal history and graduate program concerns in composition studies. The word *maverick*, although originally meaning an unbranded, orphaned, or strayed calf, has come to define someone who is unorthodox in ideas or attitudes, someone who will stray from the herd, someone who will wander off, someone who does not, or will not, get branded.

The word *mentor* holds within its boundaries many roles, some of them in opposition and all of them, I think, in need of close scrutiny in a culture that professes to value consensus over hierarchy. In its position paper on mentoring, my university's Graduate Council says that "an essential part of graduate education involves mentoring; in fact, mentoring may be the 'heart' of graduate education" (Zelditch 1). The Graduate Council defines mentors in varying roles: advisors, supporters, tutors, masters, sponsors, and models.

I have become increasingly uncomfortable with all of these roles, unexamined, thrust on me, as I suspect other women in their 40s and 50s in composition studies may feel. Most of us in this age group have not followed traditional career paths. Compounding the particular problems of specializing in composition studies—suicidal, some say, because it is woman's work, and thus devalued—has been the historical reality of male-dominated academe, including the traditional English department. *Master, tutor,* and *model* probably have defined those who have mentored us more than *advisor, supporter,* or *sponsor.*

Despite the common positive connotation of *mentor* ("experienced and trusted counsellor"; . . . "guide," according to my *Oxford English Dictionary*), perhaps the term makes me uncomfortable because of social and political ideologies residing within it. The ideal (traditional? patriarchal?) master-apprentice model may be the knowledgeable professor whose intent is to guide the student apprentice into some specialized area. At the same time, however, the master serves as a role model for the graduate student's emerging professionalism. Too much dependence on satisfying the master's demands can hamper or delay the student's growth toward autonomy and independence. And there is yet another caveat: Such role modeling—that is, the whole process of *imitatio*—is likely to be replicated when the apprentice becomes master to another apprentice.

Furthermore, some emerging gender issues in higher education intensify my concern. Women constitute about 27 percent of full-time faculty nationwide. Twenty-one percent of the faculty at research institutions are female; at four-year and comprehensive universities, about 19 percent. At liberal arts colleges, the figure rises to 29 percent and, more dramatically, at public two-year colleges to 38 percent ("Annual" 3).

These women are likely to be assistant professors, lecturers, or instructors, even when all have attained doctorates. Males are more likely to hold the rank of full professor and to have tenure. And according to the annual AAUP survey of faculty, men earn higher salaries, about 13% more than women ("Annual" 3, 4).

In rhetoric and composition, the statistics are worse. Women are the majority—or soon will be, according to the survey of 3,000 college writing teachers I conducted while preparing to write *Gender Roles and Faculty Lives in Rhetoric and Composition.* But they still do not enjoy the same status as their male counterparts: They make less, they teach more, and theirs is more likely to be the onerous burden of administrative work in writing programs where male faculty occupy most of the real positions with the real titles. All the more reason, then, we should closely examine any mentoring program to see if women are taking on a disproportionate share of the work; women who, I suspect, were not themselves mentored, except perhaps by the patriarchal master-apprentice model.

Many women writing teachers now in their 40s and 50s were first placed at the margins of their profession by graduate school experiences. They did not always choose to be mavericks. I can trace my perspective back to the early 1970s when I was working on my MA, but I believe that other women who were graduate students in the 1960s and 1970s can identify with me. Already different from my fellow students at that time—older, married, with children—I began what I now call my first academic misadventure at a central Texas university. In literature then, I began my first semester as a graduate teaching assistant in the undergraduate writing program. (Teaching writing—and liking it—placed me even nearer the margins than being an older graduate student.) All of the literature professors were men, housed in an impressive marble edifice that was also a research center for Victorian literature. Each professor's office opened into his very own classroom.

We TAs were housed in a dark, run-down building two blocks away from the English department, along with the full-time lecturers (all female, all teachers of writing). We were on the edge of the campus literally and at the margins, figuratively: mavericks.

Yes, there was one lone male in that old building: the director of composition, who reigned over his harem. But mentoring? (Wo)mentoring? There was none, unless one could make the case for the most rigid form of *imitatio*, the traditional master-apprentice model: Learn the ritual lessons of the literati and become one of them. Well, I did, and I did not.

I was not just thrown into the writing classroom, of course. Each of us TAs was assigned a buddy (one of the female writing teachers) who in the director's name explained the grading system, a system by which the program's philosophy can be summed up: two sentence fragments—F; three misspelled words—F; two comma splices—F. . . . I graded for correctness and stayed in my correct place. At my master's orals the next year, however, I opened my eyes to another perspective.

Entering the room where orals were held (actually one of the rich Victorian literature research rooms in that hallowed and marbled English department space), I took my designated place at the far end of the room's long, highly polished table, pen in nervous fingers just to have something to do with my hands. My jury of 12 White men (I am not making this up—there were 12 of them, by God) gravely entered and took their places, sitting six to a side at the other end of that long, long table. Surreal it was, that oral defense. As each examiner, in turn, asked his question so that I could perform, all of the 12, in unison, would lean forward and turn toward me, peering at me all the way down that table. I performed haltingly, poorly.

Six months after I had somehow gotten the MA, I would often wake up mid-night to replay that scary scene, anger finally submerging worries that I was an imposter, an experience—that Pauline Rose Chance described as *The Imposter Phenomenon*—I now know is shared by many women who have achieved professional success. I had not been prepared for that master's orals, which had covered Beowulf to Bellow. I had assumed that the questions would focus on my thesis topic, which was on Bernard Malamud and (ironically, again) moral redemption. In the two years I had lived as a maverick on the edges of that master's program, not one action—whether advising, tutoring, sponsoring, or supporting—had been initiated by even one of the professors to help us graduate students, at least none of the female ones, know what to expect on the oral exam, let alone how to professionalize ourselves.

The situation was not much different when I started working the next fall on my doctorate at another university in the Southwest. There were no female faculty members in that rhetoric program. I had no positive role models, and I was too much of a maverick by then to master worship, which seemed to be required of females. In fact, a female who wanted a sponsor had to initiate, then push hard for, any mentoring relationship (doing the instructor's manual, for example, for the professor's forthcoming textbook). I would not do it—not from my newfound hostile perspective. If I were a maverick, then I'd just go to hell. I'd just go it alone. (At some cost, I know now.)

What I got out of that program, I got on my own—including the writing of a dissertation on which I received no guidance. I knew that the lack of response, as I struggled to write that damn thing, was not due to my brilliant synthesis of material and polished writing. I was on my own. Not so with the very few male students in that rhetoric program. The fellowships that paid the most went to them, and they benefited from the usual male-to-male mentoring relationship.

One of the two male rhetoric professors patronized women graduate students, when he granted any of us a few minutes of his time: "What do you want to do this for [get a PhD]? You're married. . . ." Of course he didn't think he was perpetuating this familiar refrain of the 1960s and 1970s, an ideology sometimes not so much voiced as contextually implied. The other rhetoric professor lived on his own comfortable, ethereal plane, also setting himself apart from the female students, if in a different way. But he did help males get jobs in what was then a depressed job market.

In many programs now, it is much the same. Men are still more networked, still more easily accepted within English department structures, still probably younger when they enter tenure tracks, and they are still probably better paid and probably better mentored than women. However, in many programs there has been a major shift to an increase in the number of women faculty—most of them in the early stages of their careers and overwhelmed with the tenure process, motherhood, and female graduate students' needs. But some are "senior" women on composition studies faculties who have had interrupted careers or have changed careers. (Indeed, 71 percent of the female respondents to my survey considered their careers in rhetoric and composition to be non-traditional.) A little older than most, with new, or renewed, commitments to the study of rhetoric, they went back to school, where many of them, myself included, learned that we had to go it alone. That maverick strain we developed then has made us attractive role models now for younger women, and men, coming into composition studies. So here is the dilemma in which we senior women find ourselves as professors and associate professors today: our roles reversed, from mavericks to mentors.

As mentors, most composition studies faculty members are overworked because they are popular with graduate students. This is important and delightful work, usually unrecognized, and very time-consuming. But too often more of the burden falls on female writing faculty members for mentoring and role modeling, because (according to the respondents to my survey) female graduate students now make up 70 percent of the typical program in rhetoric. The burden is accepted female-to-female, often sacrificially, often preventing women faculty members from pursuing our own research. (In research universities, it takes women longer to get tenure than males: according to my survey, 6.9 years for women as compared to 5.7 years for men.) For mentoring or (wo)mentoring, then, we are penalized for our contributions to developing future scholars.

Women writing faculty also take on a heavy burden of administrative work—too often a heavier burden than our male counterparts, and without the same status derived from formal titles and commensurate compensation. And we know that such administrative work still does not count as it should in promotion and tenure decisions. In her letter of support during my tenure review, my former dean, avowing herself a victim of gender discrimination and for years nurturing a reputation as a supposed strong supporter of women, wrote disparagingly of the administrative duties I had taken on as an overload for five years, calling it "quasi-administrative work."

Actually, no other faculty members, male or female, are as burdened with administrative work as are faculty in rhetoric and composition. (The profile of Hanna in Duane Roen's chapter "Writing Administration As Scholarship and Teaching" gives a sense of this overwork.) In my survey of rhetoric and composition faculty, the subject of administrative work elicited more angry, despairing, bitter narratives than almost any other topic, the majority of these voices belonging to women. Too often women are less protective of their time than men, and (because department heads and writing program directors in our larger universities are mostly male) the faculty members with the greatest authority to make demands are male.

In view of such administrative demands on composition studies faculty, I may well ask: Should individual mentoring be required? Should it be part of one's service, as my own university's Graduate Council position statement seems to imply? Or should it be part of one's teaching, similar to directing dissertations? In times of retrenchment, both senior and probationary faculty members in composition studies need to be careful about additional demands on our time, particularly when literature faculty members are not so burdened with administrative work and especially when mentoring is not specifically included in promotion and tenure criteria.

We also need to be alert to possible dangers of mentoring. A faculty mentor may be asked by graduate students or colleagues for help or advice with problems of sexual harassment. Surely the mentor will help, but are there protections built into the mentoring program and the promotion and tenure system for those faculty members, particularly untenured faculty, who take on such support roles?

And there is yet another aspect of the dilemma here. If women faculty members do not take on this additional responsibility for mentoring—female students, primarily—then how can we change some of the deadly discriminatory practices still going on in our graduate programs? How can those of us who have considered ourselves mavericks remain mavericks, even though to step into the center, to take on even more, could bring us even more penalization?

The ideology underlying mentoring relationships is one of power. The symbolic actions of a maverick usually lead to a creative realization of self. If we apply Burkeian methods and juxtapose the two terms, *mentor* and *maverick*, in apposition not opposition, perhaps we can gain some perspective over incongruities. Here might be a beginning:

1. We can define mentoring so that its activities are not split between nurturing (female) and real work (male). In addition, mentoring functions must be both carefully delineated for, and equally distributed among, all faculty.

2. We can view required graduate papers as a succession of drafts. Despite our talk—and practice in the undergraduate writing classroom—of process and peer-group praxis, more of us can turn our graduate writing courses into mentoring discussion groups where research is seen as invention, where successive drafts of papers are brought in and discussed, rather than what I suspect is still our most usual practice: the traditional semester-end research paper where the professor, seeing it for the first time, evaluates the paper to justify the seminar grade.

3. We can create an environment where students can make the traditional research paper into a publishable paper. I would argue for

this approach instead of faculty-student co-authoring. I know important publications have come out of collaboration between faculty and student(s), and I support collaborative work. But the most generous mentoring, it seems to me, would be to create an environment where a publishable paper is the semester goal, rather than the usual summative seminar paper, which by its very nature is a record of what the student knows instead of an essay showing that he or she knows.

4. We can plan for graduate students to meet weekly with one or more faculty members for purposes of introducing students to the profession. A number of graduate programs already offer communal mentoring sessions focused on a professional agenda, rather than the usual master-apprentice model. Communal mentoring lessens possible abuses by professors who, consciously or not, use students for advancing their own research instead of their students' scholarship.

5. We can use portfolios to involve graduate students and probationary faculty more actively in reciprocally based mentoring relationships. This pedagogical tool for self-assessment, a record of changes as the person develops as both scholar and teacher, places less emphasis on the mentor as master; instead, the apprentice has a greater sense of control through the power of reflexivity.

We can work to encourage other faculty-to-faculty mentoring relationships, too. Many of these could be informal and personal—matters of senior faculty responding to and trying to anticipate the professional needs and questions of their new colleagues. On the other hand, departments could take more formal action. For instance, they could sponsor colloquia or lunch-time discussions, such as the discussions of *Scholarship Reconsidered* that Susan McLeod suggests in her chapter "A View from the Dean's Office," pair probationary and senior faculty with similar teaching or research interests, and cooperate in broader faculty development programs sponsored by the college or university.

Given the disciplinary bias composition studies faculty often experience (as they are evaluated against personnel policies developed for the literature faculty) and the gender bias still widespread in American universities, departments could work, as Richard Gebhardt suggests in his chapter "Mentor and Evaluator," to develop personnel policies and practices that help to orient and guide faculty. For those same reasons, the Conference on College Composition and Communication and the Council of Writing Program Administrators are each involved in activities that put the organizations themselves in mentoring roles. For example, the intent of the WPA's "Evaluating the Intellectual Work of Writing Program Administrators" is to mentor writing faculty involved in administration. It helps writing program administrators to articulate exactly what it is they do so that they can convince people that writing administration work is intellectual work, "requiring expertise and producing knowledge . . . not simply . . . adminis-trivia" (3). And since 1993, the Conference on College Composition and Communication has scheduled mentoring workshops before its annual meetings.

This is good, but we need more—more practica, more professional guidelines, more clear and reasonable department and collegiate guidelines for promotion and tenure. Too many of us—even senior women and men in positions to mentor graduate students and younger colleagues—are trapped in old-fashioned English departments.

I can identify, because for seven years I taught in a university that likes to call itself the "Harvard of the South." There I was, a female in rhetoric in a traditional English department! The tenure-track instructors who taught composition—15 women, three men—were assigned windowless basement cubicles. The assistant professors (seven female, two male), the associate professors (eight male, one female), and the full professors (five male, no female)—all of whom taught literature—had spacious, windowed offices two stories up. There were mentoring relationships on the master–apprentice model for the literati, but none for us in composition. In my seven years there, I taught four sections of freshman writing a semester and won a major award for teaching. I published (more than anyone else there, save one). I founded *Rhetoric Review*; I published the *Sourcebook for Basic Writing Teachers*. I did not stay in my place at the table. I did not get tenure.

Not having had mentors may have made my misadventures in academe more varied, but I have survived, and I would like to think I am stronger because I learned to see mavericks and mentoring from new perspectives. Now I am a role model. A mentor, and a maverick, still. It is scary.

I hope I have been enough of an academic maverick so that the only model (the male one, the power one) to which I was exposed has not in some way invaded my nature and infected me with the Queen Bee syndrome, of which we are seeing too much lately. The Queen Bee is the woman who, when she herself reaches a position of power, not only patronizes apprentice women workers (some call it being their mentor) but even hampers other women's career opportunities. If we initiate or enter too deeply into a role ascribed to us by others, we risk inauthenticity and self-denial. Yet, if we push our own students to the margins as many of us were pushed, we are excommunicating both them and ourselves from the community with whom we have the strongest professional ties.

WORKS CITED

"The Annual Report on the Economic Status of the Profession." *Academe* 79 (Mar./Apr. 1993). Special Issue.

Chance, Pauline Rose. *The Imposter Phenomenon*. Atlanta: Peachtree, 1985.

Enos, Theresa. *Gender Roles and Faculty Lives in Rhetoric and Composition*. Carbondale: Southern Illinois U P, 1996.

"Evaluating the Intellectual Work of Writing Program Administrators." N. p.: Council of Writing Program Administrators, 1995.

Gebhardt, Richard C. "Mentor and Evaluator: The Chair's Role in Promotion and Tenure Review." Gebhardt and Gebhardt 147–65.

Gebhardt, Richard C., and Barbara Genelle Smith Gebhardt, eds. *Academic Advancement in Composition Studies*. Mahwah, NJ: Lawrence Erlbaum Associates, 1997.

McLeod, Susan H. "Scholarship Reconsidered: A View from the Dean's Office." Gebhardt and Gebhardt 177–89.

Roen, Duane. "Writing Administration As Scholarship and Teaching." Gebhardt and Gebhardt 43–55.

Zelditch, M. "Mentor Roles." *Proceedings of the 32nd Annual Meeting*. N. p.: Western Association of Graduate Schools, 1990.

12 Mentor and Evaluator: The Chair's Role in Promotion and Tenure Review

Richard C. Gebhardt
Bowling Green State University

> *As chairs of English departments, we are given responsibility for many things . . . , but, in my judgment, none of these responsibilities is more vital to our departments, and to our colleges and universities, than the hiring and mentoring of new faculty members. I use the term "mentoring" here to refer not only, and not even primarily, to the actions of a single person—of the department chair or some other faculty member—who serves as a trusted counselor but also to the department's policies and structure for supporting teaching, research, and department service; for giving formal advice; and for carrying out formal evaluations before the mandatory sixth-year tenure review.*
>
> *—Haggard (25)*

These words by Frank Haggard, a former English Department Chair at Iowa State University, suggest several important things about the chair's role in tenure and promotion. It is an important role, of course. It is also a complex one—to provide faculty "with reasonable opportunities and *support* as well as with thorough, timely, and humane systems of *review*" (Haggard 28, emphasis added)—in which mentoring and evaluation intertwine. For instance, a chair might write that "Dr. Banks should capitalize on her success getting on the programs of major scholarly conferences by developing more papers into refereed arti-

cles"—simultaneously giving good advice for a probationer in a department which emphasizes scholarship and making an implicit criticism
part of the person's file.

As the epigraph by Haggard suggests, chair evaluations (and other
structures "for giving formal advice" and "carrying out formal evaluations") are part of the "mentoring" function of the department and the
department chair. Of course, the chair also serves as a "trusted counselor" and the administrator of "the department's policies for supporting
teaching, research, and departmental service." But these more obvious
instances of mentoring usually operate in some relationship to the
chair's responsibilities for evaluation—helping the probationer understand institutional and departmental expectations for tenure, for instance, or visiting classes and discussing the teacher's performance, or
advising whether the visibility to be gained by serving on an important
committee is worth the loss of research time. So this chapter emphasizes
the complex, simultaneous role as mentor and evaluator that the chair
plays in promotion and tenure review.

EXPECTATIONS—OFFICIAL AND ACTUAL

If faculty members are to be effectively and fairly evaluated—whether
for annual reappointment recommendations, or for tenure and promotion—chairs, personnel committees, and faculty members all need to
understand the institution's expectations regarding teaching, scholarship, and service. AAUP standards for renewal and nonrenewal emphasize that "[p]robationary faculty members should be advised, early in
their appointment, of the substantive and procedural standards generally accepted in decisions affecting renewal and tenure" (48). University
policies usually require that colleges and departments issue new faculty
members institutional handbooks and other official documents about
professional expectations and evaluation procedures, and many departments give such information to candidates during on-campus interviews.

Having copies of the department's personnel policies in their offices,
of course, does not mean new faculty members have read them, let alone
read them with care and retained key information about expectations
and evaluation standards. But understanding departmental expectations so that one can address them in one's professional agenda is
essential for the probationary faculty member. As the CCCC Committee
on Professional Guidance to Departments and Faculty put it:

> The best way, finally, to prepare for the decision of reappointment, promo-
> tion, and/or tenure is to discharge professional responsibilities to the best
> of one's ability. . . . If scholarship is an expectation of the institution, this
> means establishing a consistent line of research. . . . At institutions where

publishing is not an expectation . . . it is especially important that faculty undergo regular evaluations of their teaching effectiveness and institutional involvement . . . . (497)

The chair interested in productive mentoring and effective evaluation needs to find ways to help new faculty members actually understand the department's expectations so that they can, if they wish, try to develop professional records that will be valued by the department.

Complicating this job, however, is the fact that official criteria of promotion or merit review seldom give a complete sense of how a department values teaching, scholarship, and service. For example, although most departments stress scholarship in personnel evaluations, they do so with different nuances and emphases. Scholarship may be described in terms of its *object* of research (e.g., texts, theoretical issues, pragmatic topics), *method* of research (e.g., historical, empirical, case study), *manner* of research (e.g., rigorous, informal, applied), *genre* of publication (e.g., article, book chapter, book), *external validity* of publication (e.g., refereeing practices, reputation of publisher, citation by scholars), and extent of *individual responsibility* for the publication (see Gebhardt, "Editor's" 440–41). Moreover, those rough classifications interact with one another—for instance, the manner and validity of publication may influence evaluation so that a slight book by a marginal press might carry less weight than an article in a major refereed journal—in ways that vary from institution to institution. So it is important that department guidelines for evaluation indicate the local rules of scholarship and publishing, that probationary faculty and personnel committees understand the department's actual expectations, and that these expectations inform the department's efforts at faculty mentoring as well as evaluation.

One useful approach to this goal is to clarify abstract institutional language about excellence in teaching, research, and service by working to describe the accomplishments of a hypothetical assistant professor ready for tenure and promotion. Here, for instance, is part of a draft statement being developed by my department about the kinds of evidence that faculty members may include in their tenure and promotion applications.

Criterion 1: "Ability as an effective teacher."
EVIDENCE Applicable for Tenure and Promotion:

a. Student ratings consistently above the mid-point on the department rating form (or a pattern of improvement to that level) and student comments indicating that the person is a well-prepared, competent teacher.

b. Consistent peer evaluation as a well-prepared, competent teacher (or a pattern of improvement to that level).

c. Strong accomplishments in course or curriculum development, program administration, advising, or dissertation and thesis direction.

Criterion 2: "Research, scholarship, or creative work."
EVIDENCE Applicable for Tenure and Promotion:

a. A book published by or in press with an established scholarly, professional association, or commercial publisher.

b. 3 or more substantial articles or book chapters published in or accepted by refereed national publications of high reputation.

c. 3 or more articles or book chapters published in or accepted by less established but well-regarded publications (whether or not refereed).

d. 7 or more substantial papers delivered at refereed national or international conferences of high reputation.

e. Supporting scholarly/creative activity, including such things: work as a journal editor; book reviewing; journal refereeing; giving papers at less-established or regional conferences; consulting work growing out of scholarship and connected to one's research agenda.

f. 2 or more substantial pedagogical expressions of research or scholarship, e.g., significant curriculum development.

Criterion 3: "Service to the university and the profession."
EVIDENCE Applicable for Tenure and Promotion:

a. Membership on several committees of the department, college, university.

b. At least one significant leadership role in a national or state professional organization.

c. Consistent peer evaluation (e.g., in reappointment reviews) of active participation in the life and governance of the department. (Gebhardt Draft)

Your department's outline of criteria for promotion and tenure would probably look different—in the number of items suggested under each of the three criteria, for instance—because it would reflect the criteria in your institution's official documents and your department's local rules about relevant work for each criterion. But developing an outline of tenure criteria—and updating it periodically—would help your department understand its own expectations for faculty; it would help probationary faculty understand the department's expectations of them; and it would give chairs and other interested department members a clear basis on which to advise faculty members about their progress toward tenure.

EXPECTATIONS OF FACULTY
IN COMPOSITION STUDIES

What I have said, so far, about clarifying the departmental expectations that operate within the broad categories of teaching, scholarship, and service apply to faculty in any specialty. In most English departments, however, it is particularly important to do this for composition studies and a number of other specialties, including applied linguistics and English education. For women and men in these specialties:

- Much of the faculty member's educational impact on students comes through academic leadership (curriculum development, placement testing, staff training and evaluation, supervising student internships, etc.) rather than through the in-class contact with students often equated with teaching in personnel reviews.

- Much research is applied, rather than theoretical, and often focuses on the classroom, the workplace, the practices of writers at work, the effectiveness of pedagogical strategies, and other subjects that may not seem scholarly enough for some department members.

- Scholarship may be released through a variety of professionally accepted channels—textbooks, pedagogical articles, curriculum materials, faculty training workshops, computer software, and so forth—in addition to scholarly articles and scholarly books.

Most tenured faculty members in English departments are teachers and scholars of literature who do not have first-hand understanding of the work of their colleagues in composition studies. So chairs responsible for mentoring and evaluating composition studies faculty members face a complex task. It is not just that they need to help probationers understand departmental criteria so they can intelligently pursue tenure and promotion. They probably need to orient personnel committees and tenured faculty members so they can effectively and fairly review composition studies specialists for tenure and promotion. And they may also need to help their departments revise the professional expectations and criteria used in personnel reviews.

In most English departments, tenure and promotion criteria evolved to evaluate the work of literature professors and so may need some fine-tuning in order to allow effective and fair evaluation of probationers in composition studies. Composition studies faculty members themselves need to be involved in this effort because they are the department's experts in the nature and professional standards of the specialty. But in many departments, these are junior faculty members whose views about the criteria for their own evaluation may be seen as self-serving by senior faculty. So in most cases, leadership in the review of department personnel criteria falls to chairs and other senior faculty interested in effective, fair evaluation of colleagues.

To gain a general sense of the nature of composition studies, chairs and senior faculty on personnel committees could visit the classes—or the administrative offices—of composition studies faculty and talk with them about the special problems and satisfactions of their work with students. They could discuss publishing plans with rhetoric specialists and try to develop a feel for the ground rules and difficulties of publishing in the area. They could read self-appraisal statements and annual reappointment files of probationers attentively—looking for insights into the special approaches and professional challenges of composition studies—and then give some feedback about these documents so probationers can understand what aspects of their work they need to explain more fully in later documents. And they could consult an overview book, like Erika Lindemann's and Gary Tate's *An Introduction to Composition Studies*, and the chapters in *Academic Advancement in Composition Studies*. (Two parts of the book are addressed particularly to faculty on personnel committees: "Article Publication in Composition Studies: Some Notes for Evaluation Committee Members," the Appendix to this chapter, and John Schilb's chapter "Scholarship in Composition and Literature: Some Comparisons.")

Also, chairs and personnel committees should review departmental guidelines for merit, promotion, and tenure to see how fully they apply to faculty in composition studies and, if necessary, how they might be adjusted to allow fairer, more effective review of their colleagues. The goal might be, as I suggested before, to develop descriptive statements that clarify the institution's official criteria of acceptable work in teaching, research, and service. And the approach might be as straightforward as studying the department's personnel documents in light of professional guidelines such as these from organizations within English studies.

MLA Commission on Professional Service (1996):

Scholarship could be exemplified in the following modes and forms, among others:

- Products of original research: monographs, articles, chapters in books, review articles, edited volumes introducing new topics or ideas

- Creative professional work that is directly relevant to the faculty member's professional expertise: e.g., literature, computer software

- Published work gathering, integrating, translating, and disseminating the original work of others, enriching it through interpretive, preservative, recuperative, or critical functions:e.g., editing of journals and journal issues, research volumes, concordances, or editions of a historical work: book review, textbooks, and bibliographical essays; translations of works by others

- External documents with scholarly content: e.g., grant proposals, consulting reports

- Other forms of scholarly communication: conferences, workshops, literacy projects, participation in electronic lists.

Notice that scholarship is defined here primarily by its interactive relationship to a dynamic scholarly enterprise and participation in its community. Scholarship must be made public and open to peer criticism, but it need not be published or disseminated in traditional forums. (17)

Association of Departments of English (1993):

Scholarship should be a criterion for promotion and tenure in institutions of higher education. Different departments will have different expectations about the kinds of scholarly activities that best serve their missions and fit their institution's profiles. Publication need not be the only or even the most important measure of a faculty member's accomplishments. In evaluations of scholarship, different kinds of activities and products should be given credit. Suitable measures of excellence should be developed for nontraditional as well as for traditional forms of scholarship. ("ADE" 44)

Conference on College Composition and Communication (1989):

[P]ostsecondary institutions should count seriously certain kinds of professional activity, sometimes undervalued within current measures of scholarly achievement . . . : (l) the publication of composition textbooks as a primary form of original research; (2) collaborative research on articles and books that draw on diverse scholarly backgrounds and research orientations; (3) professional activities such as workshops and seminars for faculty at all levels; and (4) the particularly demanding administrative service that is often a regular part of a composition specialist's responsibilities. (CCCC Executive 331)

MLA Commission on Writing and Literature (1988):

1. Composition research is often disseminated in the form of textbooks . . . . While in other disciplines and even in other areas of our own discipline this form of publication is highly derivative of the scholarship that alters the field, textbooks for composition specialists frequently constitute a primary way of communicating the results of extensive research. We therefore recommend that departments consider composition textbooks as the equivalent of other scholarly books, measurable like scholarly books according to rigorous intellectual standards.

2. Similarly, research projects in rhetoric and composition are increasingly undertaken by teams of scholars, each contributing different perspectives that come from different scholarly backgrounds and research

orientations. Such collaboration needs to be respected as a legitimate way of advancing knowledge within the discipline.

3. Given the nature of this field, much of its important work is dependent on forms of dissemination that are, in fact, not published. One such form is conducting workshops, through which other members of the discipline are introduced to new developments in the field. Departments should recognize the importance of these activities and reward colleagues who conduct seminars for faculty members from other universities or from high schools. . . .

4. The professional duties of composition specialists often involve an unnaturally heavy dose of administration. This is especially true for writing program administrators (directors of composition, directors of writing centers, directors of teaching assistants, etc.). . . . In fairness, then, administrative contributions should be given significant weight during tenure and salary reviews. . . . ("Report" 73–74)

To department discussions of such guidelines by professional associations within English studies, chairs can bring relevant insights from other quarters. For instance, it may be useful for faculty reviewing personnel documents to realize that the 1989 Carnegie Foundation National Survey of Faculty found that 68% of faculty—including 69% at research institutions and 77% in doctoral departments—felt that "we need better ways, besides publications, to evaluate the scholarly performance of faculty" (Boyer 34), and for them to know that the President of the American Association of Higher Education found that 50 recent campus reports on faculty rewards revealed that many "mid-career and senior faculty clearly feel caged in by the reigning definitions of what scholarly work is valued" (Edgerton 12). Certainly, it is relevant that representatives of 16 professional associations, including MLA and CCCC, working together in the National Project on Institutional Priorities and Faculty Rewards have reached "general agreement about the characteristics of scholarly, professional, or creative work" (Diamond and Adam 13) and about the need to broaden our definition of scholarly and professional work:

Whether it be publishing the results of one's scholarly research, developing a new course, writing an innovative textbook, implementing an outreach program for the community, directing a student production, or assisting in a K–12 curriculum project, faculty on the discipline task forces agreed that there are many activities in which faculty engage that satisfy the scholarly, professional, or creative dimensions associated with promotion, tenure, and merit recognition. (Diamond and Adam 13–14)

EFFORTS TO ADVANCE
DEPARTMENT EVALUATION AND MENTORING

I cannot, of course, predict with any certainty how such guidelines might influence discussions in your department or what revisions in your department's personnel documents might come from those discussions. Generally, however, I would expect such a review to clarify the department's understanding of its own criteria for tenure and promotion; to make guidelines more useful to probationary faculty, chairs, and personnel committees; and in some cases, to trigger changes in department policies or expectations.

Policies and Procedures to Facilitate Evaluation and Mentoring

With clear and useful guidelines for tenure and promotion in place, chairs are better able to work, as mentors and evaluators, with faculty members. Rather than having to spend time explaining fuzzy expectations and abstract criteria, they can work to make sure that the department's system of review is effective and fair and to help probationary faculty build solid records of teaching, research, and service.

Perhaps the first step in that direction is to consider whether the department has a system of reasonable, timely evaluations of probationary faculty. At my institution, university policies mandate two evaluations of probationers each year—a formal departmental reappointment review by January and a chair's annual evaluation in May—in addition to annual merit review. Some in my department consider such frequent evaluation overkill, and I am not recommending this specific system. But with this sort of involvement by the chair, by an elected Promotion, Retention, and Tenure Committee, and by an elected Merit Review Committee, there is no question whether young faculty members are receiving feedback about how their work meets department expectations. Such feedback well before the time for tenure evaluation, Frank Haggard noted, is a "form of departmental mentoring of new faculty members, one that is just as important" (27) as any other. And if a department has fine-tuned its promotion and tenure guidelines and has made them more useful, it only makes sense to be sure that they are applied in as timely and effective a way as possible.

A second consideration about the department's system of evaluation is how fully individual tenured faculty members—those who eventually vote on tenure—are involved in pretenure evaluations of probationers. Haggard suggested that "every department consider it an obligation to review the teaching, scholarship, and service of untenured assistant professors about midway through their probationary periods" and that "this appraisal be conducted by the same faculty committee or tenured rank(s) that will conduct the mandatory sixth-year tenure review" (27–28). My department conducts annual reappointment reviews in which a draft of the recommendation prepared by the chair and the personnel committee is shared with the tenured faculty for response before a revised recommendation for reappointment (or for termination, or for a one-year terminal contract) is sent to the Arts and Sciences Dean. Five formal pretenure reviews may be excessive, and one midpoint evaluation may be inadequate. But either approach is better than a system that allows bitter sixth-year surprises because it does not involve the tenured faculty in evaluation in the years before the formal tenure vote.

A third issue chairs in some departments should turn to, once the department's expectations for tenure and promotion are clarified, is how well those expectations are reflected in the merit review system. Teaching may figure significantly in tenure evaluation at a doctoral university, for instance; if so, it can only be confusing and misleading for probationers if successful publishing is the only road to good raises. Publications or other professional activity to stay current in one's teaching may be an expectation for tenure at a teaching-centered college; if so, it would be confusing and misleading for new faculty if merit pay is based only on student and peer evaluation of teaching. Clearly, giving probationary faculty members mixed signals in tenure and merit guidelines neither serves them well nor advances department mentoring to help them prepare for tenure. So, where inconsistencies exist in personnel documents, it only makes sense to work toward consistency and mutual reinforcement of faculty expectations.

Communication to Facilitate Evaluation and Mentoring

Developing consistent personnel policies, fair and timely procedures for evaluation, and clear statements of department expectations for tenure and promotion are important for effective mentoring and evaluation. Perhaps equally important are the chair's efforts to help probationary faculty members understand department expectations and procedures and to help senior faculty understand the accomplishments of probationers.

Much of a department chair's communication with junior faculty is personal and informal—conferences or coffee-room conversations about a broad range of matters: delivering substantial conference papers but not revising them for publication; working on so many publishing projects that all are delayed; looking for useful ideas in student comments about one's teaching but not being paralyzed by bad ratings; taking on so many committee assignments that scholarship and publishing suffers; making sure the personnel committee has an up-to-date CV when it is working on one's reappointment review; and using the department newsletter to keep the department aware of one's publications and other activities.

In most institutions, however, department chairs are officially responsible for advising probationary faculty about tenure and promotion criteria and personnel-review procedures. So in addition to the informal advice they may offer faculty members about their work and how to build a strong record, chairs need to provide written information and guidance for probationary faculty members. Even for-the-record communications of this sort can serve the chair's joint responsibilities for mentoring and evaluation.

One such communication is an initial letter dealing with tenure requirements and personnel practices, such as one I send new faculty members a month or so before their first semester begins. Besides predictable words of welcome and good luck, the first paragraph offers some suggestions to help the new faculty member begin to connect to the institution:

> I'm pleased that you are going to be teaching in the department, and I hope you find your year professionally rewarding. Perhaps the enclosed booklet of department procedures (everything from our harassment policy and grade-challenge procedures to matters of duplication and postage) will be useful as you prepare for your fall teaching. And I hope you will participate in the university's New-Faculty Orientation on August 24 and the English Faculty Retreat on August 29.

An obligatory mention of official policies comes next, but it only serves as an introduction to more focused information about the department's expectations in research and teaching:

> Just to be sure you have them for your reference, I'm enclosing some important materials about promotion and tenure in the Arts and Sciences College. In brief, demonstrated strength in three areas—teaching, research, and service—is the basis of evaluation for merit pay, reappointment, tenure, and promotion.
>
> Scholarly publication (particularly in refereed journals and books) is the key factor the department uses in evaluating research, and substantial papers at national conferences are among other factors we consider. (The department has operated for quite some time with a broad-based view of scholarly publication—one, for instance, that includes pedagogically-related publication growing out of research or based on current scholarship.) Student evaluation, on a department form to be used in all your courses, plays an important role in all four types of evaluation (and particularly for merit); peer evaluations and a broad array of "teaching portfolio"-type materials also figure in evaluation.

Then comes a brief description of department procedures for faculty evaluation, as well as a simple suggestion about how to begin preparing for faculty evaluation:

> During the fall semester, I'll work with the elected Promotion, Retention, and Tenure Committee (and we will consult with the tenured faculty of

the department) on the first of your annual reappointment reviews. To facilitate the process, you'll need to arrange class visits by at least two faculty, to compile a dossier of syllabi and other teaching materials, and to submit an up-to-date CV and information about your scholarly work. You'll get more information about all this, later.

For now, let me just suggest that you start a "Reappointment Review" file right away and that you add to it—with reminder notes to yourself, copies of relevant materials, etc.—as the semester progresses. Besides facilitating the fall reappointment review, building a dossier this way will give you a start on the merit review file you will need to submit in January (for review by the elected Merit Review Committee). And letting this dossier grow as the semesters pass is a good way to prepare for future tenure evaluation.

And the letter concludes with another suggestion—to seek counsel and mentoring within the department:

Please feel free to contact me when you have questions about our evaluation process, the department's expectations of probationary faculty members, your successes or frustrations in the classroom, or the direction of your scholarly agenda. I'd also suggest that you get to know the other faculty who are joining the department this fall—and that you occasionally meet to discuss your successes, frustrations, and developing plans—and that you seek out one or two experienced faculty members from whom you might seek advice during this time in which you are learning about the university and its student body.

Another type of official correspondence, the annual evaluation or reappointment recommendation, can serve the chair's roles as mentor and evaluator. Clearly, both those ends are reflected in these fictional summaries from two annual reappointment recommendations of a hypothetical assistant professor whose publishing record is not developing as quickly as his teaching or service record:

Third-Year Reappointment Letter (Excerpt): I'm impressed by Dr. Patterson's very solid teaching and service and by the quality of his early scholarship (including a substantial essay in *Rhetoric Review*, one of the central refereed journals in his field). And I agree with the personnel committee that the scholarly projects Dr. Patterson is working on have considerable potential to develop, over the next two years, into the additional refereed publications that will be needed by the time of tenure review.

Fourth-Year Reappointment Letter (Excerpt): The personnel committee and I share the very positive view last year's committee had of Dr. Patterson's teaching and service and of the potential of his scholarly agenda. It's disappointing that this year brought no refereed articles to augment those from his first two years in the department. But Dr. Patterson has several substantial manuscripts circulating (revisions of papers he gave, over the past three years, at highly-competitive, blind-refereed national meetings of the Conference on College Composition and Communication). And I look forward to seeing one or two of them accepted during the ten months that remain before the department will need to decide whether to move forward with a formal tenure review.

Evaluation is clear enough, here—Patterson is solid in teaching and service and he is working at scholarship, but his record of refereed publications is a problem—and so is *mentoring*. The letters are constructive and optimistic rather than threatening, and they offer guidance (e.g., work to get one or two more articles out before the next reappointment review) and encouragement ("You can do it," one letter implies—"Remember your successes of a couple years ago?").

Because official letters of evaluation are used by administrators outside the department and may be read by senior faculty preparing to vote on tenure, they give chairs an opportunity for a special dimension of mentoring—advocacy. For instance, when the Patterson letters comment as they do about *Rhetoric Review* and CCCC's annual meeting, they provide background information that may positively influence senior faculty members voting for tenure or a dean reviewing a departmental tenure recommendation.

Chairs' official evaluations often can work, in this way, to explain a faculty member's work and orient people to specialties, like composition studies, that may not be widely understood. Instead of just reporting that a faculty member has co-authored several refereed articles, for instance, an evaluation letter could mention the frequency of collaborative research in composition studies. Rather than simply indicating that a person is studying effective means to utilize computers in writing instruction, the letter could indicate that applied research plays a central role in composition studies. And rather than stressing only the administrative duties of a faculty member who serves as writing director, an evaluation letter could discuss how the person's work with course development, staff members, and students contributes to the teaching mission of the department.

WORKING WITH TENURED FACULTY

Because the tenure and promotion decision is of such consequence for faculty—and for departments, as well—I have made it the main focus of this chapter. Clearly, however, tenure and promotion to associate professor are not the climax of an academic career. Nor do they end the chair's responsibilities as mentor and evaluator. (Indeed, the University of Kentucky's dean of arts and sciences believes that limited money for new positions, combined with the ban on a mandatory retirement age and growing demands for accountability, are leading to "increased interest in introducing formal mechanisms to review the performance of tenured faculty" [Edwards 6]. And many university and college administrators now advocate post-tenure review as a way to "identify the difficulties of floundering professors and help good faculty members perform even better" [Magner A13].)

For some faculty members, achieving tenure and promotion brings a loss of professional focus and incentive; for others, timely promotion to professor becomes a productive incentive for continuing accomplishments. In dealing with either sort of colleague, the chair has a continuing responsibility as mentor and evaluator—to help associate professors develop their potential as teachers, scholars, and department leaders.

Merit increases in salary and other rewards that chairs may be able to arrange for noteworthy accomplishments are important, both to reinforce strong professional performance by some associate professors and to motivate better work by others. Assigning a new course or arranging an interesting curriculum-development project may provide useful focus and challenge for a faculty member who lets down after tenure or burns out later. And the chair often can reinforce and shape faculty performance by making a personal investment in associate professors, for instance by asking what is going well in a class, passing on calls-for-papers or grant notices of likely interest, commiserating over a rejection letter, seeking a faculty member's advice on a sensitive department issue, and offering constructive suggestions about how a person's scholarly record is developing.

Lurking behind such discussions of an associate professor's record, of course, are the institutional criteria and departmental expectations for promotion to professor. And these can be forbidding, particularly the expectations in scholarship and publication. The following condensation of my university's research criterion is fairly typical:

> For promotion to professor, a faculty member should have an *established reputation* within the discipline or profession. This is indicated by a *significant* record of research, scholarship, or creative work—a *continuing* record of excellence normally extending at least eleven years (i.e., five years past tenure and promotion to associate professor).

That sort of standard gets elaborated, in different ways in different departments, with specific expectations—for a number of university press books, a list of refereed articles, a pattern of citation by other scholars, a record of leadership roles in national associations, and the like. These expectations can motivate pessimism and surrender, in some associate professors, rather than the further accomplishments in scholarship usually required for promotion. They also form a context for evaluation in which some associate professors who work to become professors will be judged by their departments to have inadequate records for promotion.

CONCLUSION

Both of these situations—associate professors denied further promotion and associate professors who never even try for promotion—pose morale and administrative challenges well beyond the scope of this chapter. But it is clear that responding to them, as in so much of the chair's work with faculty members, involves both mentoring and evaluation.

The chair, after all, is responsible for standards and for morale, for personnel practices that conform with institutional policy and for dealing, personally, with colleagues subject to those policies. It is a job for which there are no simple guidelines or neat conclusions. So I end with a messy generalization. Whether we are advising women and men who are preparing for tenure or we are counseling those who have been denied tenure or promotion, chairs must be sure that department expectations in teaching, scholarship, and service are *appropriate* (given the institution's standards for the position and the range of specialties within the department), *clearly stated* in department policies, and *fairly applied* in department evaluations for tenure and promotion.

APPENDIX: ARTICLE PUBLICATION IN COMPOSITION STUDIES—SOME NOTES FOR EVALUATION COMMITTEE MEMBERS

Because composition studies is a broad and growing field, its faculty members can pursue refereed, national publication in a wide variety of venues.

To begin with, tenure, promotion, and merit files of composition studies faculty may include articles published as essays or chapters in edited, special-focus collections issued by professional associations (e.g., Association of Teachers of Technical Writing, Modern Language Association, National Council of Teachers of English, Rhetoric Society of America, Society for Technical Communication); by university presses (e.g., Chicago, Florida, Missouri, Oxford, Pittsburgh, South Carolina, Southern Illinois, SUNY); and by commercial publishers (e.g., Ablex, Allyn Bacon, Baywood, Boynton/Cook, Greenwood, Jossey-Bass, Lawrence Erlbaum Associates, Longman, Sage).

Even more varied are the possibilities with journal articles. For instance, Chris Anson and Bruce Maylath have compiled a listing of more than 100 journals that (their annotations make clear) publish articles on these topics, among others: administration of writing programs, composition-literature relationships, composition pedagogy, nature and history of rhetoric, preparation of writing teachers, systematic research on writing and its teaching, technical and business communication, and writing-reading relationships (150–87).

Chairs and evaluation committee members seeking background on the journals in which their faculty are publishing could consult Anson and Maylath's guide to journals in *Teacher As Writer: Entering the Professional Conversation*. (They might also turn to current issues of the *MLA Directory of Publications* or *Iowa Guide: Journals in Mass Communication and Related Fields*—although neither provides thorough coverage of journals in composition studies). The following list is intended only as a quick orientation to the journals in the field.

Some journals in composition studies deal with a wide range of subjects and approaches. Among these are established broad-focus journals, such as *College Composition and Communication*, *College English*, *Composition Studies/Freshman English News*, *Journal of Advanced Composition* (broader than its title suggests), *Research in the Teaching of English*, *Rhetoric Review*, and *Written Communication*. There are also newer broad-focus journals, including *Dialogue: A Journal for Writing Specialists*, *Focuses*, *Issues in Writing*, and *Writing on the Edge*.

Other journals focus more sharply on one or another aspect of the various subjects and approaches within composition studies. Among these journals are: *ADE Bulletin* (on administrative and leadership matters), *American Educational Research Journal*, *Assessing Writing*, *Computers and Composition*, *English Education* (focuses on preparing teachers), *English Journal* (read by many high school teachers), *Journal of Basic Writing*, *Journal of Business and Technical Communication*, *Journal of Communication*, *Journal of Second Language Writing*, *Journal of Teaching Writing*, *Language and Learning Across the Disciplines*, *Language Arts* (read by many K-8 teachers), *Pre/Text: A Journal of Rhetorical Theory*, *Quarterly Journal of Speech*, *Reading Research Quarterly*, *Rhetorica*, *Rhetoric Society Quarterly*, *Technical Communication Quarterly*, *Teaching English in the Two-Year College*, *WPA: Writing Program Administration*, *Writing Center Journal*, and *Writing Instructor*.

Besides national journals, composition studies faculty may also have articles in publications of state affiliates of the National Council of Teachers of English (e.g., *Arizona English Bulletin*, *Illinois English Bulletin*, *Minnesota English Journal*, *Virginia English Bulletin*). Such journals typically select articles from national submission pools. And their articles may, depending on their merits, be cited by composition studies scholars and included in annual volumes of the *CCCC Bibliography of Composition and Rhetoric*.

Given the recent growth of composition studies, it is fortunate—for the field and for faculty members who need to publish—that there are so many strong venues for articles. Consider the fact that, in 1993, there were 176 composition positions advertised in the MLA's *Job-Information List* (Huber 103). Other positions were available, too, but if each of those 176 women and men were required for tenure to publish four refereed articles the result would be 704 articles to be published before 1999. That amounts to six times the number of articles that the field's largest and most competitive journal, *College Composition and Communication*, is likely to publish over those five years. In fact, 704 articles would be roughly the total number of articles published over a span of five years by *College English, Composition Studies / Freshman English News, Journal of Advanced Composition, Journal of Basic Writing, Research in the Teaching of English, Rhetoric Review, Rhetoric Society Quarterly, Writing Program Administration*, and *Written Communication* combined. Add into the equation the 159 composition positions advertised in 1992 (another 632 articles needed by 1998) and the 180 positions from 1991 (yet another 720 articles by 1997). And do not forget to calculate the impact of assistant professors hired more recently, associate professors working toward promotion, and senior faculty who are submitting their articles.

Clearly, composition studies is lucky to be served by a growing number of well-regarded book publishers and journals. However, for some people, the number and variety of publishing opportunities available to faculty in composition studies may raise questions about the prestige of journal and book articles included in a tenure, promotion, or merit dossier. It is not difficult, if such questions arise, to examine the experience of journal or book editors or to check on editorial board membership and manuscript-reviewing practices; also, the judgments of external evaluators can be very helpful in providing a professional view of a journal or a publisher in question. But too many faculty members are now required to publish (see Boyer 12) for most departments to count only articles in a short list of acceptable journals. As Donald Jarvis acknowledged in his 1991 MLA book, *Junior Faculty Development*:

> The strongest research universities may be able to continue to demand that junior professors publish with the best presses and the best refereed journals. It is impossible, however, for the average institution to make this demand for all of its junior faculty members. Since there are nearly half a million professors in the United States, every professor cannot publish every year with the best publishers. (26)

For some people, the number of composition journals and essay collections that include pedagogy in their editorial interests may also raise questions about the substance or seriousness of the articles in a personnel file. Teaching and scholarship, however, are very closely related in this particular field; as two of the leading bibliographers of composition studies have put it, "[t]he major concern of most composition specialists is teaching writing well" (Lindemann and Tate v).

This relationship of pedagogy to research is widely understood and supported by professional associations, such as the Modern Language Association. For example, the MLA's "Report of the Commission on Writing and Literature" provides a useful perspective on the place of pedagogy in composition studies research, and a report of the MLA Commission on Professional Service considers teaching to be no less a site of intellectual work than research/scholarship (see note 4 in my chapter "Evolving Approaches"). Another good resource is the "Statement of Good Practice: Teaching, Evaluation, and Scholarship," issued by the MLA's Association of Departments of English. It ends with these words: "Scholarship on teaching—its methods, assessment procedures, and ways to improve it—should be valued on a par with traditional forms of scholarship" ("ADE" 45).

WORKS CITED

AAUP Council. "Statement on Procedural Standards in the Renewal or Nonrenewal of Faculty Appointments." *Academe* 76 (Jan./Feb. 1990): 48–51.

"ADE Statement of Good Practice: Teaching, Evaluation, and Scholarship." *ADE Bulletin* No. 105 (Fall 1993): 43–45.

Anson, Chris M., and Bruce Maylath. "Searching for Journals: A Brief Guide and 100 Sample Species." *Teacher As Writer: Entering the Professional Conversation.* Ed. Karin L. Dahl. Urbana: NCTE, 1992. 150–87.

Boyer, Ernest L. *Scholarship Reconsidered: Priorities of the Professoriate.* Princeton: Carnegie Foundation for the Advancement of Teaching, 1990.

CCCC Committee on Professional Guidance to Departments and Faculty. "Draft Statement of Professional Guidance to Junior Faculty and Department Chairs." *College Composition and Communication* 38 (Dec. 1987): 493–97.

CCCC Executive Committee. "Statement of Principles and Standards for the Postsecondary Teaching of Writing." *College Composition and Communication* 40 (Oct. 1989): 329–36.

Diamond, Robert M., and Bronwyn E. Adam. "Describing the Work of Faculty." *The Disciplines Speak: Rewarding Scholarly, Professional, and Creative Work of Faculty.* Ed. Diamond and Adam. Washington: American Association for Higher Education, 1995. 1–14.

Edgerton, Russell. "The Re-Examination of Faculty Priorities." *Change* Jul./Aug. 1993: 10–25.

Edwards, Richard. "Toward Constructive Review of Disengaged Faculty." *AAHE Bulletin* 47.2 (Oct. 1994): 6–7, 11–2, 16.

Gebhardt, Richard C. Draft Statement of Promotion and Tenure Evidence. 1994.

——. "Editor's Column: Scholarship, Promotion, and Tenure in Composition Studies." *College Composition and Communication* 44 (Dec. 1993): 439–42.

——. "Evolving Approaches to Scholarship, Promotion, and Tenure in Composition Studies." *Academic Advancement in Composition Studies.* Ed. Richard Gebhardt and Barbara Gebhardt. Mahwah, NJ: Lawrence Earlbaum Associates, 1997. 1–19.

Haggard, Frank E. "Hiring and Mentoring New Faculty Members." *ADE Bulletin* No. 95 (Spring 1990): 25–28.

Huber, Bettina J. "Recent Trends in the Modern Language Job Market." *Profession 94*. New York: MLA, 1994. 94–105.

Jarvis, Donald K. *Junior Faculty Development: A Handbook*. New York: MLA, 1991.

Lindemann, Erika, and Gary Tate, eds. *An Introduction to Composition Studies*. New York: Oxford UP, 1991. v–vi.

Magner, Denise K. "Beyond Tenure." *Chronicle of Higher Education*. 21 July 1995: A13, A16.

MLA Commission on Professional Service. "Making Faculty Work Visible: Reinterpreting Professional Service, Teaching, and Research in the Fields of Language and Literature." 1995; accepted by the MLA Executive Council 1996.

"Report of the Commission on Writing and Literature." *Profession 88*. New York: MLA, 1988. 70–76.

Schilb, John. "Scholarship in Composition and Literature: Some Comparisons." *Academic Advancement in Composition Studies*. Ed. Richard Gebhardt and Barbara Gebhardt. Mahwah, NJ: Lawrence Erlbaum Associates, 1997. 21–30.

13 The Importance of External Reviews in Composition Studies

Lynn Z. Bloom
University of Connecticut

"A slow sort of country!" said the Queen. "Now, here, you see, it takes all the running you can do, to keep in the same place. If you want to get somewhere else, you must run at least twice as fast as that!"

—Lewis Carroll, *Through the Looking-Glass (127; ch. 2)*

A tenure review, as Sam Johnson observed of an impending hanging, wonderfully focuses the mind. During one particularly interesting period in my life, in the course of several moves to accommodate a dual-career marriage, I underwent four tenure reviews in seven years. In recent years, comfortably tenured, I routinely serve as an external evaluator of English Departments and writing programs, as well as an external reviewer of scholarship in numerous cases of tenure and promotion—not to mention grant proposals, fellowship applications, and submissions to journals and presses. In the immortal words of Ann Landers, I've "been there, honey." As my mind wonderfully focused on the nature of these myriad reviews in preparation for this chapter, I was forcibly reminded of how variable and subjective the process is, how political, and ultimately, how helpful reviews, of individual scholarship and of entire programs, can be to both candidate and institution, if done well.

ELASTIC CRITERIA FOR TENURE AND PROMOTION

Whatever the local departmental or institutional definitions of *teaching*, *scholarship*, and *service* may be, their actual meaning resides in interpretations more or less variable, as determined by diverse review committees, chairpersons, deans, and other administrators. Because the nature of academic work is diverse and ever-changing, God (or Godot, if you prefer) has to be in the details. There's no way a school, or a department, or for that matter a discipline, can anticipate the wide range of developments in the field or in the possible work its faculty will do from one year to the next. Individual reviewers and committees must have enough flexibility to exercise their sense of the current state of the art, the cutting edge, the retrograde.

In scholarship, for instance, what is the *right* amount and nature of publication? What is the pecking order among journals and presses—and is it different for composition and rhetoric than for literature? If not refereed, is a publication beyond the pale? Are single-authored works worth more than collaborations? How are edited volumes or collections to be weighted? What is the status, if any, of online "publications"? Do reviews "count"? Do textbooks? Workbooks? Software? Instructional videos? Or are the latter four evidence of teaching rather than scholarship? Or some hybrid? How, if at all, should a personnel review treat work submitted but not accepted, work in progress, unfunded grant proposals? Each of these questions has, perforce, innumerable temporary answers, each embedded in a particular context. Although we wouldn't have it any other way, this necessary flexibility requires continual fine-tunings that depend on a complicated confluence of subjective judgments.

The elastic nature of such standards may be even more conspicuous in rhetoric and composition. Here diverse research methodologies (including case studies, ethnographies, and quantitative empirical investigation) and emphasis on teaching and administration, although normative, are not necessarily understood by peers in more traditional literary fields. Should directing a writing program be considered teaching, because the director usually trains teachers, develops curricula, and may offer consultations or workshops to other faculty members and public school teachers? Or service, for everything provided is a service to the program's constituents? Or—as Boyer might argue—scholarship, reflecting the theoretical and intellectual basis, and biases, of the discipline and applying them to diverse student populations, inside and outside of traditional classrooms? How can such teaching (or service or scholarship) be evaluated? Through students' progress—in the course, throughout their undergraduate studies, or on the job? Cost of delivery of services? The director's ability to keep the program under control and out of the hair of the other faculty? Community outreach and articulation with the area high schools?

The fact remains that, despite the best efforts of schools and professional organizations to establish and enforce uniform, objective standards for tenure and promotion, departments and institutions still have the flexibility, borne of criteria that are variable of necessity, to retain and promote the people they want to keep and to wash out the rest. To rephrase a signal idea from *Alice in Wonderland,* my guess is that in most reviews for tenure and promotion, the verdict is reached first, implicitly, and the justification is adduced afterward, when the evidence is formally examined. These may be fighting words in a litigious era when people talk in code instead of making the reasons explicit. Nevertheless, I would contend after having served as department chair and on numerous committees at relatively benign schools, internal reviewers are in for no surprises, although the candidates themselves may be, for their decisions will reflect the prevailing norms of their intramural culture (see Torgovnick, Chapter 4; Bloom "Teaching"). In such a culture, external reviews—of programs and of individuals' work—are necessary.

THE NECESSITY OF EXTERNAL REVIEWS

External reviews are necessary, not because external reviewers are any more objective than individual departments or institutions—they're not—but because they're removed from them, and therefore at least in theory, free of local concerns, including alignments in departmental feuds and current priorities. Although many English departments now hire specialists in composition and rhetoric, in most departments their numbers are not large. Thus their tenure and promotion will be determined by colleagues from another culture, most likely literary studies. It is particularly important for such candidates' work to be commented on by external experts in composition and rhetoric chosen, through suggestions from both the candidates and the department chair, because of their national reputations. These external reviewers can be expected not only to know a great deal about the discipline they represent and to understand its national, perhaps international, implications, but also to be highly partisan toward it. How could they be otherwise?

In the course of the review—whether on a site visit to a writing program or in a letter evaluating the candidate's scholarship—the reviewer becomes an advocate for the discipline, although not necessarily for the individual candidate. The external reviewer's primary task, although I have never seen it stated in any departmental or institutional charge to a reviewer, is to interpret the nature of the candidate's work or program for the actual and potential readers of the report, the department, the dean, the university review committee(s), the provost—and, should tenure be denied, for anyone else who might read the documents during appeal.

If done with thoroughness and care—following, for instance, the ADE and WPA standards for external reviews—a thoughtful reviewer's report will educate its readers, even those who think they already know what the rapidly changing field of composition studies is, or does, or can do. (If it better fits your needs, substitute *writing program, freshman English,* or another alternative for *composition studies* in that sentence.) As Rowe notes, "Even the writing of ephemeral evaluations . . . helps constitute a national and an international scholarly community." This is an extension of "our teaching mission both in the classroom and in our professional exchanges" (48–49). The reviewer's interpretations of anyone's work will need to explain to specialists in other areas of English studies, or in other disciplines entirely, the nature of that work, its actual and potential dimensions, and its implications and consequent significance at the departmental and institutional levels and in the profession at large. This may involve translation of the candidate's normative language, concepts, and values into those the readers can understand and appreciate.

A CHARACTERISTIC CASE

Let us consider the issues involved in a characteristic case. Often—some would argue too often, although I would not—a new PhD, let's call her Alice,[1] with a specialization in composition studies is hired to direct the English Department's, and so the college's, writing program. A minimalist list (after all, you readers are busy people) of her duties follows.

Alice plans the freshman composition curriculum, coordinates it with upper-division writing courses, revises it annually, and oversees the summer placement of incoming students into the appropriate courses. She appoints and teaches the new TAs and adjuncts (a modest ten per year) how to teach composition, formally through a one-semester course each year and informally through a mentoring program which involves the more experienced part-timers (some 25 in all). Every year she evaluates the writing portfolios of all the new teachers' students, and she provides both a conference and a written personnel evaluation of each teacher every year. She writes institutional grants to secure computer classrooms and a campus-wide writing center and then, because funds are tight, teaches and monitors the TAs assigned to work in these areas. She chairs the English Department's Freshman English Committee, and she serves on the university committee inaugurating a writing-across-the-disciplines program. She is continually trouble-shooting, as well as negotiating with the department chair and the dean over class size, program funding, and hiring.

Alice is given one course released time each semester, a twenty-hour-a-week graduate assistant throughout the academic year, a work-study student for ten hours per week during the summer, and pay for one extra summer month. She shares department secretarial services. Like other faculty members, she is expected to attend professional meetings, to publish, and in other ways to be professionally active. Although she is a new faculty member, Alice is in fact expected to do as much administrative work as her department chair, although without his institutional power.

If Alice does her work well, much of it will be invisible or buried in reports and statistical compilations. Only those who have held comparable positions, including most of the external evaluators whose judgment might be called on during a tenure review, can fully understand the demands, pressures, potential, and constraints under which Alice works.

External Review of the Writing Program

Because Alice's work as WPA is remote from the experience of many who will evaluate her tenure file, it can be extremely helpful to have an external review of the writing program the year before tenure review, in order to put on the record a knowledgeable, fair-minded, yet sympathetic analysis of the director's work. Two reports are crucial in such a review: the program self-study, prepared in advance of the visit, usually written or coordinated by the writing director; and the response of the external evaluator (or evaluation team) to both the report and the campus visit.

The program self-study customarily addresses such matters as curriculum (including philosophy, courses, instructional methods and materials, responses to student writing, and assessment), faculty working conditions and development, and various aspects of program administration (see the WPA self-study guidelines in White, 304–13). It highlights program goals, strengths, problems, and inadequacies. The evaluator's report should address the same issues and others, if necessary, as well as commend successes and suggest solutions to difficulties (see Beidler; McLeod; and White, Chapter 12).

The self-study anatomizes the writing program and lays out the director's track record, and the evaluator's response assesses both. So the external evaluator (or evaluation team) is collaborating with the writing director and the department to strengthen the program and, if the evaluation is being conducted the year before a tenure vote, to provide evidence for the director's tenure review. External program reviews are not necessarily or uniformly favorable. But their analysis of existing deficits and problems often deflects potential criticism of the director by identifying institutional difficulties, such as underfunding and lack of administrative support.

External Review of Scholarship

Alice's scholarship, as well as her work as writing director, figures in her review for tenure and promotion. Some people might ask whether she should be judged according to the same criteria afforded faculty peers who teach somewhat more but have few if any administrative duties. I believe that, to prevent composition studies specialists from being stigmatized by a double standard, the same qualitative criteria must apply to all. Of course, such criteria, and the relative weighting of individual areas of scholarship, teaching, and service, may—and should—be adjusted by the department and university review committees when a candidate carries the sort of administrative burden Alice does.

In reviewing candidates' work for tenure and promotion to associate professor, I use the following criteria, applicable equally to scholarship in composition studies and literature:

1. Is the candidate aware of the major and some minor dimensions of his/her research area, including pertinent research issues, methodologies, and significant literature?

2. If so, in what ways does the candidate draw on the established body of research in the field?

3. In what ways is the candidate contributing to the ongoing research in the field? Synthesizing, summarizing, or interpreting the research of others to audiences unfamiliar with it? Using others' research as the basis for investigations into new areas? Making innovations in methodology or theory?

4. If either of the latter, how significant does the candidate's ongoing research appear to be? *Minor* (either going over old ground, or dealing with peripheral or trivial issues or with trivial aspects of a potentially significant issue)? *Middle-level*, representing some solid contributions to the existing state of knowledge or state of the methodological art? (Such research can usually be extended or expanded, or it can lead to additional areas; it's good work on which to build.) *High-level*, representing innovative thinking or innovative methodology that will be on the cutting edge of the field, that will influence the work of subsequent researchers, and that will engender other significant related research projects, of the candidate as well as others?

5. Has the candidate made significant contributions to the discipline through participation in national and/or regional professional organizations, establishment of a teaching or critical canon or curriculum, and/or aided in the professional development of others, faculty or students?

How the candidate's review committee and department employs and weights these, or any other criteria, is beyond the outside evaluator's control. The evaluator can only be clear and emphatic about the quality and the importance of the candidate's work. When, as in Alice's case, a WPA is a candidate for tenure/promotion, the evaluator also has an obligation to demonstrate how each criterion is applicable to the work the writing director has been hired to do. Thus, my view of materials to be evaluated expands considerably the conventional materials that Rowe expects the external reviewer to address. If Alice has developed a freshman curriculum, for instance, the external reviewer should be supplied with materials that will indicate its philosophy, underlying scholarship, and quality. In addition to conventional publications in scholarly journals and books, these could include textbooks, instructional software, workshop handouts, curriculum guides, advice to teachers in the writing program, syllabi, writing assignments, graded papers, portfolio summaries, and student evaluations—preferably written commentary.[2]

By increasing the scope of materials reviewed beyond the conventional books, articles, and conference papers, the external reviewer of candidates in composition studies, affirming Boyer's views, is implicitly lobbying for their legitimacy in a tenure review. The home team may, at any level, elect to ignore these materials and may, consequently, discount the external reviewer's evaluation. Nevertheless, these materials become and remain part of the candidate's record, for all to consider—or to reconsider if a negative decision is appealed.

CONCLUSION

That English departments are changing to incorporate experts in composition studies into their mainstream faculty is unmistakable, as Bettina Huber's recent reports to the ADE and MLA indicate. That the criteria enabling the tenuring of such experts are being expanded and revised is less certain.

Conventional literary faculty members should derive their view of composition studies research from the major work—intellectual, theoretical, pedagogical—in the field. Instead, far too many adhere to the view represented in Richard Marius's surly indictment of the work in composition studies as essentially pragmatic and unintellectual:

> I maintain that, against the background of the present *practical* state of the discipline, all the research going on in composition and rhetoric matters not at all. I can think of no book or article devoted to research or theory that has made a particle of difference in the general teaching of composition for the past twenty or thirty years—and I can think of a great many commonly held assumptions in the discipline that are supported by no major research at all.

> One cannot therefore consider in any realistic way the state of scholarship in composition without calling attention to the woeful condition of the discipline itself that renders all scholarship merely ornamental. Composition remains overwhelmingly practical . . . the most important books are textbooks [atheoretical and uninformed by research]. (466)

In this myopic reading of the discipline, composition studies is a lost cause. If Marius were right, either prevailing criteria for tenure and promotion would have to change dramatically to reward atheoretical, unimaginative recycling of stale, ineffectual pedagogy or else no specialist in composition studies would be tenurable. Fortunately, this is not the case.

To rebut Marius is beyond the scope of the discussion here; Donald McQuade's essay on "Composition and Literary Studies," following Marius's in *Redrawing the Boundaries*, provides a necessary corrective. And a wealth of notable composition research books and articles provide *prima facie* evidence of sophisticated theory, wide reading, keen critical intelligence, and humane understanding of politics, philosophy, and pedagogy. Three prizewinning works published since 1990 are representative of current scholarship in composition studies at the highest level included in Criterion 4, mentioned earlier: Kurt Spellmeyer's *Common Ground: Dialogue, Understanding, and the Teaching of Composition*; Susan Miller's *Textual Carnivals: The Politics of Composition*; and Lester Faigley's *Fragments of Rationality: Postmodernity and the Subject of Composition*.

Academia, however avant garde intellectually, is in governance wedded to tenure and promotion review procedures that make it, as Lewis Carroll's Queen observed, "A slow sort of country" where "it takes all the running you can do, to keep in the same place. If you want to get somewhere else, you must run at least twice as fast as that!" Composition studies faculty members, whether candidates for tenure and promotion or their external reviewers, know this running metaphor all too well. In both research and administration, as current work indicates, we are of necessity on a fast track. There is no other place.

NOTES

[1]The choice of a woman for this example is deliberate. (See Holbrook, Bloom "I Want," and also Miller, Chapter 4, "The Sad Women in the Basement: Images of Composition Teaching.") The following list of duties is an embellishment of the typical composition specialist's job described in Slevin. See also the Council of Writing Program Administrators' guidelines for WPA positions; Carter and McClelland; and Roen.

[2]Conventional, institution-wide course evaluations are based on an efficiency model rewarding large-scale lecture courses that deliver large amounts of material in a clear, organized fashion with little interchange between students and lecturer. This

model does not apply very well to the messy, improvisatory, collaborative nature of many writing classrooms. Moreover, short- or long-term, small- or large-scale, institution-wide assessment programs are freighted with difficulties. (See Witte and Faigley; White, Chapters 11–13; and Greenberg et al.; and the WPA self-study guidelines.)

WORKS CITED

Association of Departments of English. *A Checklist and Guide for Reviewing Departments of English*. New York: ADE, 1985.

Beidler, Peter G. "The WPA Evaluation: A Recent Case History." *WPA: Writing Program Administration* 14.3 (Spring 1991): 69–73.

Bloom, Lynn Z. "I Want a Writing Director." *College Composition and Communication* 43 (May 1992): 176–78.

——. "Teaching College English As a Woman." *College English* 54 (Nov. 1992): 818–25.

Boyer, Ernest. *Scholarship Reconsidered: Priorities of the Professoriate*. Princeton: Carnegie Foundation for the Advancement of Teaching, 1990.

Carroll, Lewis. *Through the Looking Glass*. 1871. *Alice in Wonderland*. Ed. Donald J. Gray. New York: Norton, 1971. 101–209.

Carter, Duncan, and Ben McClelland. "WPAs Assess the CCCC's 'Statement of Principles and Standards.' " *WPA: Writing Program Administration* 16.1–2 (Fall/Winter 1992): 71–88.

Council of Writing Program Administrators. "Guidelines for Writing Program Administrator (WPA) Positions." *WPA: Writing Program Administration* 16.1–2 (Fall-Winter 1992): 89–94.

——. "Guidelines for Self Study to Precede a Writing Program Evaluation." White 304–313.

Faigley, Lester. *Fragments of Rationality: Postmodernity and the Subject of Composition*. Pittsburgh: U of Pittsburgh P, 1992.

Greenberg, Karen L., Harvey S. Wiener, and Richard A. Donovan, eds. *Writing Assessment: Issues and Strategies*. New York: Longman, 1986.

Holbrook, Sue Ellen. "Women's Work: The Feminizing of Composition." *Rhetoric Review* 9.2 (Spring 1991): 201–29.

Huber, Bettina J. "The Changing Job Market." *Profession 92*. New York: MLA, 1992. 59–73.

——. "The MLA's 1991–92 Survey of PhD Placement: The Latest English Findings and Trends through Time." *ADE Bulletin* No. 108 (Fall 1994): 42–51.

——. "Recent and Anticipated Growth in English Doctoral Programs: Findings from the MLA's 1990 Survey." *ADE Bulletin* No. 106 (Winter 1993): 44–63.

——. "Women in the Modern Languages, 1970–90." *Profession 90*. New York: MLA, 1990. 58–73.

McLeod, Susan H. "Requesting a Consultant–Evaluation Visit." *WPA: Writing Program Administration* 14.3 (Spring 1991): 73–77.

McQuade, Donald. "Composition and Literary Studies." *Redrawing the Boundaries: The Transformation of English and American Literary Studies*. Ed. Stephen Greenblatt and Giles Gunn. New York: MLA, 1992. 482–519.

Marius, Richard. "Composition Studies." *Redrawing the Boundaries: The Transformation of English and American Literary Studies*. Ed. Stephen Greenblatt and Giles Gunn. New York: MLA, 1992. 466–81.

Miller, Susan. *Textual Carnivals: The Politics of Composition*. Carbondale: Southern Illinois UP, 1991.

Roen, Duane H. "Writing Administration As Scholarship and Teaching." *Academic Advancement in Composition Studies*. Ed. Richard C. Gebhardt and Barbara Genelle Smith Gebhardt. Mahwah, NJ: Lawrence Erlbaum Associates, 1997. 43–55.

Rowe, John Carlos. "The Ethics of Professional Letters: Eleven Theses." *Profession 90*. New York: MLA, 1990. 48–51.

Slevin, James F. "The Politics of the Profession." *An Introduction to Composition Studies*. Ed. Erika Lindemann and Gary Tate. New York: Oxford UP, 1991. 135–59.

Spellmeyer, Kurt. *Common Ground: Dialogue, Understanding, and the Teaching of Composition*. Englewood Cliffs: Prentice Hall, 1993.

Torgovnick, Marianna De Marco. *Crossing Ocean Parkway: Readings by an Italian American Daughter*. Chicago: U of Chicago P, 1994.

White, Edward M. *Teaching and Assessing Writing*. 2nd ed. San Francisco: Jossey–Bass, 1994.

Witte, Stephen F., and Lester Faigley. *Evaluating College Writing Programs*. Carbondale: Southern Illinois UP, 1983.

14 Scholarship Reconsidered: A View from the Dean's Office

Susan H. McLeod
Washington State University

Before I became one, I thought administrators were part of the problem with the academic review process for faculty members in composition studies. I viewed deans and provosts as individuals with more power than understanding; the further up they were in the academic chain of command, the narrower and nastier I imagined administrators to be in their views of the criteria for tenure and promotion and in their views of what constituted acceptable scholarship in a discipline—especially in my discipline. In a hierarchical institution like a university, I reasoned, these individuals were the ones who needed to be enlightened about the nature of the work in composition. Then the too-frequent tales about wonderfully qualified colleagues denied promotion or tenure would cease.

From the dean's office, however, I have a rather different view. In point of fact, the administrators above me are remarkably inclusive and generous in their notion of scholarship and research. The higher on the organizational chart an administrator is, the more open she or he seems to be to a broad definition of what it is that constitutes scholarship. Collaborative work, creative work, publications on administrative issues, textbooks, computer software—all are acceptable evidence of professional growth in the eyes of most upper-level administrators I know. When one stops to think about it, the reason is fairly obvious. During the review process for tenure and promotion, these administrators must read (and watch and interact with and listen to) materials from many disciplines, taking into account the fact that research and scholarship in, say, microbiology is going to take quite a different form than it will in theater arts. No single definition of scholarship or professional growth paradigm fits all the units in any institution.

From my middle-level position, I can see that although administrators have to write the letters that confirm or deny tenure recommendations, it is at the department level that promotion and tenure difficulties in our field occur. Composition scholars, especially if there are just a few of them in a department, are often viewed as *other* by their literature colleagues. Their scholarship often looks applied rather than theoretical. They publish in different journals, they sometimes do collaborative work, and they often have administrative duties that eat up their time but fall in the underappreciated category of service.

All these difficulties have been detailed elsewhere, most eloquently by Maxine Hairston in her call for independence from English Departments. Whereas breaking away as a separate unit might be a solution for some, the fact remains that most composition faculty members are going to be evaluated for tenure and promotion within English departments. If we want fair treatment for composition studies faculty members in the institutional review process, recognition of our field's particular contributions to scholarship must come first at home, in our departments. The key to an effective review process for composition faculty, then, is for members of the English department to be educated about how the work of composition scholars fits into the larger picture of academic scholarship. Administrators can and should play a role in helping these colleagues broaden their notions of scholarship before it is time to cast ballots during the review process. And a useful resource for administrators in this endeavor is an influential 1990 book published by the Carnegie Foundation.

SCHOLARSHIP RECONSIDERED

Ernest Boyer's *Scholarship Reconsidered* calls for an overhaul of the notion of academic scholarship. Boyer begins by noting the renewed attention being paid to undergraduate education in institutions (evidenced in general education reforms, for example) and the accompanying interest in good teaching. He points out that there has been no move to change the faculty reward system, a change which should—indeed, must—go with a renewed commitment to areas beyond research in the institutional mission. More inclusive definitions of scholarship are needed:

> [T]he most important obligation now confronting the nation's colleges and universities is to break out of the tired old teaching versus research debate

and define, in more creative ways, what it means to be a scholar. It's time to recognize the full range of faculty talent and the great diversity of functions higher education must perform. (xii)

After a historical review of the expectations for faculty, in which he points out that research is a latecomer to the reward system, Boyer argues that it is time to rethink what it means to be a scholar—to "give the familiar and honorable term 'scholarship' a broader, more capacious meaning, one that brings legitimacy to the full scope of academic work" (16). In other words, Boyer does not propose that we do away with the present reward system for faculty, only that we expand our notion of the basis for it. He proposes thinking about the work of the professoriate in four separate—but overlapping—areas: the scholarship of discovery, the scholarship of integration, the scholarship of application, and the scholarship of teaching.

The *scholarship of discovery* is the most familiar of his categories—it is what academics usually refer to as research. This sort of scholarship involves expanding the boundaries of knowledge, contributing to the understanding of a field through work no one has done before. The prototype of such scholarship is work in the sciences and medicine, from which Boyer draws his examples (the isolation of a virus, the sighting of a new comet, the unlocking of the genetic code), but of course other disciplines produce discoveries as well. Although it is difficult to classify composition scholarship in tidy ways, Shirley Brice Heath's ground-breaking *Ways with Words* and Janet Emig's *The Composing Processes of Twelfth Graders* might be thought of as examples of the scholarship of discovery in the field.

By *scholarship of integration* Boyer means the kind of work that makes connections between ideas across the disciplines, or puts specialties in larger contexts—work which "seeks to interpret, draw together, and bring new insight to bear on original research" (19). Often this is interdisciplinary work at the boundaries where fields come together. In composition, we might think here of the work Linda Flower and John R. Hayes did to make connections between cognitive psychology and the composing process, and of writers like William Wresch and Cynthia Selfe who brought composition and computers together. In the category of integration Boyer also includes work that is strictly interpretative—the fitting of research (one's own or that of others) into larger conceptual or intellectual frames. Instead of asking, "What is this?" integration scholarship asks, "What does this mean?" Scholars like Wayne Booth, Edward Corbett, and Kenneth Burke come to mind, here, in the field of composition studies.

Boyer's third category, the *scholarship of application*, involves applying the research and interpretative elements of the first two categories to problems of consequence in the larger community. Boyer makes a distinction between the activities that make one a good department or university citizen (usually defined as service) and activities that are tied to and flow from one's field of knowledge. The latter activities, Boyer argues, are

> serious, demanding work, requiring the rigor—and the account-
> ability—traditionally associated with research activities. . . . New intel-
> lectual understandings can arise out of the very act of
> application—whether in medical diagnosis, serving clients in psychother-
> apy, shaping public policy, creating an architectural design, or working
> with the public schools. In activities such as these, theory and practice
> vitally interact, and one renews the other. (22–23)

Writing program administrators may recognize this argument as one made by Richard Bullock in 1987—that administration can and should be considered scholarship. *WPA: Writing Program Administration* is a composition journal which publishes the scholarship of application almost exclusively. James Gray, the driving force behind the Bay Area Writing Project—which became the National Writing Project—is one of many figures who exemplifies this strand of scholarly work.

Boyer defends his last category, the *scholarship of teaching*, as the culmination of the other forms of scholarship: "In the end, inspired teaching keeps the flame of scholarship alive . . . . Without the teaching function, the continuity of knowledge will be broken and the store of human knowledge dangerously diminished" (24). This scholarship is the most difficult to document for the review process, but it appears in many venues, among them textbooks, software, how-to articles on teaching topics, curriculum guides, in-house documents, and teaching portfolios (on the last item, see Edgerton et al.). Donald Murray and Peter Elbow, among others, practice scholarship of teaching in composition studies.

Boyer goes on to call for a thorough revision of the faculty reward system to take into account the rich diversity of faculty contributions to scholarship. It is inspiring reading, but such a revolution is not likely to occur soon, in my institution or in yours, so I would like to consider how his ideas might be used by administrators in the present climate—one in which many institutions, for good or for ill, still emphasize research and publication. It is up to deans and other administrators to help nurture and guide new faculty members whose research may not fit the traditional definition and to help senior faculty members broaden their definition of what constitutes acceptable research and publication in composition. (Richard Gebhardt deals with these ideas in his chapter "Mentor and Evaluator.")

For faculty to be able to use Boyer's ideas, it is essential that upper-level administrators take *Scholarship Reconsidered* off the shelf and get it into the hands of English department chairs, who should in turn share it with their faculties. (As any good administrator knows, this must be done with tact and discretion—faculty members are suspicious, often rightly so, of ideas that come down from administrative offices as if from Mount Sinai. A bottom-up approach would be preferable: Boyer's ideas will be more acceptable to those who discover them for themselves.) Once the expansion of the notion of scholarship and the validation of the importance of teaching is being discussed among the faculty, administrators can announce their support of those ideas and ask for help in implementing them within the faculty evaluation process.

PREPARING FOR TENURE OR PROMOTION REVIEW

From the candidate's perspective, the most crucial part of preparing for tenure or promotion review is building a strong, well-documented application; just as important, perhaps, is the process by which that application is evaluated. To suggest how these two factors work together in successful personnel evaluations, I present here three hypothetical cases in which mid-level administrators, taking their cues from Boyer, establish a fair and flexible review process and work with candidates over time, both to educate English department faculty and to help candidates build strong applications. We will consider the promotion case for a Director of Composition, and tenure cases for a Writing Center Director and an English Education specialist, all located in an English Department.

Our setting is Ideal State University. English Department Chair Vera E. Savvy has attended a series of chairs' workshops held by the dean of the college, and she has managed during her term of office to raise the morale of the department considerably. Knowing that one of the ways to increase faculty productivity and morale is to get faculty members talking together about common concerns, she has encouraged frequent collegial interaction among the members of the department. There is a yearly departmental retreat for all faculty members, where they discuss the direction of the department; at the beginning and the end of the year, Chair Savvy and the graduate director take turns giving parties for department members (including, of course, the graduate students). After reading Lucas's *The Department Chairperson's Role in Enhancing College Teaching* (the text for one of the chairs' workshops given by the dean), Savvy started a colloquium series in which teaching as well as research is discussed. At one of these sessions she asks a respected faculty member (with whom she has shared her copy of *Scholarship Reconsidered*) to present Boyer's ideas for discussion, indicating during the discussion that she thinks the department could take a leadership role in the institution in redefining the concept of scholarship. The department has a system of course rotation, so that no one owns a course—thus, the new faculty members have a chance to teach graduate seminars immediately, and all faculty members (including the chair) take their turn at teaching lower-division, upper-division, and graduate classes. As a result of these practices, careful nurturing by the chair, and some judicious hiring, the faculty are a diverse group of people who tolerate differences among themselves; the department is a collegial place.

The historic mission of Ideal State is teaching, research, and service. In the last two decades, however, there has been an increased emphasis on grants and research; faculty members are expected to develop a focused research program and publish their work. To attain tenure in the English Department, one must show evidence of a growing body of scholarship (usually, this means articles in refereed journals); to be promoted to full professor, one needs to attain national recognition (usually, this means a book).

The tenure and promotion process, established by College Dean I.M. Wise, involves a careful series of dry-run ballots before the real thing occurs. Each untenured member of the department puts together a file that is evaluated yearly by the tenured faculty; the dean's office sponsors workshops for untenured faculty members to help them put this file together. The evaluation takes the form of a straw vote; faculty members must write comments supporting their vote, citing evidence from the candidate's record (ballots with no comments are discounted). Chair Savvy uses these yearly comments to give feedback to candidates, but she also scrutinizes the ballots carefully to see if she needs to educate some of the tenured faculty about new developments in the field.

At the end of an untenured candidate's third year in the department, there is a dry run that goes beyond the department. The candidate's file is also evaluated by the College Tenure and Promotion Committee (made up of representatives from departments within the college), the Dean, and the Academic Vice President. An advisory letter is then sent to the candidate, stating either that the progress toward tenure is satisfactory or pointing out the areas that need improvement. The chair meets with the dean and then with the candidate to discuss the dry-run review and to give counsel if needed.

To ensure fairness during the final tenure and promotion process, Dean Wise requires letters from five outside reviewers; Chair Savvy has encouraged faculty reviewers to rely on the evaluations of the outside experts when they are not familiar with the area of a candidate's work. Two peer evaluations of teaching are included in all tenure and promotion materials. Dean Wise has established guidelines to assure all that these class observations are meant to be positive experiences for both junior and senior faculty; senior faculty members occasionally report in their letters that they learned something about teaching from observing the class. There is a college-wide mentoring program in place to help support new faculty. A seasoned member of the department helps the newcomer understand teaching and research expectations, serves as one of the two peer evaluators of teaching, and is the candidate's advocate when the case comes before the tenured faculty in the department. The existence of a College Tenure and Promotion Committee ensures that candidates have other colleagues who can comment on the worth of their work, a factor that is especially important for those in small departments. (Dean Wise also uses this committee as a place to mentor some senior faculty about the breadth of possibilities for scholarship in the College.) According to a policy encouraged by the dean, new faculty members are first in line for travel money so that they can present papers at national meetings and begin to establish professional networks outside the institution. Dean Wise's often-expressed sentiment about the tenure and promotion process is that it should be supportive rather than adversarial, on the premise that professional growth occurs best in an atmosphere of positive expectation.

Promotion for a Writing Program Director

The Director of Composition, an energetic woman named Leslie Grammar (known as "Les"), was hired at the associate professor level with tenure; because Chair Savvy felt the position's heavy administrative responsibilities would interfere with a junior faculty member's progress toward tenure, she persuaded the Dean that the director position should always be at the level of associate or above.[1] During her four years as Director, Les Grammar has overhauled the Teaching Assistant Training program, established a portfolio system to certify writing competency, taught graduate and undergraduate classes, developed a new curriculum in Freshman Composition, retooled the basic writing course, directed faculty seminars on writing across the curriculum, and published a composition textbook. She has also won a campus teaching award.

Grammar's mentor is Professor Oldheimer, a senior literature person who once ran the writing program as interim director. Oldheimer met with the Dean and the Chair when Grammar was first hired, and the three discussed how he could best help her; he and Grammar have met regularly since that time to discuss her progress toward promotion. Although she has a number of publications that predate her hiring, Les Grammar needs to show that her professional growth is continuing in her new position; each time she has launched an initiative in the writing program, she has followed Oldheimer's suggestion that she document what she was doing, preferably in a published article. She now has pieces in a number of journals, especially in *WPA: Writing Program Administration*, the *Journal of Teaching Writing*, and the *Journal of Basic Writing*. Helped by Dean Wise's policy on travel money, Grammar has presented at national conferences and has made contacts that have resulted in invitations to write book chapters.

The volume of Writing Director Grammar's work is impressive. Still, her publication record seems to be all over the map, with pieces on TA training, basic writing, curricular reform in composition, writing across the curriculum, and portfolio assessment. She, Oldheimer, and Savvy meet with the Dean to discuss how best to present her case, and they decide that her focus is really the scholarship of teaching. She writes a narrative to include with her promotion file, showing that her work as Director of Composition and as leader of the WAC faculty workshops is primarily that of a teacher of teachers. Drawing together the various pieces she has published (and citing Boyer), Grammar shows how they reflect the major focus of her work, the scholarship of teaching. She also includes in her promotion materials the nomination letters for her teaching award and a videotape of one of her classes so that she can be seen in action.

One danger signal occurred during the first dry-run tenure balloting on Grammar's promotion application, when the usual few grumpy colleagues declined to count her textbook as a real book, even though it had been reviewed in a respected journal and declared to be ground-breaking.[2] Chair Savvy takes them out to lunch and chats with them in a friendly fashion about the issue, giving them the MLA's 1988 "Report of the Commission on Writing and Literature," which recommends that composition textbooks be considered the equivalent of other scholarly books. She works into the conversation a reminder of the broadened definition of scholarship recently discussed in the faculty colloquium. Thinking in particular of these colleagues, the Chair asks Grammar's outside reviewers to comment on the textbook as evidence of scholarship, referring them also to Boyer's work.

The promotion file in its final form contains a narrative, written by Grammar (with advice from Oldheimer and Savvy); five very positive outside letters; documentation of her teaching excellence in the classroom and as a teacher of teachers, including the videotape of a class; peer reviews of her teaching; her articles; and her textbook. When it comes time for the ballots to be counted, the majority of Grammar's colleagues vote to promote her. Chair Savvy writes a glowing summary, explaining that the two diehard faculty members who voted against the promotion are "out of touch with the field." The College Tenure and Promotion Committee concurs, and Dean Wise writes a recommendation to promote.

Tenure for a Writing Center Director

Ernest Modesto was hired to set up and then direct a writing center. A quiet, unassuming person, he has worked with Grammar to set up a splendid center, dovetailing it with both the TA training effort and the preservice training of high school English teachers (using both groups as tutors). Thanks to his efforts, the center serves students in all disciplines and has attracted much positive support from grateful teachers across campus. He has also secured a large donation for the department—a roomful of computers from a large computer company—to support the work in the center. (In typically modest fashion, he credits the university's development officer and Chair Savvy for the gift, even though his interest and expertise were the reasons the company made the donation.) He has been instrumental in integrating the computers into writing instruction, setting up networked stations for tutoring, for example, and devising an electronic bulletin board for students enrolled in writing classes.

Modesto's research interests are twofold: collaborative work (especially peer collaboration), and computers and writing. He has published several articles on collaboration and writing with other colleagues in such journals as *Computers and Composition*, the *Journal of Computer-Based Instruction*, *Composition Studies*, and *College Composition and Communication*. In the area of computers, he has authored software that connects in-house the composition curriculum and the writing center. A major publisher has expressed interest in Modesto's integrative software.

Modesto's mentor is the department chair herself. Chair Savvy's training is in literature, and she is committed to the literature curriculum in the department. She also sees the importance of the writing program in that it keeps the department at the center of the university curriculum. Her long-range plan is to strengthen the writing program, which touches almost every student in the university, and to use the program's importance to argue for more resources for the department as a whole. Modesto's position is part of her strategy to build links to programs across campus (she and Dean Wise created the position, with help from central administrators), and she wants to ensure that the writing center director's bid for tenure is successful.

Modesto's collaborative work has presented his colleagues with problems in the dry-run stage of the tenure process; because they do not do collaborative work themselves, they cannot determine what amount of the work is really his. Savvy makes several suggestions to Modesto: collaborate with different individuals; put his name as first author when he does the bulk of the work to ensure that he gets the citations; and submit several articles that he has written by himself. She also talks to the faculty members in question over lunch about the fact that collaborative work is the norm in many disciplines (including that of the Academic Vice President, a scientist), and that a solo-authored piece on collaborative work would seem at the least rather odd. When a few of his colleagues are still not satisfied, Modesto (with prodding from Savvy, who has identified his tendency to erase his own authorship) writes an explanatory preface for his tenure file that describes the process by which several of his collaborative pieces were written, underscoring his role as chief author.

Modesto's work with computers is also unfamiliar to his colleagues. Savvy consults with Dean Wise on strategy, and they agree that the value of the ccmputer donation can be listed under "grants and research" in Modesto's file. The English Department has received few grants of that size, so it is an impressive figure. Since Modesto's in-house software is also difficult for his colleagues to evaluate, Savvy persuades him to talk with the book representatives who have been pestering him, and he subsequently signs a contract with a major publisher. The contract goes into his tenure application file, along with the letters from the reviewers who responded positively to Modesto's software.

When the time comes to write his candidate's narrative, Chair Savvy works with Modesto to present his work as the scholarship of integration. Referring to Boyer, he presents his work as being at the boundaries between disciplines, as cutting edge work. The fact that he has published in a variety of refereed journals (and has finally produced a single-authored piece to satisfy his singletarian colleagues) and the contract for and positive reviews of his software present a convincing case to the department.

Tenure for an English Educator

Constance Smiley is a cheerful woman who taught for many years in the public school system before deciding to go back to graduate school. She was hired by Ideal State to be the English Education expert in the English Department; as such, she is a liaison between the subject-matter department and the College of Education and the advisor for all English Education majors. She teaches the English Methods classes, works closely with the writing center (where her Methods students tutor as part of their practicum), and during the summer runs the local affiliate of the National Writing Project. Smiley also coordinates the English department's teaching-emphasis MA program, many of whose students she has recruited from the Writing Project. Her research interest is bilingual education, in which she occasionally teaches courses.

Smiley's mentor is Professor Keene, a department member trained in linguistics and known for his interests in educational research. Keene is very taken by the work Smiley does with teachers, but is concerned that department members will view much of it as "just service." He has a strategy session with Chair Savvy and Dean Wise; they advise that Smiley present her work as both the scholarship of application and the scholarship of discovery, using the latter to bolster the former. She has done several studies, stemming from her doctoral research, on bilingual education in different settings. Keene reads over Smiley's manuscripts, helps her with the journal submission process, and encourages her to resubmit when manuscripts come back. He even collaborates with her on one piece that unites their respective interests in linguistics and second language acquisition. Smiley begins to build up a body of published research in journals like *Research in the Teaching of English* and *American Educational Research Journal*. Mentor Keene also encourages Constance Smiley to submit pieces on her work with the Writing Project to venues like *English Journal*.

When it becomes apparent during her dry run that some of her colleagues do not know some of the journals in which she has published articles (in fact, one was put off by the nonscholarly nature of the pieces in *EJ*), Smiley writes a section for her narrative describing each journal, including the national organization with which it is affiliated, its acceptance rate, and the audience at which it aims. Using Boyer's categories, Smiley explains how she does primary research—the scholarship of discovery—and then translates that scholarship for teachers. Chair Savvy chooses outside reviewers from prestigious programs in English Education, asking them to comment on Smiley's work with the Writing Project as well as her research program. Smiley sails through the tenure process.

The Importance of Administrative Leadership and Support

The cases of Grammar, Modesto, and Smiley are hypothetical, but they are not fantasy. Some of the elements of the promotion and tenure review process at Ideal State University already exist in many English departments, and they could exist anywhere—given the right support and the right leadership.

Chairs are key figures, as is Savvy in the previous narrative, in creating departmental cultures that nurture and support all faculty (see Massy et al.). Most of the effective chairs I know are made, not born; they work hard learning management skills, attend ADE Summer Seminars, read *ADE Bulletin* and publications from the American Council on Education (such as John Bennett's *Chairing the Academic Department*). They are people who can get things done, but they also have certain personal qualities—a collegial streak and a warmth that makes others look to them for advice as well as leadership.

Deans can also help departments establish collegial cultures that support diverse areas of scholarship. They can set the tone for the college, as Dean Wise did, by indicating that professional growth, not a competitive weeding out, is the goal of the tenure and promotion process. They can set up professional development workshops for chairs, in addition to working with chairs individually to put into writing departmental tenure and promotion criteria that ensure fairness and evenhanded treatment of faculty members as they climb the academic ladder. They can hold meetings for all new faculty members to demystify the tenure and promotion process. And deans can also make it clear, by supporting junior faculty members who are working to grow professionally, that they expect to promote and tenure the people they hire.

CONCLUSION

Not all chairs are savvy, of course, and not all deans are wise. And even if they were, individual faculty members still have important roles to play in their own promotion and tenure reviews. (Richard Gebhardt discusses many of these in his chapter "Preparing Yourself for Successful Personnel Review.")

To achieve a broader understanding of the details of academic personnel evaluation, I suggest that probationary faculty read *Scholarship Reconsidered*. Boyer's views will help you keep the notion of scholarship in perspective which, in turn, will reduce the chance of your getting mired in a publish or perish mode of thought, a mode sometimes encouraged when institutions emphasize numbers rather than quality when evaluating promotion and tenure application files. To think about scholarship as the social constructionists do will also be useful to you—as a way of joining the ongoing conversation and sharing your own unique insights into the field of composition studies. Publication does provide external validation of the quality of your work, but that is secondary to the true reason for publishing—to help the rest of us think through important issues.

Let me close by coming back to the view from the dean's office. Management at the middle and upper levels in academe is very different from management in corporations; university administrators have much less power than faculty members imagine. Individual cases for promotion and tenure must be made at the department level.

The tradition of faculty hegemony and the newer power faculty members have through unionization have made some administrators wary of trying to use their still-considerable authority of moral suasion. This does not mean, however, that university administrators will let nature take its course in the promotion and tenure review process. Quite the contrary. Proactive deans recognize that a critical component of their jobs is to put in place policies and procedures for academic personnel evaluation that are formative and fair, as well as summative and legal. These policies and procedures should include the dean's creating a collegial climate for working with department chairs to help educate faculty about scholarship as Boyer has re-envisioned the concept.

ACKNOWLEDGMENTS

I want to thank the members of my writing group—Professors Marie Glynn, Rachel Halverson, and Lori Wiest, all of WSU—for their helpful comments on drafts of this chapter.

NOTES

[1]*College: The Undergraduate Experience*, in which Ernest Boyer sees good writing skills as a major factor insuring success in college, was the linchpin for the chair's argument that convinced the dean to fund the position at a higher level.

[2]These are the same faculty who believe the department has been in a death spiral since Anglo Saxon was dropped as a requirement for English majors. Savvy visited them the year before to discuss the work of an assistant professor who publishes on post-colonial literature; a few years earlier, she had similar conversations with them about the work of a junior colleague who publishes feminist theory. She is slowly bringing them around.

WORKS CITED

Bennett, John B. *Chairing the Academic Department: Leadership Among Peers.* 2nd ed. New York: ACE/Macmillan, 1984.

——. *Managing the Academic Department: Cases and Notes.* New York: ACE/Macmillan, 1983.

Boyer, Ernest L. *College: The Undergraduate Experience.* New York: Harper, 1987.

——. *Scholarship Reconsidered: Priorities of the Professoriate.* Princeton: Carnegie Foundation for the Advancement of Teaching, 1990.

Bullock, Richard H. "When Administration Becomes Scholarship: The Future of Writing Program Administration." *WPA: Writing Program Administration* 11 (Fall 1987): 13–18.

Edgerton, Russell, Patricia Hutchings, and Kathleen Quinlan. *The Teaching Portfolio: Capturing the Scholarship in Teaching.* Washington: American Association for Higher Education, 1991.

Gebhardt, Richard C. "Mentor and Evaluator: The Chair's Role in Promotion and Tenure Review." *Academic Advancement in Composition Studies.* Ed. Richard C. Gebhardt and Barbara Genelle Smith Gebhardt. Mahwah, NJ: Lawrence Erlbaum Associates, 1997. 147–65.

——. "Preparing Yourself for Successful Personnel Review." *Academic Advancement in Composition Studies.* Ed. Richard C. Gebhardt and Barbara Genelle Smith Gebhardt. Mahwah, NJ: Lawrence Erlbaum Associates, 1997. 117–27 .

Hairston, Maxine. "Breaking Our Bonds and Reaffirming Our Connections." *College Composition and Communication* 36 (1985): 272–82.

Lucas, Ann F. *The Department Chairperson's Role in Enhancing College Teaching.* San Francisco: Jossey-Bass, 1989.

Massy, William F., et al. "Overcoming 'Hollowed' Collegiality." *Change* July/August 1994: 11–20.

"Report of the Commission on Writing and Literature." *Profession 88.* New York: MLA, 1988. 70–76.

Afterword: Re-Envisioning Tenure in an Age of Change

Elizabeth Tebeaux
Texas A & M University

At the risk of seeming to veer from the subject of this book, I open this chapter with a prediction: Within a decade, tenure, specifically the number of tenured faculty positions, will be waning dramatically. A growing percentage of new faculty members will be hired under contracts that can be renewed repeatedly or terminated at the end of any contract period. Major university systems will be actively discussing and looking for ways to eliminate the tenure system as we now know it. And traditional tenure will only be granted to outstanding faculty members and to faculty members coveted by other institutions.

TENURE AND THE NEW IRREVERENCE
FOR HIGHER EDUCATION

The reason for my prediction is simple: For the first time in American history, the public is becoming skeptical about the value of higher education. Criticism centers on such issues as the value of a college degree, which may no longer lead to meaningful or secure employment, and the idea that tenured faculty members are guaranteed lifetime employment. Since the mid-1980s, the public, state legislatures, and boards of trustees have been asking, with increasing persistence, how money for higher education is being spent and what universities have to show for this money.

From the public's perspective, tenure is the most distasteful aspect of the way colleges do business. (Why, many ask, should faculty, almost alone among the professions, be immune to global competition, economic downturns, and loss of job security affecting us?) My thesis is this: If faculty members do not begin to reform tenure, we may find it changed or eliminated for us, and we will probably not like the results. To avoid this, we have to re-envision both tenure and the way our graduate programs prepare students for careers as faculty members.

I have come to these conclusions through my experiences as a 20-year veteran in technical communication and as the editor of a recent collection of guidelines and perspectives on tenure and promotion.[1] In this essay I comment on current tenure requirements in technical communication and propose what I believe should be the requirements for tenure; I also suggest changes that would allow our graduate programs to better prepare students for life in a new academic culture.

TENURE CRITERIA AND ACADEMIC CULTURE

Tenure Criteria: The Status Quo

Tenure-track faculty members in technical communication typically are required to publish a substantial number of articles in recognized refereed journals, or a monograph-length study with a reputable commercial or academic press.[2] These publications focus on theory of technical communication, application of literary theory to technical communication, classical rhetoric and technical communication, social theory as applied to technical communication, history of technical communication, gender and technical communication, ethnographic studies, work-based research, computers and composing, document design, editing, collaboration, and research in the pedagogy of technical communication.

In addition to fulfilling requirements for original, significant publishing, faculty members are evaluated on teaching and their responsibilities for program administration or program and course development. Excellent teaching and program leadership, although often expected, may not be rewarded. Excellent teaching and administration can help a person whose publication record is acceptable, but not outstanding. Questionable teaching can result in a negative tenure evaluation unless the faculty member's research record is brilliant. What always counts is the publication list.

All too often, because of its applied nature, technical communication, like composition studies as a whole, has been regarded as an ugly step-sister by English departments. Aspiring to become more beautiful members of the family, technical communication faculties have adopted traditional scholarly criteria for tenure and have begun to publish in a written discourse—arcane, esoteric, opaque, and detached from that which exists in nonacademic (work) settings. This situation, to my mind, is not professionally wholesome. It is neither conducive to faculty development nor justifiable to the public, to legislatures and governing boards, or to students.

Restructuring Tenure for a New Academic Culture

Because of the crisis of confidence now facing higher education and the status quo I just described, I believe American higher education needs to take a hard look at faculty attitudes toward teaching and scholarship, and at what these attitudes suggest about our values. I also believe that faculty members in technical communication, and in composition studies as a whole, are uniquely positioned to respond to the current crisis in confidence. If we base our response on the ways our discipline serves human understanding and communication, we may find that we survive rather well the changes that new economic realities are making in the academy and, ultimately, in tenure.

Too many faculty members believe that financial Nirvana will soon return and that they can ignore the economic vice that now grips higher education. But many analyses of higher education costs (e.g., Massy and Zemsky, Dill, Johnstone, Mingle, Ingram, and Levin) attest to the pervasiveness and the seriousness of the problem. In short, legislatures and governing boards are no longer convinced that campuses need more money, more degrees, more programs, and higher tuition.

Major universities—such as Stanford, Michigan, Illinois, Minnesota, and Tennessee—have begun restructuring in earnest. If Kenneth Ashworth, Texas's Commissioner of Higher Education, gets his wish, Texas will soon embark upon an accountability-driven funding formula that will link higher education funding to measurable outputs (see Ashworth 11–13). Criteria based on accountability formulas and used for program evaluations will measure numbers of degrees awarded; effectiveness of remediation; numbers of minority students enrolled and retained; numbers of community college transfers who graduate; scores on professional licensing exams; numbers of tenure-track faculty teaching lower-division courses; contributions of faculty to communities, public schools, and business; the employability of students completing a program; student and employer satisfaction with the program; and the relationship of faculty achievements to the goals of the program (Ashworth 14).

Noticeably absent from such criteria for formula funding are numbers of published articles in scholarly journals and other traditional criteria for tenure. In her 1994 "State of the College" address, Julia M. Davis, Dean of the College of Liberal Arts at the University of Minnesota-St. Paul, explains why:

What we are facing is a real shift in the priorities of state governments and in the expectations of the public about higher education. We are no longer the only game in town for people who wish to further their education, either by seeking degrees or by taking a series of courses of special interest. . . . In many ways, universities face a changing market much as the privately owned small town banks, pharmacies, and grocery stores have experienced. Research universities are not outlet stores, nor should they be. But outlet education, if you will allow me to use such a phrase, is growing all around us in the form of corporate based educational programs, specialized courses that are vocationally oriented, and provision of courses in areas quite removed from an institution's campus. Close inspection of the allocations for higher education throughout the United States reveals a trend toward increased support for community colleges, technical schools, and state colleges where the emphasis is on teaching rather than research.

Widespread public demand for quality undergraduate instruction rather than graduate instruction puts at special risk those faculty members and departments who see teaching undergraduate courses as merely a stepping stone to the real work of producing graduate students. But public dissatisfaction is wider still.

The public blames tenure for faculty resistance to accountability and cost controls, and it questions the need for faculty to have guaranteed lifetime employment. According to participants in the 1994 Pew Round-table—senior officers of 400 universities—tenure is perceived as the cause of universities' becoming "havens for a privileged class that has forgotten its responsibilities to others," as well as "tar pits of political correctness, inefficiency, and self-serving attitudes and practices." Moreover, tenure is believed to create a faculty that is a "self-perpetuating oligarchy openly disdainful of the opinions of others" (*Policy Perspectives* 6A).

If we are to change these perceptions of tenure, I believe there are five things we should do to reform and restructure tenure.

Develop New Criteria for Faculty Evaluation.   Basing tenure review—and other forms of faculty evaluation—on the antiquated categories of research, teaching, and service disproportionately rewards faculty members for earning prestige in their disciplines. Instead, we need to create procedures and standards that encourage departments and their faculties to recognize the importance of doing business in new ways—in a word, to innovate. Accountability requires us to measure ourselves in terms of our contributions to the university, to the publics it serves, and to students. Therefore, more realistic—more context sensitive and accountability responsive—tenure criteria would follow a new model of interrogatives, rather than prerogatives:

- What has the faculty member done to further the welfare of the institution and contribute to the achievement of its mission?

- What has the faculty member done to serve the community and the public?

- How has the faculty member's teaching changed students? What have they specifically mastered or learned that they did not know?

- What is the value of the faculty member's intellectual work to students, to the community, and to the institution?

Within such a model, faculty members could describe the prestige they have earned within their disciplines, but these achievements would be only one segment of the evaluation.

Encourage New Approaches to Research and Scholarship. As Clark Kerr, President Emeritus of the University of California has argued, ethical knowledge must have value beyond the prestige it generates for the faculty member within his/her discipline ("Knowledge Ethics"). In today's and tomorrow's high tech environment, an accounting of published books and articles will no longer be the sole measure of a faculty member's worth. Faculty who develop alternatives to standard courses, faculty who program software and design computer-based teaching methods, and faculty who respond to high-tech with applications that improve productivity and yield effective learning within and beyond classrooms will be deemed worthy of tenure or its successor.

Encourage Applied Research. Donald Kennedy, President Emeritus of Stanford University, describes the academy's endemic resistance to any research or field of study that has "been contaminated by practice" (136). Attempting to avoid this contamination, writing research has developed new nomenclatures, new postures, and new theories to improve its intellectual thrust. The results have, all too often, moved away from the product—literate students—and toward pure intellectualism.

As higher education researchers have pointed out (e.g., Kennedy; Massy; Kerr *Higher*), a balance between pure theory and mere application must be attained. Technical communication and composition studies as a whole are in a particularly good position to do this. Research that seeks to find new ways of improving writing instruction and then designs qualitative and quantitative research to document the effectiveness of these efforts should be welcomed.

Encourage Teaching That Uses the Information Superhighway. Computer-aided classrooms have become more commonplace than a decade ago, and a move away from traditional classrooms to distance learning has begun. English has been among the last of academic departments to adopt computer technology. But English faculty, particularly technical communication faculty, should realize that the information superhighway will influence how we teach and how we define our discipline. Of course, such efforts can themselves lead to applied research in how to make distance education effective. Proactive research can ensure that English departments and composition and technical communication programs become part of the process by which teaching is examined and redefined by technology. This type of proactive research would show the relevance of English studies to the new academic culture.

See Service As Public Outreach and Reward Faculty for It.   Composition and technical communication faculty members can provide public service workshops in report writing, documentation development, and policy and procedure writing. They can help high schools incorporate technical communication into composition curricula and improve the instructional methods of high school teachers. Such projects that link university faculty with public education can provide important applied research opportunities that yield new methods for teaching writing to a new range of students. Such efforts should be rewarded in the new academic culture, for as Richard Ingram and Robert Gale of the Association of Governing Boards of Universities and Colleges both have shown, it is time that universities stop criticizing public schools and reach out to help them.

PREPARING GRADUATE STUDENTS
FOR A NEW ACADEMIC CULTURE

Efforts to restructure tenure criteria must also involve changes in the graduate programs in which the faculty of the future develop habits and expectations that influence their work for years to come. I offer the following admonitions to suggest ways that graduate programs should change to better prepare students for faculty work in a new academic culture.

First, take a hard look at your existing graduate programs. Are your students getting jobs? What kinds of jobs are they getting? How do your graduates feel about their educational experience and their preparation? What changes would they like to see?

Next, restructure graduate programs so that they allow students flexibility in developing expertise in a broad range of fields. Any new PhD in rhetoric, composition, or technical communication should have extensive computer expertise, writing lab credentials, and an understanding of distance education. Consider developing degree options that allow students multiple career opportunities inside and outside the academy. Students with backgrounds in computer science, marketing, educational technology, distance education, and ESL—to name a few currently popular fields—will likely have improved employment odds in both nonacademic and academic settings as institutions attempt to cover more tasks with fewer faculty members.

Third, encourage work-based research that is publishable in academic journals but grounded in the realities of the workplace. In a shrinking job market, graduate students who focus on purely arcane theory are not preparing themselves for job markets outside the university.

Fourth, be sure your graduate students can speak two—or even three—languages fluently and also understand business and social protocols of the countries in which these languages predominate. Modifying language examinations to focus on knowledge of current business, technical, and cultural publications would enhance students' cultural as well as linguistic knowledge.

Fifth, educate graduate students about the realities of the academic job market, as well as the economic pressures higher education is facing because of the rising costs of K through 12 education, health care, crime prevention, and replacing decaying urban infrastructures.

Finally, limit the number of your PhD graduates. As academic jobs in composition studies and technical communication decrease in the future, a glut of PhDs available for part-time teaching will add to the ability of universities to do without tenure-track positions. Departments that continue to flood the market with PhDs for which an insufficient number of jobs exist are themselves exhibiting lack of accountability. As Stuart Brown and Jack Selzer made clear in two separate *ATTW Bulletin* articles, comfortably-tenured graduate faculty members cannot continue to think only about themselves.

IMPLICATIONS OF THE NEW REALITY—
ACADEMICS AND ECONOMICS

Donald Kennedy sees today's problems in higher education as early premonitions of coming fiscal exigencies. Faculties, he believes, can either work in partnership with university administrators to deal with these exigencies or risk having boards of regents take control of institutions (Kennedy 153). Indeed, in a new academic culture shaped by demands for cost control and accountability, faculty members will no longer be able to assume that they are the sole arbiters of what should be taught and how. Nor will disciplinary prestige be a paramount criterion on which faculty members are measured for promotion, tenure, and other rewards. Instead, governing boards will become increasingly more active in monitoring costs, measuring outcomes, and defining quality, while expecting faculty to be more dedicated to the goals of the institution than to individual successes within disciplines.

Confronted with mandates to cut costs, institutions will seek to capitalize on cost advantages offered by technology.[3] And they will seek other efficiencies, too. For instance, members of the American Association of Higher Education (AAHE), such as SUNY Chancellor Bruce Johnstone, and of the Wingspread Group have advocated changes that could have profound implications for composition and technical communication programs: re-engineering the 130-hour undergraduate degree into a three-year degree, with general education courses placed in the high school curriculum; eliminating fixed semester- or quarter-hour requirements for courses; and replacing traditional courses with shorter courses that teach higher-order thinking skills (see Johnstone and Wingspread). Also, as I predicted at the beginning of this essay, institutions will reduce the numbers of faculty in tenure-line positions.

English departments, with the powerful intellectual tools of rhetoric and composition studies, can be at the forefront of a new academic culture—if they will adapt to and even exploit the changes that are coming in American higher education. To do this requires re-envisioning faculty work and the way it is rewarded by departments, colleges, and universities.

NOTES

[1]In 1995, the Association of Teachers of Technical Writing (ATTW) issued a collection of essays, *Issues in Promotion and Tenure for Faculty in Technical Communication*, written by senior faculty in technical communication. It is a statement of sorts, offering guidelines about what can be or is being required for tenure in various institutions that offer technical communication courses and programs.

[2]A technical communication faculty member who has 8 to 12 substantial articles in print or a monograph-length study in press and 4 to 5 articles in print will have little difficulty satisfying most departments' publication requirements for tenure. A well-reviewed scholarly book in print will do nicely. Articles in conference proceedings and book reviews are not generally considered substantial publications, and assistant professors are encouraged to devote their energies to academic articles and books focusing on current theory or scholarly explorations of a current topic in technical communications research.

A substantial article is defined as one that reviews existing literature, posits an extension of the topic or provides new information or a new approach to the topic, and illustrates effectively written analysis. The ATTW can recommend to departments and colleges external reviewers who will help assess the quality of publications. Technical communication reviewers are generally interested in publications that will show original approaches to current topics and will likely make an impact on (be extensively cited by) other scholars.

[3]As the 1994 Pew Roundtable reported, new distance learning consortiums are providing education that is cheaper, more accessible, and more state-of-the-art than traditional college classes (see *Policy Perspectives*). These new educational providers are not bound by monolithic bureaucracies that take years to respond to needed curricular change; they are not bound by rigid semester-hour requirements that

assume that students need the same time for a writing course as for a calculus course; and they are able to show that distance learners perform as well on exams as students in traditional classes.

WORKS CITED

Ashworth, Kenneth H. "Performance-based Funding in Higher Education: The Texas Case Study," *Change* Nov./Dec. 1994: 8–15.

Brown, Stuart C. "Caveat Emptor: Academic Prospects for New Ph.D.'s in Technical and Professional Communication." *ATTW Bulletin* 5.1 (Fall 1994): 5–7.

Davis, Julia M. "The State of the College." College of Liberal Arts of the U of Minnesota-St. Paul. Fall 1994.

Dill, William R. "When Are You Going to Get Rid of Tenure?" *Trusteeship* Sept./Oct. 1993: 6–10.

Gale, Robert L. "Scanning the Future of Higher Education." *AGB Reports* Nov./Dec. 1992: 6–13.

Ingram, Richard T. "The End of Sanctuary." *AGB Reports* May/June 1992: 19–23.

Johnstone, D. Bruce. "Enhancing the Productivity of Learning." *AAHE Bulletin* Dec. 1993: 2–4.

Kennedy, Donald. "Making Choices in the Research University." *Daedalus* Fall, 1993: 127–56.

Kerr, Clark. *Higher Education Cannot Escape History: Issues for the Twenty-first Century*. New York: SUNY P, 1994.

—. "Knowledge Ethics and the New Academic Culture." *Change* Jan./Feb. 1994: 9–15.

Levin, Henry M. "Raising Productivity in Higher Education." *Journal of Higher Education* 62.3 (1991): 241–62.

Massy, William F., and Robert Zemsky. "Cost Containment: Committing to a New Economic Reality," *Change* Nov./Dec. 1990: 16–22.

Mingle, James R. "Faculty Work and the Costs/Quality/Access Collision." *AAHE Bulletin* Mar. 1993: 3–13.

Policy Perspectives 5.3 (April 1994). Report on the 1994 Pew Higher Education Roundtable.

Selzer, Jack. "Some Noise from a Spoilsport." *ATTW Bulletin* 5.1 (Fall 1994): 7–9.

Tebeaux, Elizabeth, ed. *Issues in Promotion and Tenure for Faculty in Technical Communication: Guidelines and Perspectives*. N.p.: ATTW, [1995].

Wingspread Group on Higher Education. *An American Imperative: Higher Expectations for Higher Education*. N.p.: Johnson Foundation, 1993.

Author Index

Subject Index